I0816558

CANNIBAL HOLOCAUST
AND THE SAVAGE CINEMA OF RUGGERO DEODATO

This revised and updated third edition published by FAB Press, November 2021

Second edition published May 2011

First published March 1999

FAB Press Ltd.
2 Farleigh
Ramsden Road
Godalming, Surrey
GU7 1QE
England, U.K.

www.fabpress.com

text by
Gian Luca Castoldi
Harvey Fenton
Julian Grainger
Xavier Mendik
Kim Newman
Julian Petley

A CIP catalogue record for this book is available from the British Library.

ISBN 9781913051129

Printed in Czech Republic

CANNIBAL HOLOCAUST
and the savage cinema of
Ruggero Deodato

Gian Luca Castoldi
Harvey Fenton
Julian Grainger
Xavier Mendik
Kim Newman
Julian Petley

CANNIBAL HOLOCAUST

and the savage cinema of Ruggero Deodato

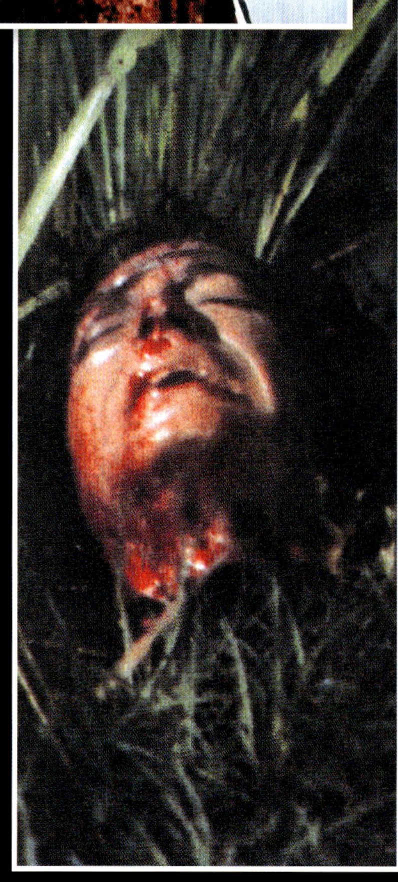

illustrations:

front cover, frontispiece & title page:
Cannibal Holocaust

above:
The Yamamomo shrine, constructed from the remains of the Yates team:
Cannibal Holocaust

right:
A bizarre form of ritual execution:
Last Cannibal World

bottom right:
Cut and Run

back cover top:
Cannibal Holocaust

back cover middle:
Massimo Foschi finds redemption in cannibalism:
Last Cannibal World

back cover bottom:
A Yacùmo warrior engages in cannibalism in an attempt to drive white men spirits from the jungle:
Cannibal Holocaust

edited and designed by
Harvey Fenton

interviews
Gian Luca Castoldi
Xavier Mendik

reviews
Gian Luca Castoldi
Harvey Fenton
Julian Grainger
Kim Newman

research
Julian Grainger
Francis Brewster

censorship notes
Julian Petley

Special Thanks to **Deborah Bacci** for translating Gian Luca's texts from Italian into English, and to **CoCo** for help with image scanning.

Thanks to the following for essential research assistance:
Nathan Bradbury, Francis Brewster, Kenneth Eriksen, Kris Gavin, Manlio Gomarasca, Craig Ledbetter, Marc Morris, Adrian Luther-Smith

Illustrations are from the collections of:
Martin Beine, Bill Bennett, Gian Luca Castoldi, Martin Coxhead *(Flashbacks)*, **Mitch Davis, Ruggero Deodato, Harvey Fenton, Adrian Luther-Smith** *(Delirium Collection)*, **Marc Morris, Ezio Palaggi** *(Videotel Service, Roma)*

CONTENTS

LE DERNIER MONDE CANNIBALE
(THE CANNIBALS)
un film de RUGGERO DEODATO

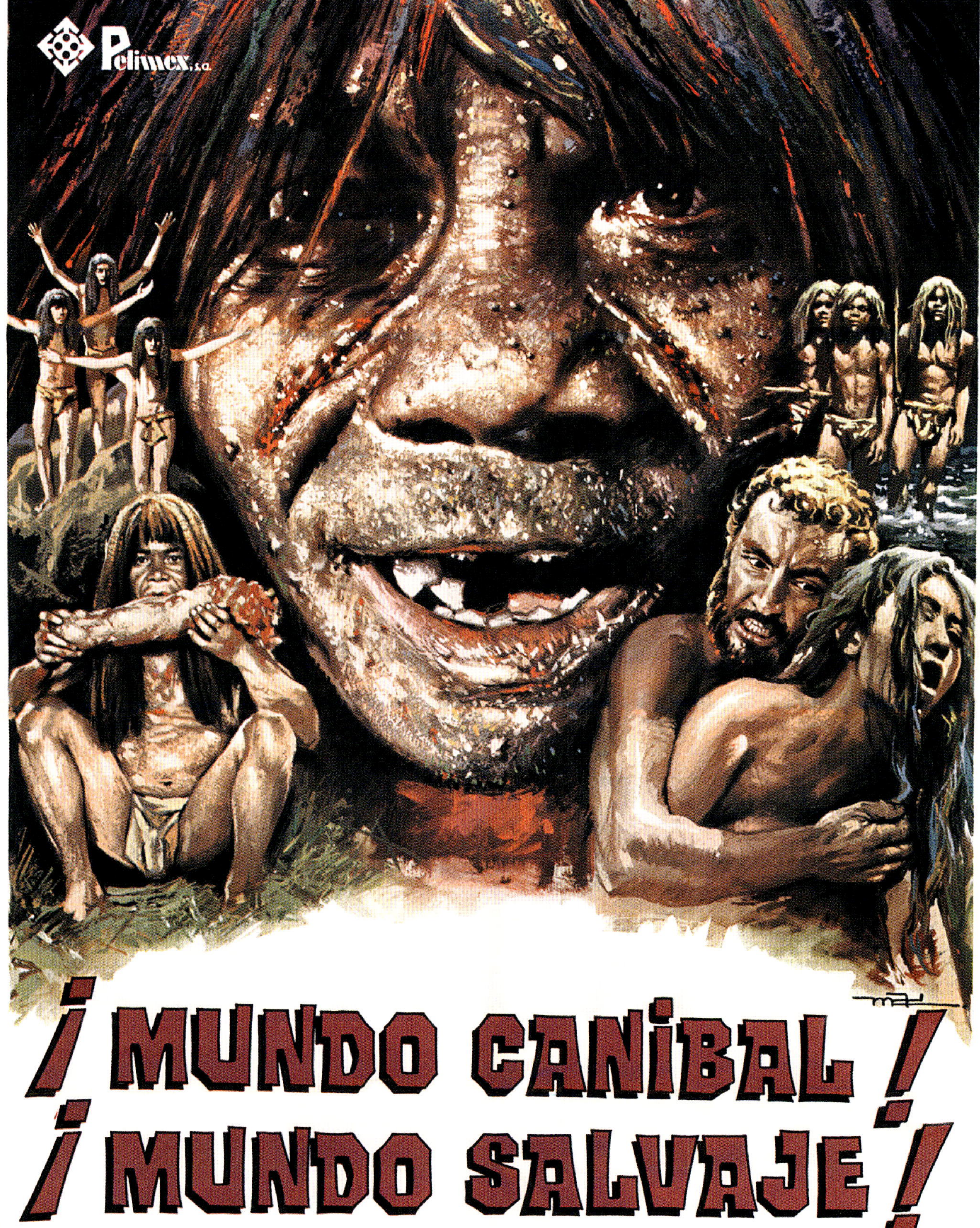

Spanish theatrical poster for 'Last Cannibal World'

RUGGERO DEODATO

Ruggero Deodato has the dubious honour of being the man who created one of the most infamous horror movies ever made. **Cannibal Holocaust** is Deodato's most celebrated movie, and he is fully aware of this fact; during the course of the interview featured in this book, he says, *"The best one for me is **Cannibal Holocaust**. It is impossible to equal that film..."* Deodato will never live down the legacy of this stunning film, and one gets the impression that he is content with this state of affairs, hence this book rightfully devotes a large proportion of its pages to documenting every aspect of Deodato's brutal, distressing masterpiece. However we are also here to thoroughly document the entire career of one of the busiest men in the film-making industry. He has survived in this most turbulent of environments for over forty years by being ever-adaptable, willing to try his hand at any genre: along with two further jungle-adventures – **Last Cannibal World** and **Cut and Run** – his filmography includes cop thriller **Live Like a Cop, Die Like a Man**, claustrophobic slasher **House on the Edge of the Park**, apocalyptic adventure movie **The Atlantis Interceptors**, costume fantasy film **The Barbarians**, plus an impressive array of comedies, erotic thrillers and prime-time Italian TV serials.

This book is the most comprehensive analysis of Deodato's work ever published. It is our intention that the career-spanning interview and detailed filmography printed in these pages will serve as a valuable, lasting source of reference for everyone who takes an interest in this increasingly important figure in the world of cinema.

above: Ruggero Deodato in 1991, at home in Rome.
right: Deodato filming in 1998, in Zimbabwe during the making of the TV series **Sotto il cielo dell'Africa**.

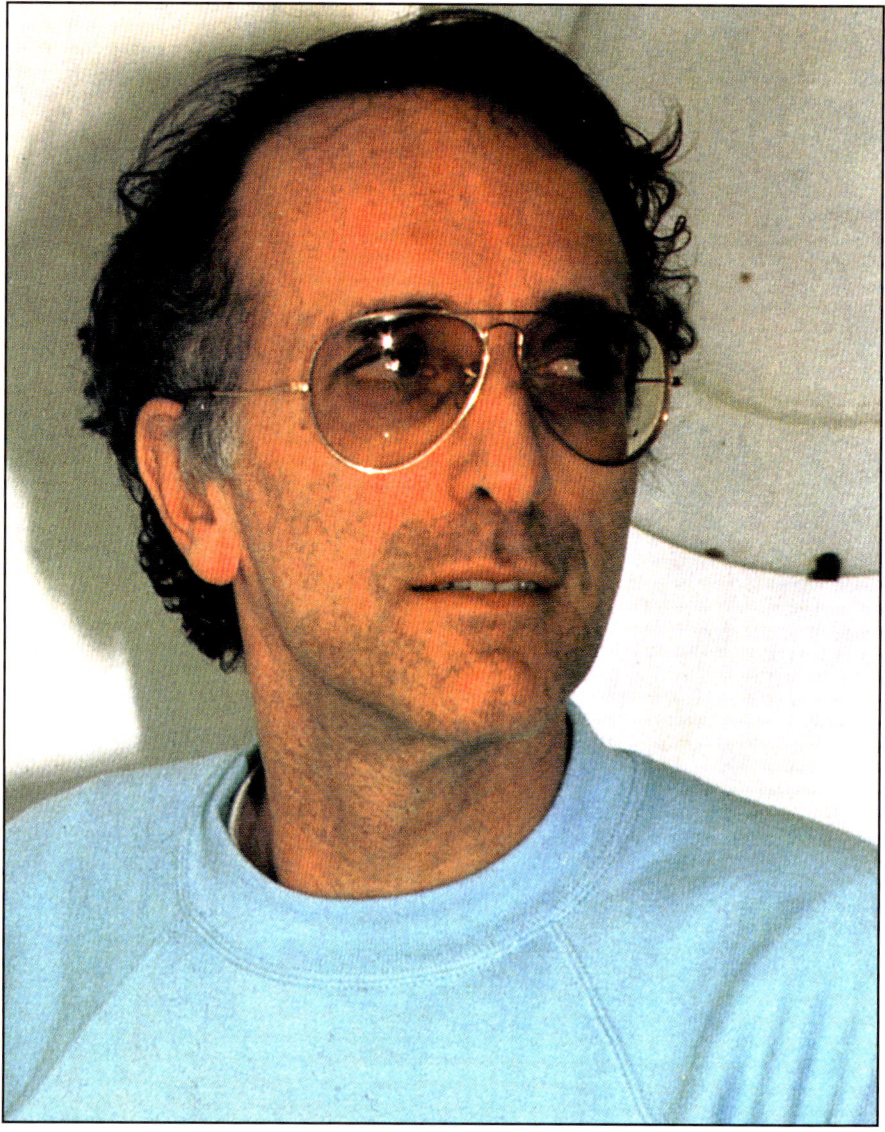

above from the top: Deodato somewhere in South America ; With a lion whilst making **Sotto il cielo dell'Africa** ; With Mario Adorf during the making of **Ocean**.

top right: Deodato photographed in 1988, during the making of **Un delitto poco comune** (aka **Phantom of Death**).

below: Deodato operates an elephant-trunk 'hand puppet' during the filming of **Sotto il cielo dell'Africa**.

Ruggero Deodato was born on 7 May 1939 in Potenza, Italy. He grew up in the Parioli region of Rome, which happened to be home to many of the prime movers in the vibrant 1950's Italian movie industry. Due to this cultural background, Deodato was naturally drawn to the world of cinema, becoming good friends with the son of the great neo-realist director Roberto Rossellini at an early age. This friendship opened the door to Deodato's film-making career when, in 1958, Rossellini asked him to undertake third assistant director work on the French / Italian co-production **Il generale della rovere** (released 1959). Deodato's work on this film was uncredited, but he very quickly became one of the most sought-after assistant directors in Italy, amassing an impressive total of more than forty credits in the eight year period up to 1967.

In addition to working on half a dozen Rossellini movies, he collaborated with many more top directors of the time including the likes of Renato Castellani, Sergio Corbucci,

left: Deodato directing **Ocean**.
below: Relaxing in Paris with Michela Rocco.
bottom: Filming **The Atlantis Interceptors**.

Carlo Ludovico Bragaglia, Mauro Bolognini, Antonio Margheriti, Riccardo Freda, Carlo Lizzani and Joseph Losey.

Deodato's breakthrough came in 1964 when, two weeks into the shoot, he took over from Antonio Margheriti as director of **Ursus il terrore dei Kirghisi**. Upon completion of the film, also known as **Hercules, Prisoner of Evil**, direction was credited to Margheriti. Deodato had to wait until 1968 for his full directorial debut, **Phenomenal and the Treasure of Tutankamen**, which he uncustomarily decided to sign with the pseudonym 'Roger Rockfeller'. From this point on there was no stopping the talented young director, who tried his hand at a wide variety of genres.

Deodato's key works for the cinema have often been termed 'misanthropic', and this angry strand first really emerged during his 1975 erotic thriller **Waves of Lust**, which amongst the softcore sex scenes deals with violent psychological warfare leading to a double murder. The following two years saw the stakes raised further, the intense cop-thriller **Live Like a Cop, Die Like a Man** asking us to side with a couple of cops who are basically criminals operating on the 'right' side of the law, and the lyrical back-to-nature survivalist fable **Last Cannibal World** being the first Deodato movie to confront the viewer with images of actual animal butchery. These images provoke many complicated debates, some aspects of which are considered in these pages. This hard edge continued – legendarily – into **Cannibal Holocaust** and **House on the Edge of the Park**, but Deodato's angry late-Seventies stance was interrupted by the sentimental 1978 'weepie' **L'ultimo sapore dell'Aria** (aka **Last Feelings**), a film for which – unlike the majority of his fan base – Deodato has a great deal of fondness.

In recent years Deodato's work has lost the primal edge of screaming, fearful barbarism, but if anything it is more technically accomplished than ever, case in point being the daft B-movie exploitation of **Dial: Help**, in which the ever so decorative Charlotte Lewis is implausibly menaced by a homicidal, love-sick telephone amongst some of the most bafflingly atmospheric lighting and set-designs ever seen in Deodato's movies. Sure, it makes no sense, but it doesn't half look good...

One last thing. Deodato pops up on-screen in most of his films. Some of his cameos are even speaking roles. We have listed as many of these cameos as possible in the credits accompanying each film review, so you know where to look out for him next time you watch one of his films. Try to spot him in **Live Like a Cop, Die Like a Man**, **Concorde Affair**, **Cannibal Holocaust**, **Phantom of Death**, **The Atlantis Interceptors**, **Dial: Help** and **The Washing Machine**, but for the most fiendishly clever, downright audacious cameo of all, just check out **Cut and Run**. Deodato's movies are full such of moments, which reward careful viewing, but his cameos are merely a playful diversion; he is at his most impressive when deadly serious. For the alert viewer who is prepared to be mentally challenged and emotionally assaulted, his best films can prove to be both cathartic and inspirational. The unprepared invariably feel insulted, cheated and confused. By making films with such resonance and power, yet still managing to survive in an arena so profoundly undermined by lowest-common-denominator compromise, Ruggero Deodato has earned my utmost respect.

(Harvey Fenton)

INTERVIEW

Ruggero Deodato

interviewed in 1999 by Gian Luca Castoldi

You first came into contact with the world of cinema during the nineteen fifties, as Roberto Rossellini's assistant director. How was it that you had this opportunity?

I have been a friend of the great director's son ever since childhood. Despite being born in Potenza, I have always lived in Parioli *(area of Rome)* and many of the people who worked in cinema lived in my area. From an early age I gravitated towards the world of cinema; I very soon found myself with some small jobs at the studios, and being a very good friend of Lorenzo *(Rossellini)*, I was often at his house in Santa Marinella. One day out of the blue his father said to me "Ruggerino, why don't you come with me to be my assistant".
I would never have imagined this request, but I went and made my first film as third assistant director, then soon I was second assistant and so on, each time I went up in the hierarchy. Rossellini was a genius and his children also had great qualities. Lorenzo could have done much more but his father never helped him very much so it was me who became his first assistant director.
I worked on six films shot by Rossellini: **Il generale della rovere**, **Ere notte a Roma**, **Viva l'Italia!**, **Vanina Vanini**, **Anima nera**, and the episode **Illibatezza** *(his contribution to **RO.GO.PA.G**)*.

In that period did you work exclusively with Rossellini?

No, I had a bout of good fortune. For a time I found it impossible to detach myself from Rossellini's team; Rossellini was a genius but he was surrounded by mediocre people, and there weren't any great opportunities to emerge from this situation. However, the director Carlo Ludovico Bragaglia asked me to work with him and I had to work very hard to detach myself from the group. That was my good fortune; with Rossellini you could not learn, he was an artist who worked from impulse. There was no need for cinematographic technique. The first friction between Rossellini and myself was when I had to film a race and I tried to portray the event in the most spectacular way possible. When he saw what I had filmed he eliminated everything and said that I had not understood anything about cinema and that my approach was just a "mannerism". After this disagreement we parted and I went to shoot films with Freda, another master. The first of these films was **Romeo e Giulietta**.

top: Deodato with Gian Luca Castoldi at the time of this interview.
above: in 1969, during the making of **Il triangolo rosso**.
right: in 1990, filming **Ocean**.

What do you remember about Freda?

He was a real genius. His genius is not actually seen in the films, which are not all that innovative anyway; it was in his style of filming. He had a sense of the shot and the editing that were incredible. He is extremely cultured; a man of great refinement.

You have worked with some great masters.

Before shooting a film of my own I had worked with Rossellini, Bragaglia and Freda, and we must not forget that I also made a great many films with Corbucci; the first film with him was **Il figlio di Spartacus**. But at the same time I was also working with Mauro Bolognini, Renato Castellani, Antonio Margheriti... I made a great many films but all of them were concentrated in the space of maybe six or seven years, this period starting from my first experience with Rossellini, when I was 19 years old.

*One of the films in which you collaborated with Margheriti as assistant director is **Danza macabra**.*

A delicious film. I have made many films with Antonio but that one is certainly the best.

I have read an interview with Margheriti, in which he said that it was thanks to you that he was able to have Barbara Steele for that film.

I used to flirt with Barbara Steele quite a bit. At that time I was about twenty four years old and she, after having made lots of horror films with Bava and Freda, had just shot **Fellini's 8 1/2** and wanted to escape from the horror star cliché. Sergio Corbucci, who was the original choice as director of that film, knew of my relationship with Barbara, and therefore asked me to talk her into shooting **Danza macabra**.

Yes, there is a legend which says that she, after having worked with Fellini, became big-headed and no longer wanted to do horror films.

It is true. It was me who convinced her to do another terror film.

What sort of person was Barbara Steele?

A wonderful woman, exceptional. Although I was flirting with her, it was absolutely platonic. She was not a cold woman; it seemed as if she were from the South. She loved cats and she lived in a splendid house full of them.

Whilst working on Margheriti's fantasy films you worked with many young novice Italian actors: Franco Nero, Lisa Gastoni...

Franco Nero was a great friend of mine, we were inseparable to the point that it was actually me who convinced Sergio Corbucci to call in Franco for **Django**. He had already chosen another actor, Mark Damon, for that part but I was telling him to choose Franco. I didn't manage to convince him until I managed to show him to Nori, Sergio's wife, who then imposed him on her husband.

*Where was **Django** filmed, Madrid or Almeria?*

In Madrid. Franco and I spent several weeks working together in Spain. Now he has forgotten about me. He even pretends not to know me.

What memories do you have of the science-fiction films of Margheriti?

They were well-made. Margheriti used to personally work on the special effects, together with *[Cataldo]* Galliano. They did a good job, and they certainly did not need to envy American films.

*Your first job as director came to you when you took over from Margheriti in the direction of **Ursus il terrore dei Kirghisi**.*

He filmed for the first two weeks and I filmed for the last two. The film featured Reg Park, Ettore Manni – who was also the producer – and Mirielle Granelli, who was his wife.

Do you like the peplum genre?

I had already worked on **Ursus nella valle dei leone** by Bragaglia, but no, the peplum was not my genre. I have never even seen **Ursus il terrore dei Kirghisi**. I left it at the editing stage and [Otello] Colangeli finished it. I don't even remember how it was signed. I was a young lad and I don't think of it as one of my films.

*We can therefore consider your first film to be **Donne... botte e bersaglieri**.*

My first film was **Gungala, la pantera nuda**, the sequel to another film *(**Gungala la virgine della giungla** by Romano Ferrara)*. We filmed it in Kenya, and part of it in Italy in the De Paolis style *(incredibly famous theatre of Roman mime)*. After having looked at the scenes shot in Italy we decided to go to Kenya for three weeks to finish the film. After this I filmed **Fenomenal e il tesoro di Tutankamen** with Lucretia Love, who was amongst other things the wife of the producer and actor Mauro Parenti. Do not ask me the story because I don't remember it. There is a curious anecdote attached to the making of that film. Whilst we were shooting a scene in Paris, on the Champs Elysees, whilst panning the camera I framed Rex Harrison

top: Deodato worked with Antonio Margheriti during 1963 on the gothic horror film **Danza macabra**. The film was released in the USA under the title **Castle of Blood**. *middle:* Deodato claims it was he who suggested that Barbara Steele (*right*) should be given the role of Elizabeth. *bottom:* Italian "locandina" poster design.

Promotional designs for two of Deodato's collaborations with Antonio Margheriti: **Danza macabra** & **The Virgin of Nuremberg**. Deodato also collaborated with Sergio Corbucci during the making of **Django**, filming exteriors in Madrid for two weeks.

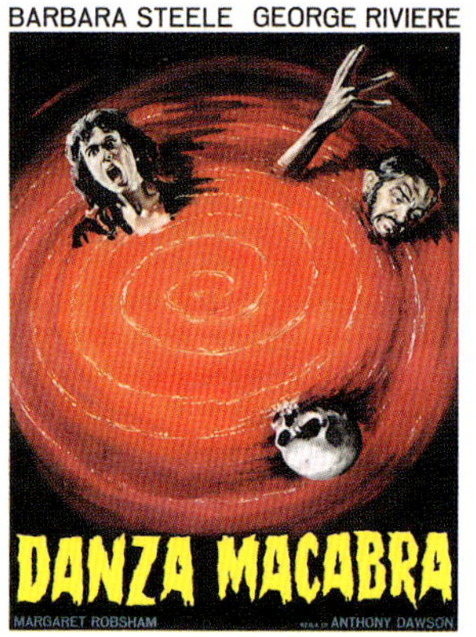

who was passing there by chance. After finishing the shot, I immediately asked him, disconcerted, if I could use that footage for my film. He gave me his approval and so in my film I also have Harrison *(laughter)*.

After **Gungala** I started work on a film which I never made. A producer sent me to Ethiopia for three months with two fantastic scriptwriters. One was Franco Solinas, the other Giorgio Allorio. We never wrote that script but we enjoyed ourselves like maniacs. I could tell you so many of those adventures... betrayals, escapes, jokes, risks of every type.

Straight after that Sergio Corbucci called me from Spain where he was filming, because he had an assistant director who was not working properly, and I worked for two weeks with him. It was whilst I was in Spain, I think, that I was called by *(Edmondo)* Amati to shoot those two films for him. They are the two musicals, **Donne... botte e bersaglieri** and **Vacanze sulla Costa Smeralda**. Back then, one did not think very much about genre. Bolognini had just made **Guardia, guardia scelta, brigadiere e maresciallo**. At that time the specialisation one sees today did not exist. In fact, I have always tried to change genre, as I do not wish to become typecast as a director specialising in a particular form.

If you were to make films purely with regard to your personal taste, which direction would it take you?

The cinema of adventure. I like costume films; the details. But then I also like dramatic films. There is not a particular genre; I have made a sentimental film and I liked it.

What do you enjoy reading?

I read everything. I like historical books, the biographies of Gianni Granzotto; I have read

Giulio Cesare and *Annibale*. I love history, the customs of societies, the historical detail. Making those two comedy films was not the pinnacle of my aspirations, nevertheless I enjoyed them because I have a great humorous vein in me. In any case it is not easy to make a comedy, a director by trade cannot make a comedy, it doesn't come out well, it doesn't come out naturally. The camera must be organised, the lighting must be correct, and whilst organising these details one can lose the spontaneity of the comic performance, which is what makes the film. I believe that the comic director does not exist, it is the actor who makes the comedy film.

Yet you have helped launched the careers of a lot of comic actors. For example Enrico Montesano.

Yes, and [Paolo] Villaggio, [Oreste] Lionello, [Lino] Toffolo. They were all in **I quattro del Pater Noster**. Montesano had a very small part in **Donne... botte e bersaglieri**, it was his first film. He did the rounds of the production houses in search of small roles. He was a very likeable type. Villaggio though had already done some cabaret. Many people involved in **I quattro del Pater Noster** have become important names in Italian cinema; the film had a screenplay written by Maurizio Costanzo, the music was by Luis Enriquez Bacalov, who has since gone on to win an Oscar for his musical score to **Il postino**. The actors included Montesano and Villaggio. To make it now it would cost five billion just for the music *(laughter)*.

***Zenabel** is a romantic adventure film with Lucretia Love and John Ireland...*

It's a very enjoyable film which unfortunately was plagued by bad luck. For example, the première screening of the film coincided with the bomb at the Banca dell'Agricoltura di Milano in 1969. So nobody went to the cinema. A crazy situation. The film did not make a lira. It was at this time that I left Rome, even though I had been asked to make a film, and went to Milan to make advertisements. It was the only thing that I could do. My wife *(Silvia Dionisio)* had become a star – the producers would only invite me to the social events if she was there. I had to change everything to prove that I was worth something. In that period I made a great many advertisements. I made six spots for Amaro Cora *(a brand of liqueur)* which were incredibly successful; the actors were Silvia and Jean Sorel and they were like small films. I had to stop doing them when **Ondata di piacere** came out because Umberto Cora was shocked by the film; there was a shot of Dionisio next to a bottle of liqueur and this sent him into a towering rage. Also from that period is the series **All'ultimo minuto**, one of the best things ever filmed for Italian television. It had an American rhythm and dynamism. Those tele-films have disappeared from circulation and I do not own a copy of even one of them because the producer Jacopo Rizza died. He was a famous journalist, he was the first to interview the bandit [Salvatore] Giuliano. Jacopo was an adorable person as well as the husband of Gisella Sofio. Perhaps we should ask her. I worked with some excellent actors on that series: Adriana Asti, Andrea Checchi, Maurizio Merli...

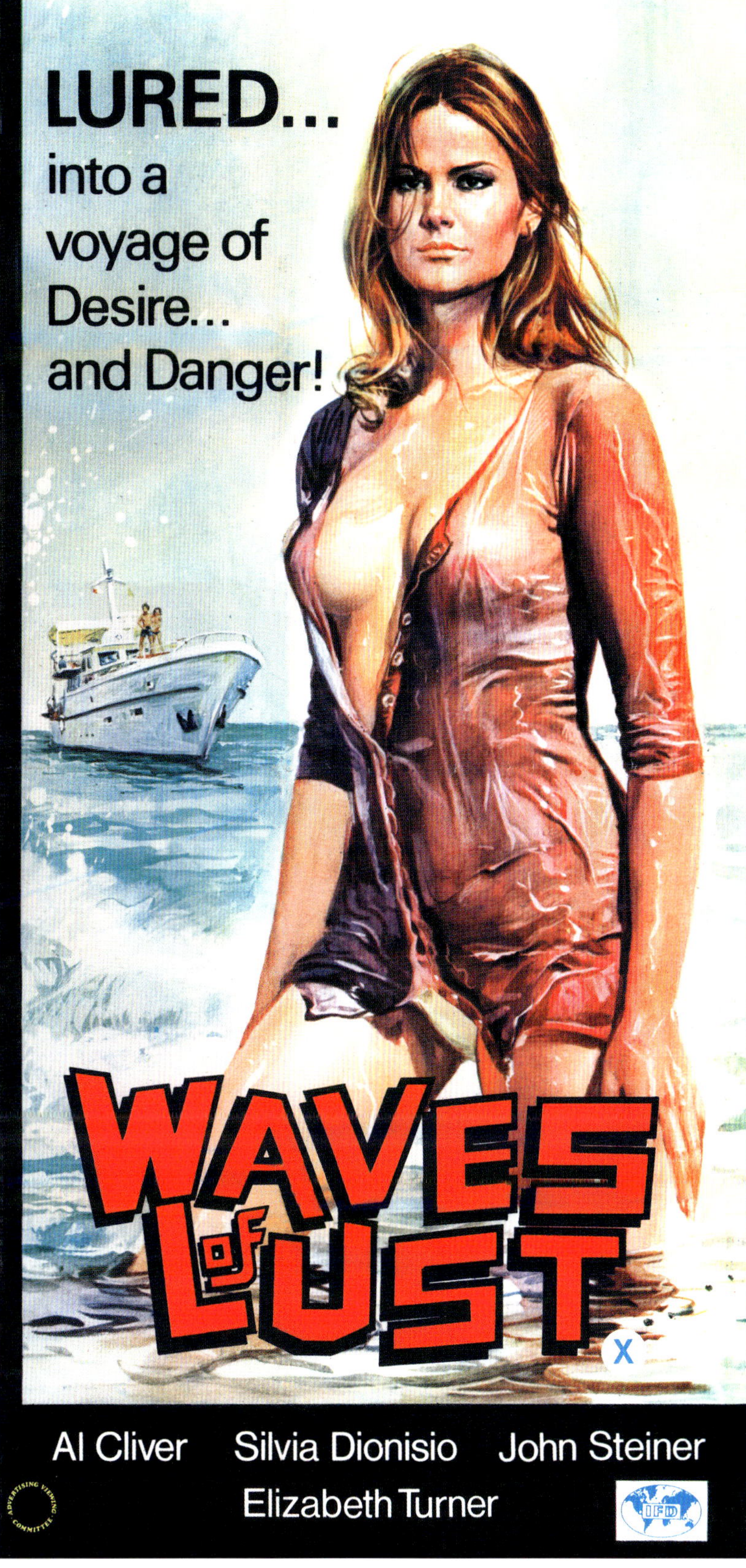

Waves of Lust was the export title for **Ondata di piacere**, Deodato's successful contribution to the erotic thriller genre which was very popular in Europe during the early Seventies.

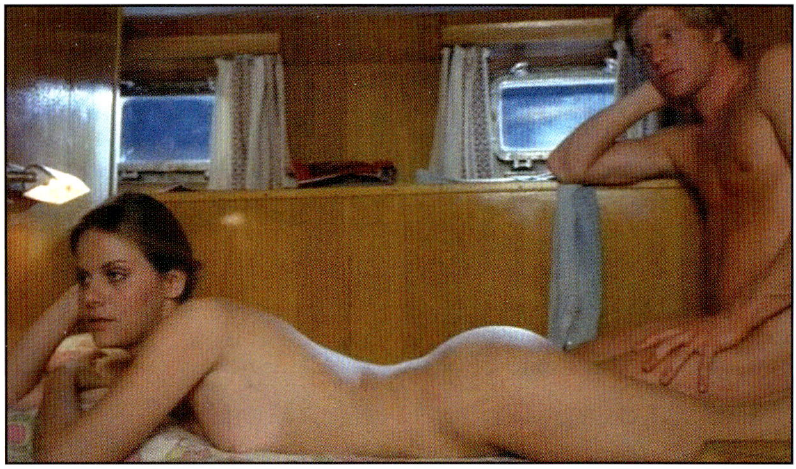

above: Marc Porel (left) and Ray Lovelock (right) in the violent, cynical cop thriller **Uomini si nasce, poliziotti si muore** (aka **Live Like a Cop, Die Like a Man**).

opposite page, top left: Deodato shifted genre yet again with his next film, **Ultimo mondo cannibale** (aka **Last Cannibal World**), which starred Massimo Foschi and Me Me Lai.

top and below: **Ondata di piacere** (aka **Waves of Lust**) starred Silvia Dionisio, who was Deodato's wife at the time of filming.

*In the same period you also filmed **Il triangolo rosso** for television.*

It was the Italian tele-film which inaugurated **Il maresciallo Rocca** *(famous Italian TV series about the traffic police starring Luigi Proietti)*. The stars were Jacques Sernas, Riccardo Garrone, Elio Pandolfi. Amongst the special guests I had Ottavia Piccolo, Alessio Orano... The first series was very successful and was also sold to Germany. I filmed many of the episodes for that series. Then I made the pilot episode for a proposed series **Il segreto di Cristina**, which unfortunately didn't eventually lead to a series.

*After all this television work you returned to cinema with **Ondata di piacere**.*

The producers, [Alberto] Marras and [Vincenzo] Salviani, asked me to make an erotic film; this style of movie was in fashion at the time. [Ornella] Muti, [Eleonora] Giorgi and Agostina Belli were the pioneers and then everyone started doing it. I had planned to shoot that film with another actress, who at the last minute refused to be filmed naked. So I put forward my wife's name to the producers; at that time she was a star and had never undressed for the cameras. She accepted the part only because all her peers were doing this sort of film at that time.

Where was the footage on the yacht filmed?

At Cefalù. Amongst the actors was Al Cliver *(Pier Luigi Conti)* who was a very distinctive character. He was not a real actor, he had another career; furniture restoration or carpentry. The film was very successful.

*Next you made a splendid cop film, **Uomini si nasce, poliziotti si muore**, about a very effective police partnership.*

Ray Lovelock and Marc Porel were truly a winning couple. There was a symbiosis between the two of them which worked perfectly, the hard man and the more humane one. The whole thing had an ironic touch, which set it aside from the other productions of that genre. And it was extremely violent, so much so that it had problems with the censors and was cut. We had also planned a sequel for that film, but during that same period Monnezza *[a comic, anarchic cop played by Tomas Milian in a series of films]* had turned up, so the spell was broken. They were completely different types of characters.

How did you become the director of ***Ultimo mondo cannibale****? Did you get in on someone else's project or did the producer come directly to you?*

There was already an outline written by Renzo Genta, then Gianfranco Clerici contributed to it as well, as did a couple of actors. The producer of **Ultimo mondo cannibale** had **Il paese del sesso selvaggio** *(Umberto Lenzi's 1972 cannibal adventure film* ***Deep River Savages****)* in distribution together with my **Uomini si nasce, poliziotti si muore**, which was much more successful, therefore he thought he would let me shoot the cannibal film.

It was my idea to use Massimo Foschi because I wanted a great actor with an ordinary face, but also a very energetic, physical actor. Someone wrote that he was too theatrical, but I think he was very good for that role, he gave much more truth to the character. In Massimo's absence Ivan Rassimov would have had the role of the protagonist.

top: Locandina for the first Italian cannibal adventure film, Umberto Lenzi's **Il paese del sesso selvaggio**. Deodato's **Ultimo mondo cannibale** followed four years later, and was a success all over the world. Posters on this page are from Italy *(left)*, USA *(above)* and France *(below)*.

top left and middle: **Ultimo mondo cannibale** features many acts of animal butchery, a staple ingredient of all the Third World cannibal movies.
above: The film also featured a great deal of frank male and female nudity.
top right & inset: Deodato takes a dip during the making of the film. In the foreground is script continuity assistant Lamberto Bava.

Did you have any problems shooting those scenes of full-frontal nudity?

We spoke about it in advance and I explained that they were fundamental for the film. As I have already said, Massimo is a great actor and he understood perfectly.

The film was originally intended for Lenzi, why then did you shoot it?

As I said, the producer wanted me, and perhaps at that time Lenzi looked down on that sort of film.

There have been many criticisms regarding the animal killings in your cannibal films.

All the animals which were killed were then eaten by the natives. For example, they were greedy for crocodile meat, and when we killed one they always went for the paws, which were the first parts to disappear. It leaves a much greater impression on me when, for example during a race, an injured horse must be killed. A horse, like all domestic animals, leaves an impression. Not a crocodile. It is also important to consider the fact that the natives ate these animals because that is their food. The animals we killed in the various films were rodents, wild boars, perhaps we over-did it a bit with the turtle, however that also was eaten. Then there were the little monkeys, which made an impression on me because when one of them was killed the others died of heartache. Nowadays I wouldn't do it anymore, times have changed. When I was a child I lived in the country and it was normal to see a chicken, a rabbit or a pig being killed. Today my daughter sees it and she becomes distressed. Even when there was a dead person in the family, in previous times all the family used to watch over the corpse, today when somebody dies their body is hidden straight away. Before, death was a natural fact, and now it has become a taboo.

Have the films of [Gualtiero] Jacopetti inspired you?

Jacopetti managed to intuitively know, twenty years in advance, everything that's happening now. His films were truly beautiful.

top left: Carlo Lupo and Vittorio Colcazzi in **L'ultimo sapore dell'aria** (aka **Last Feelings**), Deodato's sentimental love story.
above from the top: Deodato relaxes in the jungle ; At the Brussels Horror Festival with British director Clive Donner (**Thief of Baghdad, The Caretaker**) ; With Carlo Ludovico Bragaglia during the director's 102nd birthday celebrations.
below: Behind the scenes with Miles O'Keeffe in 1986 during the making of **The Lone Runner**.

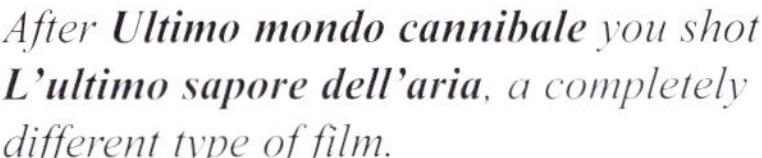

*After **Ultimo mondo cannibale** you shot **L'ultimo sapore dell'aria**, a completely different type of film.*

That film was commissioned from abroad. At that time Italian directors had a good reputation and we were hired unseen. Nowadays nobody wants us anymore, our market has thrown us completely to the ground. Some of my films have never been released in Italy, but I receive video cassettes from all over the world.

Sometimes you hear these critics who come out of the cinema after having seen a film by one of today's directors, one of the so-called minimalists, who comment amongst themselves, "it is well filmed." But I say, what does it mean, "well filmed"? They should be more concerned about the non-existent story. The films of today are very poor as regards screenplays; to shoot the films which we used to make one needed physical strength and not jokes. When I was shooting my films about the cannibals everything was problematical; there were problems of communication, of location, of hygiene, of health. Every day was a new adventure. In the film which I have just finished shooting with Bud Spencer, in Costa Rica, we were once again breathing that same air. Unusual situations; one had to deal with it.

Didn't you work with a screenplay?

Yes, there was always a screenplay, but there is something which I have learned right from my very first film. Supposing I have to shoot a scene in Piazza di Spagna and another one under the Viminale. I prepare all the story boards for the scenes which I have to shoot and then I start filming. Then, what often happened was that I was sent away from there and made to go somewhere else. What do you do in that case? You have to organise things all the same. We could not wait, we had to shoot in another area and perhaps pretend to be in Piazza di Spagna. That is the difference between us and the directors of today. We used to know how to improvise if we needed to.

*Let's go back to **L'ultimo sapore dell'aria**.*

I had a very good budget at my disposal provided by the Japanese producers, and I had a cast of unknown youngsters. All the means were at my disposal. That was a very beautiful picture. We filmed in Holland, at Asti, Rome, and Varazze. I didn't have any problems making that film.

So in your case one cannot speak of financial problems when shooting a film?

Look, I don't think I have ever had any economic problems. Little films, so to speak, perhaps I have shot one or two of them. For example the one which I made in Morocco, **Lone Runner**. I don't think it was ever released in Italy.

above: Danish video cover for **Concorde Affair**. *above right:* Deodato in Rome outside the Adriano cinema, which hosted the première screening of **Concorde Affair**. *bottom:* Outrageous poster for **Cannibal Holocaust** on public display in 1980 outside a cinema in Cartagena, Colombia. *below & opposite page:* **Cannibal Holocaust**.

__Concorde Affair '79__ had an excellent cast and seems to have been shot with adequate means.

If I had had a hundred million lire more, it would have been a masterpiece. It was more successful than the film about Concorde starring Alain Delon, which came out at the same time as mine *(__Airport '79: The Concorde__)*. Universal, who distributed the Delon film, took legal action against us and lost. British Airways had given us permission to use Concorde while Air France had given permission to the other film, which was flop. If the producer, Giorgio Carlo Rossi, had given me a little bit more money it would have been comparable with the American films of that era.

Any problems in having to work together with all these big names?

No, there was only James Franciscus, who was convinced that he could play predator with Mimsy Farmer, but she was very European and very high-brow, so she scorned him straight away.

Was __Cannibal Holocaust__ made in response to the success of __Ultimo mondo cannibale__?

At that time all the German distributors were buying our films unseen. Some Germans arrived with 90,000 Marks to help finance the shooting of a film. Then there were Japanese investors, who paid a great deal. For my own part I searched for other producers to complete the budget. We shot in Leticia, on the border between Colombia and Peru.

At that time on the television we were always seeing death scenes, they were the years of terrorism and my film was also a condemnation of a certain type of journalism. The technique and the basic themes of the film have since been appropriated and adapted by many others, the most recent example being Oliver Stone, who certainly has seen the film, and it's obvious. *(I think that Deodato is referring to* ***Natural Born Killers****)*. The resulting reaction for him was the same; partly it was our own fault because we went too far in expressing a moral standpoint. For example the final punchline "who are the real cannibals?" leaves the door open to doubt. We should have left no room for doubt in the minds of the spectators about the moral stance of the film. They make me laugh, some of the critiques against me, when they speak of the "gratuitous pleasure" of certain scenes, the turtle... then they even said that I had really impaled a woman to shoot the scene of the executed native. In Colombia they spread the word that Deodato is mad, that I did incredible things. The truth is that the guide whom we had at that time organised safaris in the South American style for German tourists. The Peruvian Indios got killed, thrown in the Amazon river, and after a hundred metres they didn't exist any more, nobody would ever find them; that river is full of piranha, crocodiles... When I found out about it, I denounced him and in fact he was arrested. From then on the guide, who now is out of prison, has promised that if I return to Colombia, he will kill me.

Were the tribes with which you worked really cannibals?

Yes, they were cannibals and they devoured the killed enemy, often due to hunger. The only cannibals who undertook ritual cannibalism, for religious reasons, were the ones from Belize. The Amazonian cannibals practically devoured people raw. In Asia, by contrast, they cooked them with glowing hot stones, they stuffed them with banana leaves and then they ate them from the inside, never from the outside.

How were the conditions while you were shooting?

Leticia is an incredible place. It's in Colombia but it's a hundred metres away from Brazil, and the equivalent distance from Peru. The difference is in the Indios: the Brazilian ones are very intelligent, the Colombian ones stupid, and the Peruvian ones even worse. The Alcuma tribe, who are based only a hundred metres from the town, live as if they were thousands of kilometres away from civilisation. All the drugs in the world pass through Leticia, but we never had any problems with the traffickers.

all images this page: **Cannibal Holocaust**. Faye Daniels (Francesca Ciardi) was the only female member of the doomed documentary team led by Alan Yates (Gabriel Yorke). She is seen here disturbed by the sight of the impaled native woman *(above)* and terrified when, earlier during the expedition, she discovers a huge spider crawling on her shoulder *(centre)*. Despite being the only member of the team to show any sign of restraint or humanity at all, her fate at the hands of the vengeful Yamamomo is particularly protracted and brutal.

Is what is seen in the film true, about the peaceful tribes and the cannibal tribes?

Completely. The names of the tribes, and their peculiarities as shown in the film are all real. The incredible thing is that each tribe speaks its own language. The Ticuna do not understand the Anamaru, who live very near by, yet they do understand the language spoken by another group of Ticuna thousands of kilometres away. They are nomads who, from one stock, have moved around the whole of Amazonia.

How did you make the decision to use those unknown actors?

The youngsters were all found at the Actor's Studio in New York. I needed somebody with an Italian background, so I took on Luca Barbareschi who was studying there and spoke English perfectly. Francesca Ciardi was a girl from Rome, and she also spoke English perfectly. The film was shot in English. The very controversial role of the impaled native was actually played by our Colombian costume-maker.

How did you manage to contact Robert Kerman?

He had played a small part in **Concorde Affair '79**; he was a flight controller in the scenes shot at the airport in London. He was a good actor. I only recently found out that he was a porn actor, and I was very surprised because I saw him naked and he had a tiny thing... They probably only used his face in the porn films and the body of somebody else. It is strange because he wasn't even a bad actor. He was perfect for his role in **Cannibal Holocaust**, he represented an ordinary man, the university professor, the studious one, thrown into that incredible adventure.

What are your thoughts on this ever so controversial film?

The film has brought me good luck and bad luck. I adore it and I like the way it has been made. Even watching it today it is a masterpiece. It is a film that never gets boring. But it has given me lots of problems, proceedings, sequestrations, reportings, censorship, and persecutions. In Italy it was released to massive financial success but after a few days it was confiscated. It was re-released years later, but by then it no longer had the impact it had when it first came out.

The film did very well abroad.

It has made two hundred million dollars. In Tokyo alone it made seven million dollars, second only to **E.T. the Extra-Terrestrial**. I believe it has been the greatest ever Italian success abroad. It is possible that maybe the films of Bud Spencer and Terence Hill have made more money, but I am not sure.

It is interesting that in Italy the film was originally released in its entirety, but was cut in the version that was released theatrically after its confiscation, whereas on video the film is more or less complete.

Well, I have a French video cassette which I think is complete.

all illustrations this page: **Cannibal Holocaust**.
top: At home with the feared Yamamomo, also known as "The Tree People".
middle: Professor Monroe's guide Chaco (Salvatore Basile) discovers the partially-decomposed remains of Felipe, the Yates team's unlucky guide.
bottom: Retribution. The Yamamomo hack Jack Anders's decapitated torso to pieces.

There is a story that you can no longer visit Colombia. Is this true ?

No, it's not true.

*After working on **Cannibal Holocaust**, you made **La casa sperduta nel parco**.*

The film was shot in three weeks. It's a claustrophobic movie: everything takes place in one night inside a villa. We shot in New York and Rome. It's completely different to **Cannibal Holocaust**.

The principal actor was David Hess. What type of person is he?

David is a great actor but as a man he is not very pleasant. He is a blackmailer. I asked him to appear in the film which I shot recently with Bud Spencer (***Noi siamo angeli***), and the day that we were due to shoot he came to me to tell me that he wanted more money. I told him literally where to go. However, when we are filming he has a great presence, he is an excellent actor for just one particular type of role.

opposite page: All illustrations are from **La casa sperduta nel parco** (aka **House on the Edge of the Park**). *top left:* American video cover *top right:* Ricky (Giovanni Lombardo Radice) gets his way with Gloria (Lorraine De Selle). *centre:* Promotional artwork for the film's Spanish release features typical censorship of nipples, whilst deeming the razor-slashing of faces and breasts to be acceptable! *bottom left:* Alex (David Hess) beats up Howard (Gabriele Di Giulio).

this page, left: Lisa (Annie Belle) flirts with danger by provoking the violence-prone Alex (David Hess) in the kitchen at the **House on the Edge of the Park**. *below:* British video cover for **The Atlantis Interceptors**, aka **I predatore di Atlantide**. *bottom:* Roaming bike gang terrorises the inhabitants of small-town America in **The Atlantis Interceptors**.

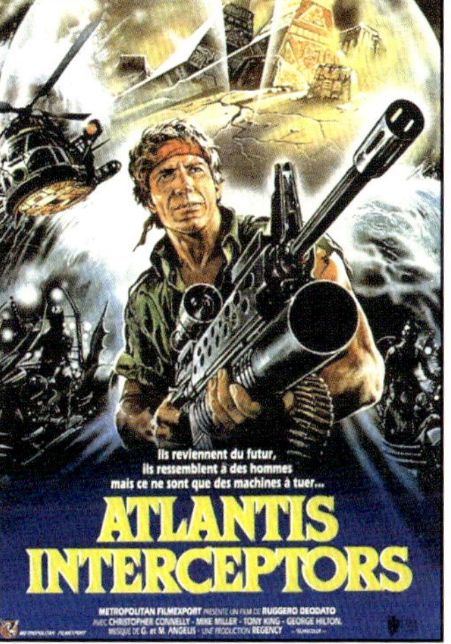

*Your next film was **I predatori di Atlantide**.*

I chose Christopher Connelly, who had done **Martin Eden** with Giacomo Battiato for television. It wasn't one of my most successful movies because there wasn't much money, however it was pleasant to make. I remember it with great fondness as I enjoyed making it so much. We filmed it in the Philippines; it was co-produced by the local government, and Imelda Marcos provided us with everything that we wanted.

above: Belgian poster for **Inferno in diretta** under both its French language title, **Amazonia, la jungle blanche**, and its English language title, **Cut and Run**.

One of your best action films is ***Inferno in diretta****. The film has an excellent cast: Richard Lynch, Leonard Mann, Gabriele Tinti, John Steiner, Karen Black, etc...*

That film, unfortunately bears the traces of a great deal of disagreement between myself and the producer Alessandro Fracassi – an excellent person who I like very much –

however, he and all the production team wanted to make a new **Cannibal Holocaust**, whereas I refused, so inevitably this conflict had repercussions on the film. It's a hybrid, but seeing it again now I can say that I made it very well and I like it better now than I used to. In the past I undervalued it, whereas now I consider it one of my better films. The best one for me is **Cannibal Holocaust**. It is impossible to equal that film, then **Inferno in diretta**, then **Ultimo mondo cannibale**, **Concorde Affair** and **The Barbarians**...

***Inferno in diretta** started life as a project by Wes Craven, originally called **Marimba**. At what stage did you become involved?*

all illustrations this page: **Inferno in diretta**. *top:* Italian fotobusta. *above:* Carnage during the film's violent opening sequence. *left:* Deodato on location.

Inferno in diretta:
Michael Berryman leaps into action *(right)*. Torture at Colonel Horne's base camp *(below)*. Italian video cover *(bottom left)*.

bottom right: Michael Berryman as he appears in **The Barbarians**.
opposite page, top: Deodato with some of the cast and crew of **The Barbarians**.
middle: **Camping del terrore** was retitled **BodyCount** in English-language territories.
bottom: Deodato outside a cinema in Madrid which was showing **Un delitto poco comune** (aka **Phantom of Death**) in 1988.

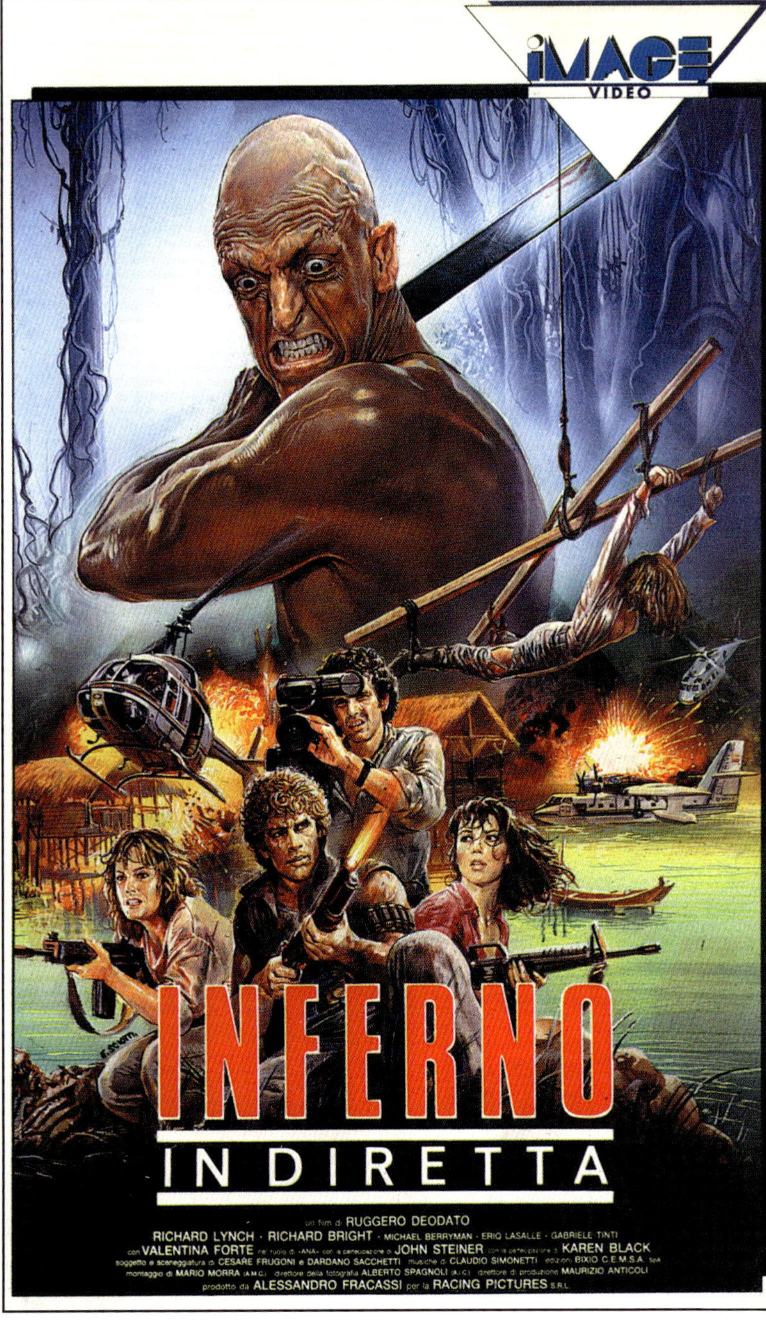

The film should have been shot by Wes Craven. The producer had contracted him to do it and the film was due to be shot in Colombia. Before production commenced there were some problems, and they called me in as Craven's replacement. I took the screenplay which Craven and a collaborator had produced, and which was at that stage called **Marimba**, and I changed it completely, working on it together with Cesare Frugoni and Dardano Sacchetti. We decided to shoot it in Venezuela. Wes Craven did not shoot any scenes in that film.

The cast features both Richard Lynch and Michael Berryman.

Berryman is a little lamb who would not hurt a fly. He was born prematurely so has that 'incomplete' aspect, he is very thin-skinned but he is a wonderful person. The only one with whom I did not get on was Leonard Mann. In the role played by Lisa

Blount I should have had Linda Fiorentino, but at that time Lisa had recently appeared in **An Officer and a Gentleman** with Richard Gere, and I chose her on the strength of that. The problem was that there were too many stars, one didn't want to do one thing, one was always drunk, and I (who neither drink nor smoke) had to battle against everybody.

The Barbarians *was shot on a low budget.*

Cannon had hired a director for the production, with whom they were having great problems. They called me in and I changed everything. The director who had started the shoot had planned it in a classical way. I decided instead to do a work of fantasy, something almost surreal. It turned out to be a film which was more ironic than dramatic.

The lead actors certainly haven't gone on to great things...

They were two big American brothers, completely mad and full of steroids.

Camping del terrore *was a move towards the American-style slasher movie.*

That type of film was forced on me by the producer, who wanted to do something for the foreign market. The setting is beautiful, we filmed it in Abruzzo. The scriptwriter Alessandro Capone makes me laugh; he tells people that he wrote that film. "But what do you take pride in it for?" I say to him, "there was no story in that film!" The best part is the music by Claudio Simonetti.

Even for this one, the cast was rich: Mimsy Farmer, David Hess, Charles Napier...

I took him *(Napier)* on because he had done **Rambo** and this made it possible for us to export the film.

Lone Runner?

We shot in Morocco intending to release the film in 70mm but it never was released in Italy. There was such a fragile story, invented on the spur of the moment, that I don't even remember what it was about.

Your next film is one of the most interesting that you made in the Eighties; ***Un delitto poco comune****.*

The story is very beautiful, written by Gianfranco Clerici and Vincenzo Mannino, but when [Edwige] Fenech enters onto the scene... the problem is not her as such, because she is good there's no doubt, but the audience is not used to seeing a film like that one which features Fenech in the cast. *(Although Fenech is well-known amongst horror and giallo fans for her work in these genres during the Seventies, at the time of* ***Un delitto poco comune*** *she was mostly familiar to contemporary Italian audiences for her comedy roles.)* I would have wanted to do a well-made film in every sense. There's the scene with the child on the swing which is really beautiful, there's this atmosphere... I had Pleasence who is an exceptional actor, then when Fenech arrives it's as if I had introduced Lino Banfi! She is good but she has nothing to do with that film.

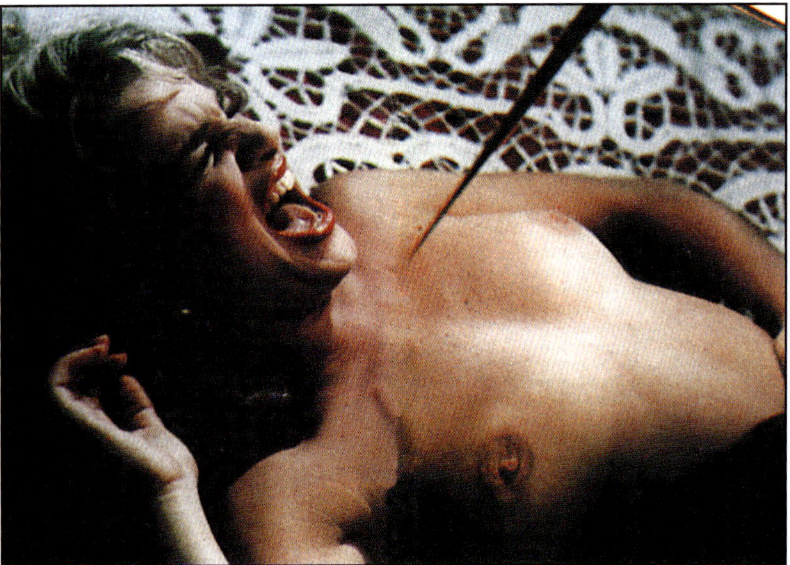

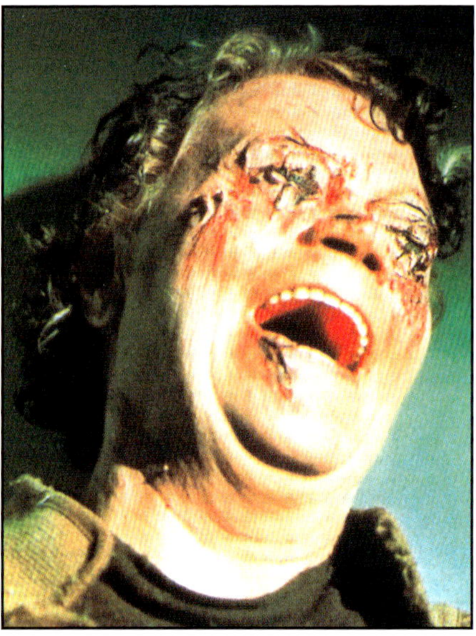

above: A violent scene from **Un delitto poco comune** (aka **Phantom of Death**).
top right: The mess that results after a pay-phone spits out coins as projectile weapons in **Minaccia d'amore** (aka **Dial: Help**).
below: Dutch DVD cover for **Dial: Help**.
bottom right: Deodato sets up a shot with Marisa Berenson whilst making **Ocean**.
opposite top: Deodato sets up a tracking shot on the epic **Ocean** shoot.
opposite right: Back to exploitation cinema with **The Washing Machine**.

Were you obliged to hire Fenech for that role?

Kelly LeBrock should have had her part. But I do not want to be misunderstood, Fenech is an excellent professional, it is simply that she was not right for that particular role. One must consider that the public often goes to see a film basically because there is a star who attracts them to it; it can be Fenech, [Alvaro] Vitali, [Lando] Buzzanca, Banfi...

You returned to horror in 1989 with ***Minaccia d'amore*** *(aka* ***Dial: Help****).*

It was given a theatrical release in Italy and it was bought by [Silvio] Berlusconi for Mediaset. It's a delicious film. It's a fantasy film and this is the reason that I like it. The story concerns a telephone which falls in love with a girl who is trying to make a call to her friend, and which kills all the people who hang around the girl. This is the type of fantasy film which I like. Zombie films don't interest me, a telephone which falls in love, yes. Hard horror is not my genre, I far prefer fantasy.

Another of the television productions you have directed is ***Oceano****.*

It's a splendid story, beautiful, that will unfortunately never be released. I wrote it with Alberto Vazquez Figueroa, and it has an awesome cast: Mario Adorf, Irene Papas, Ernest Borgnine, Martin Balsam, Senta Berger, Marisa Berenson... The film was bought by Fininvest. Every television company in Italy must have a wealth of programmes, films etc. which they must hold unused. Amongst this wealth is this series which, being set in the sixties, does not age. We shot it in Venezuela and in the island of Lanzarote in the Canaries. It's the story of a family of fishermen during the reign of Franco. The beautiful daughter gets raped by the son of the boss of the island, the brother of the girl takes revenge and kills him, and to escape the wrath of the boss he

has to escape to Venezuela, retracing the route taken by Columbus. It tells of all the adventures during the crossing of the ocean and of his arrival in Venezuela. It's a beautiful film.

*After working on **Oceano** you stayed in television with **I ragazzi del muretto**, which was very successful. Did you expect such an outcome?*

I made it with mad love. I camc to it aftei the first series, which was good for nothing. I made a much richer, more beautiful series of programmes. The critics have taken it to the stars. Even the third series, which I didn't make, reached that level.

After that series?

I made a very beautiful film called **Mamma ci penso io**, shot in Venezuela, which won the second prize at the 1991 Berlin festival, in the films for children section. It also went to the Giffoni Film Festival. It's a delightful film which was developed from an old project of mine and re-adapted as a comedy.

*Next you made **The Washing Machine**, your most recent horror film.*

The film was developed from a theatrical piece and was shot in Budapest. I wasn't very happy with **The Washing Machine** because I was never convinced that the casting was correct, and the film was made too quickly.

right: Deodato in Madagascar "working on ideas for a new film"...
below: During the making of the children's film **Mamma ci penso io**, which was adapted from a more hard-edged script entitled **Los gamines**.

below from the top:
Bud Spencer *(left)* and Philip Michael Thomas (*right*) in **Noi siamo angeli** ; Deodato in India with Michela Rocco ; Deodato with Michela Rocco during a break in the filming of **Sotto il cielo dell'Africa**.

*After **The Washing Machine** you made a film in South America with Bud Spencer.*

It's a television series which I made for transmission on RaiUno, it's called **Noi siamo angeli**, and it stars Philip Michael Thomas, Bud Spencer, Erik Estrada. Very nice. It's the story of two escaped prisoners who dress up as friars and end up in a mission. The little friars help solve a whole series of situations and adventures. The screenplay was written by [Sandro] Moretti in collaboration with Capone and two others.

You have often worked with Rai.

Yes, they call on me despite the fact that I do not have great political merits in their eyes. But it's not specifically RAI, it's the producers. I have never been out of work thanks to the support of television.

*Tell me about the latest television production which you shot in Zimbabwe: **Sotto il cielo dell'Africa**.*

It consists of twelve self-contained episodes of about ninety minutes each, interlinked by the story of a doctor who travels to Zimbabwe in Africa, to manage a hospital. The protagonist is Carol Alt, while the chief nurse, who is also her best friend, is played by Michela Rocco. In each episode there is a different guest star: Tomas Arana, Bert Young, Daniela Poggi, Marco Leonardi and others.

What are these episodes about?

They are stories of adventure and of love, but there is also one which is a thriller in which a patient in the hospital, who is terminally ill, hires someone to kill her. Later on however she changes her mind, but by now it is too late and the man is already hot on her heels. There is a fabulous epilogue inside the hospital in which he takes some people as hostages.

Ruggero Deodato was interviewed by Gian Luca Castoldi. The text was translated from Italian by Deborah Bacci.

la F.D. CINEMATOGRAFICA presenta

DAVID A. HESS · ANNIE BELLE in

LA CASA SPERDUTA NEL PARCO

con CHRISTIAN BORROMEO
e con la partecipazione di LORRAINE DE SELLE
musica composta e diretta da RIZ ORTOLANI
regia di RUGGERO DEODATO
colore LV LUCIANO VITTORI
distribuzione ADIGE FILM 76

STAMPA FOTOCROM - ROMA

L' OCEANO SI SQUARCIÒ E TUONARONO...
I PREDATORI DI ATLANTIDE

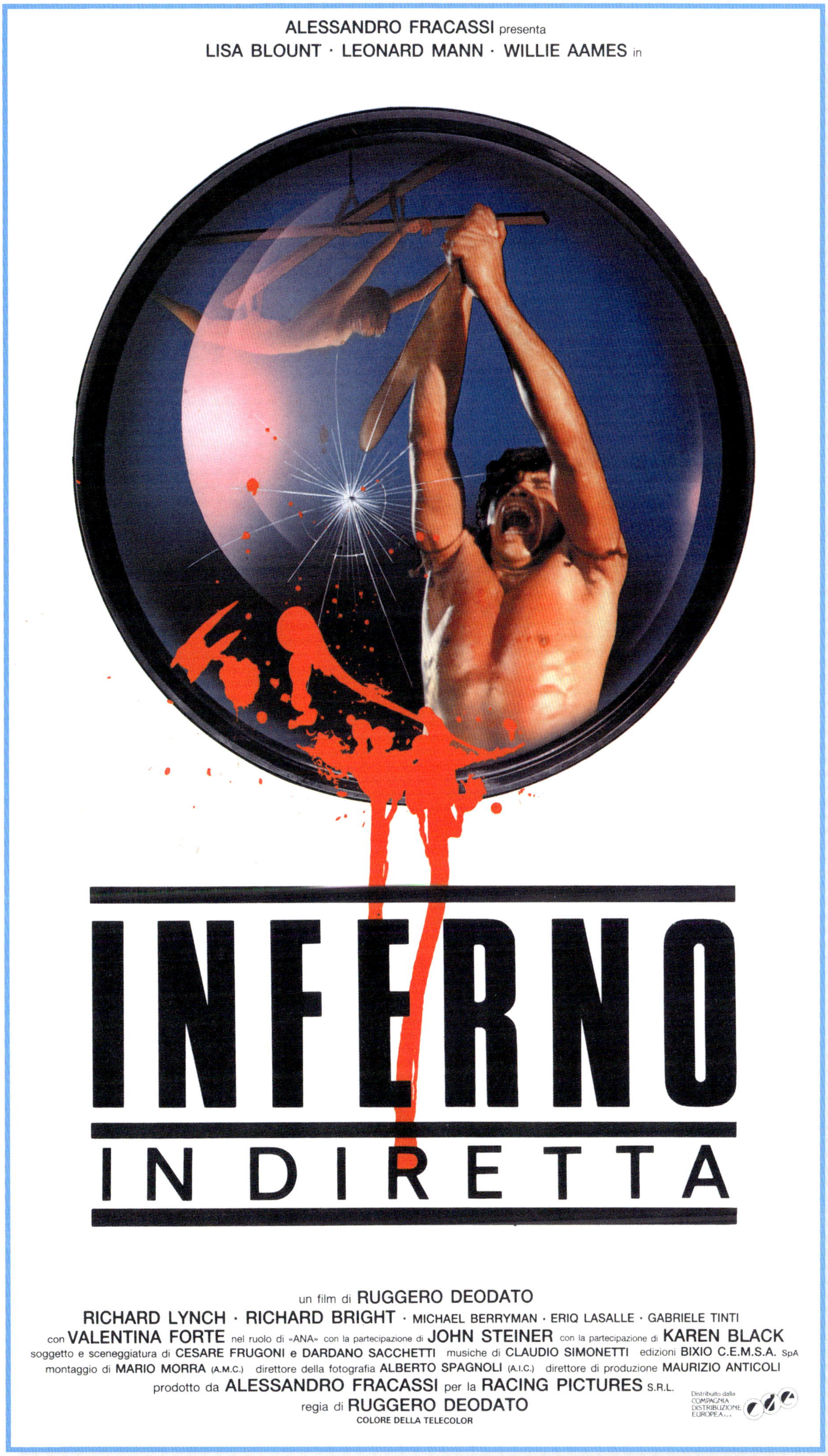

ALESSANDRO FRACASSI presenta

LISA BLOUNT · LEONARD MANN · WILLIE AAMES in

INFERNO
IN DIRETTA

un film di RUGGERO DEODATO

RICHARD LYNCH · RICHARD BRIGHT · MICHAEL BERRYMAN · ERIQ LASALLE · GABRIELE TINTI

con VALENTINA FORTE nel ruolo di «ANA» con la partecipazione di JOHN STEINER con la partecipazione di KAREN BLACK

soggetto e sceneggiatura di CESARE FRUGONI e DARDANO SACCHETTI musiche di CLAUDIO SIMONETTI edizioni BIXIO C.E.M.S.A. SpA

montaggio di MARIO MORRA (A.M.C.) direttore della fotografia ALBERTO SPAGNOLI (A.I.C.) direttore di produzione MAURIZIO ANTICOLI

prodotto da ALESSANDRO FRACASSI per la RACING PICTURES S.R.L.

regia di RUGGERO DEODATO

COLORE DELLA TELECOLOR

Distribuito dalla COMPAGNIA DISTRIBUZIONE EUROPEA s.p.a.

PIETRO INNOCENZI - TANDEM CINEMATOGRÁFICA s.r.l. - D.M.V. DISTRIBUZIONE s.r.l. E RETEITALIA s.p.A. presentano

MICHAEL YORK EDWIGE FENECH
DONALD PLEASENCE

UN DELITTO
POCO COMUNE

UNA PRODUZIONE GLOBE FILMS s.r.l. · TANDEM CINEMATOGRAFICA s.r.l.
D.M.V. DISTRIBUZIONE s.r.l. · REALIZZATA DA PIETRO INNOCENZI

MUSICA DI PINO DONAGGIO DIRETTORE DELLA FOTOGRAFIA GIORGIO DI BATTISTA
EDIZIONI MUSICALI GIPSY MONTATORE DANIELE ALABISO
DOLBY STEREO® IN SELECTED THEATRES COLORE "LV" LUCIANO VITTORI S.p.A.

UN FILM DI
RUGGERO DEODATO

Distribuzione
DMV srl

NESSUNO TORNA VIVO DAL
CAMPING
DEL TERRORE
ALESSANDRO FRACASSI PRESENTA
BRUCE PENHALL · MIMSY FARMER · DAVID HESS
IN "CAMPING DEL TERRORE"
UN FILM DI RUGGERO DEODATO
LUISA MANERI · ANDREW LEDERER · NICOLA FARRON
STEFANO MADIA · JOHN STEINER
NANCY BRILLI · CYNTHIA THOMPSON · VALENTINA FORTE
IVAN RASSIMOV · ELENA POMPEI
E CON CHARLES NAPIER NEL RUOLO DELLO SCERIFFO
CREATURE IDEATE E REALIZZATE DA FRANCESCO E GAETANO PAOLOCCI
PRODOTTO DA ALESSANDRO FRACASSI PER LA RACING PICTURES S.r.l.
REGIA DI RUGGERO DEODATO
Titanus
DISTRIBUZIONE

CHARLOTTE LEWIS

MINACCIA D'AMORE

UN FILM DI RUGGERO DEODATO

con MARCELLO MODUGNO - MATTIA SBRAGIA
CAROLA STAGNARO - VICTOR CAVALLO con CARLO MONNI
e con WILLIAM BERGER

prodotto da METROFILM S.R.L. SAN FRANCISCO S.R.L. in collaborazione con RETEITALIA S.P.A.
musiche di CLAUDIO SIMONETTI regia di RUGGERO DEODATO
colore della TELECOLOR S.P.A.

DISTRIBUZIONE europa cine tv

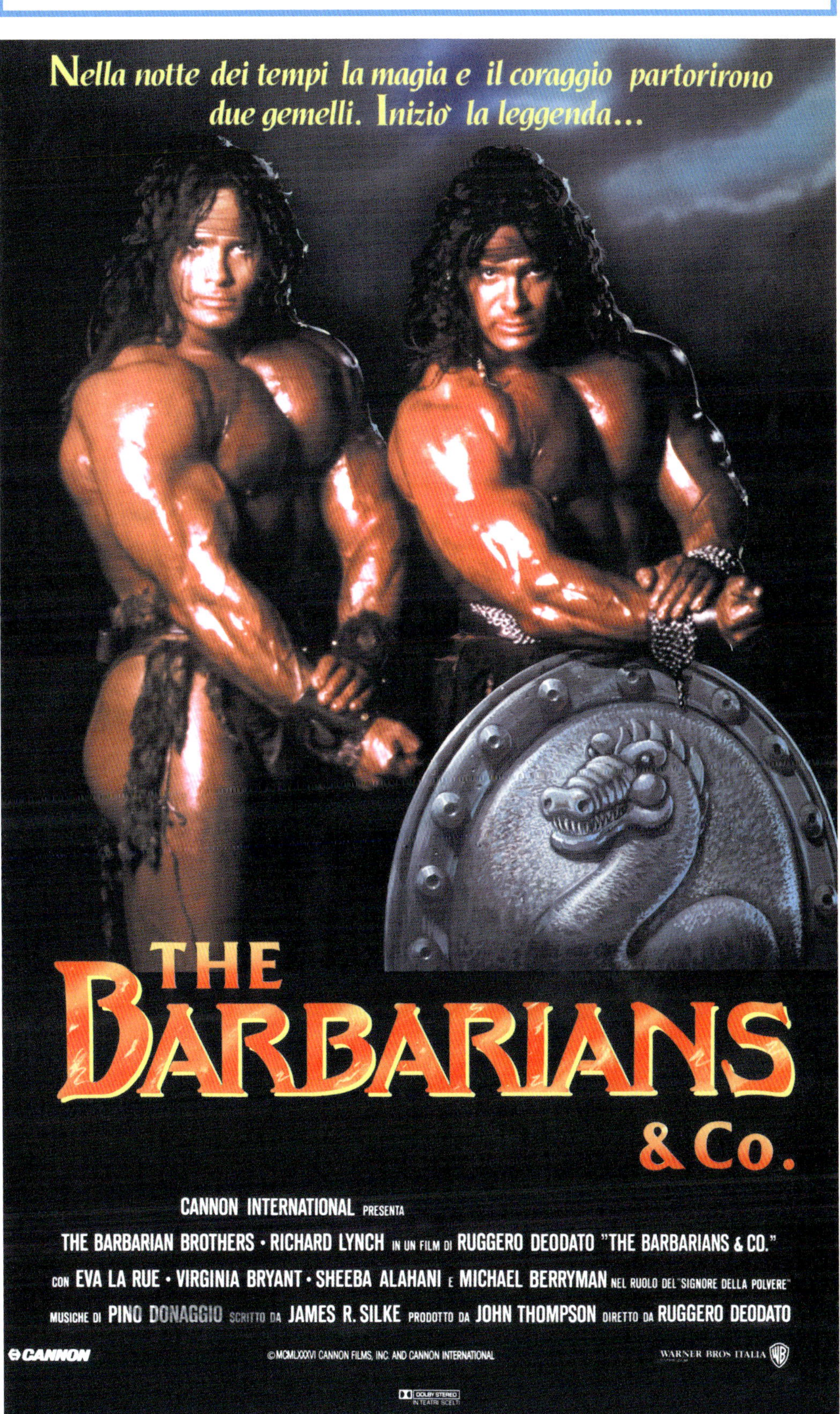
Nella notte dei tempi la magia e il coraggio partorirono
due gemelli. Iniziò la leggenda...
THE
BARBARIANS
& Co.
CANNON INTERNATIONAL PRESENTA
THE BARBARIAN BROTHERS · RICHARD LYNCH IN UN FILM DI RUGGERO DEODATO "THE BARBARIANS & CO."
CON EVA LA RUE · VIRGINIA BRYANT · SHEEBA ALAHANI E MICHAEL BERRYMAN NEL RUOLO DEL "SIGNORE DELLA POLVERE"
MUSICHE DI PINO DONAGGIO SCRITTO DA JAMES R. SILKE PRODOTTO DA JOHN THOMPSON DIRETTO DA RUGGERO DEODATO
CANNON
©MCMLXXXVI CANNON FILMS, INC. AND CANNON INTERNATIONAL
WARNER BROS ITALIA
DOLBY STEREO
IN TEATRI SCELTI

locandina gallery

FILMOGRAPHY as director

HERCULES PRISONER OF EVIL

1964
Italian theatrical title: **Ursus il terrore dei Kirghisi**
US theatrical title: **Hercules, Prisoner of Evil**
French theatrical title: **La terreur des Kirghiz**
Italy
director: Anthony Dawson [Antonio Margheriti]
actual director [uncredited as such]: Ruggero Deodato

produced [uncredited] by Ettore Manni for Adelphia Compagnia Cinematografica/S.A.C. – Società Ambrosiana Cinematografica.
registration number: 3.276. visa number: 43366 (14/7/64). Italian takings: L114,761,000
colour by Eastmancolor. in Totalscope

cast: Reg Park (Ursus). Ettore Manni (Ido). Mireille Granelli (Aniko). Furio Meniconi (Zereteli). Maria Teresa Orsini (Katia). Lilly Mantovani (slave). Serafino 'Nino' Fuscagni (Mico). Ugo Carboni. Giulio Maculani (Varos). Piero Pastore (Amko). Claudio Scarchilli (Lava). Gaetano Quartararo (Kirghiso Officer).

NOTE: Character names are sometimes changed when a film is dubbed into English. In this case Ursus became the better known Hercules and Zereteli became Zara.

story by Marcello Sartarelli. director of photography: Gabor Pogany. music: Franco Trinacria [Franco Mannino]. editor: Otello Colangeli. art director & set dresser: Dick [Riccardo] Domenici. production supervisor: Natalino Vicario. production manager: Luciano Cattania. 1st assistant director: Ruggero Deodato. 2nd assistant director: Nino Fruscella. continuity: Eva Koltay. cameramen: Claudio Ragona & Mario Capriotti. make-up: Maurizio Giustini. hairdresser: Jolanda Conti. assistant editor: Maria Napoleone. sound technicians: Giulio Tagliacozzo & Mario Morigi. English language version by Robert Spafford. weapons: Rancati. costume house: Antonelli. wigs: Maggi.

Italian theatrical distributor: Titanus Distribuzione (1st public showing on 31 July 1964). running time: 90 minutes. length: 2,750 metres.
French theatrical distributor: S.N.A. (released on 21 April 1965). running time: 100 minutes.

This film's scenario unfolds against the backdrop of guerrilla warfare between the 'Circassi', led by Ursus (Reg Park), and the 'Kirghisi' of the reigning prince Zereteli (Furio Meniconi). The conflict has continued for many years, following the death of the old Khan.

These turbulent lands are tormented by the bloody raids of a monstrous being called The Vulture, who assaults peaceful caravans of passers-by, spreading panic and death. The scheming daughter of the murdered Khan, Aniko (Mireille Granelli), is making her claim to the throne. The death of Ursus would serve this purpose, so she sends a hired assassin to kill the hero, but Ursus escapes the attack.

The arrival of the shrewd Ido (Ettore Manni), brother of Ursus, provokes a battle between the two communities. One night when Ursus is absent because he has kept an appointment with Aniko, Ido is resting in Ursus's tent, when he is attacked by The Vulture, only just managing to save himself. Later, Aniko tells Ido of her relationship with Ursus and about their future marriage, which will be a prelude to their crowning at Sura, the capital of the Kingdom.

During a bout of hunting Ursus is attacked and wounded by The Vulture. Meanwhile the Kirghisi, taking advantage of the fact that all the town's warriors are away, attack Meliva (the Circassi village) killing the remaining inhabitants. The Vulture is accused of this massacre, while Zereteli and his men drag Ido to Sura, and imprison Aniko in a cave where the monster dwells. While he is in prison, Ido discovers everything about Zereteli's schemes and, after escaping, he warns the Circassi, who attack Sura to avenge the massacre of Meliva. After having captured Zereteli, they force a confession from him in which he reveals that Aniko is not the heir to the throne, a right which is due to the real daughter of the Khan, Katia (Maria Teresa Orsini), now Ursus's servant, who had lost her memory after the death of her father. It turns out that Aniko is a cruel witch who controls a potion which causes her victims to transform into the monster; The Vulture was in fact Ursus, or whomever drunk the potion. The perfidious woman thus spreads panic in the region, destabilising the power of Zereteli and provoking the clash between the Circassi and the Kirghisi. Exposed by the astute Ido, Aniko takes her own life, throwing herself into the void.

Deodato's debut as director happened in unexpected circumstances. For this film he collaborated with Antonio Margheriti. The respected director's numerous commitments meant that he had to limit his presence on the set. Responsibility for day-to-day shooting therefore passed over to Ruggero. During the day he shot the scenes and in the evening he watched the rushes together with Antonio, who also occupied himself with working on the special effects. (The most striking moment in a film which is particularly sparing of tricks is a fire which appears in the foreground while we witness a flood in the background. Unfortunately the two images blend very badly, and the make-up is not convincing.) These are the final scenes which were filmed by Margheriti, who for contractual reasons signed the film whereas Deodato is credited as the first assistant director.

The film is pleasing despite not being a masterpiece. The many ethnic influences place it geographically in the region of Russia at the border between Europe and Asia – notable instances of local colour include Cossack dances and the parties at the palace of the Khan. Reg Park, with the physique of a modern body-builder is an Ursus who does not have the charisma of Ettore Manni, far more effective as Ido, the brother of Ursus. The suggestion of class-based élitism on the part of Ursus – who does not so much as look at Katia, until he realises that she does not belong to the 'common people' of his community – is a fairly standard trait to find in a 'peplum' movie.

Following his work on **Hercules Prisoner of Evil** it was almost four years before Deodato would claim the full directing credit for a film.
(Gian Luca Castoldi)

Films are presented in the order in which they were released.

They are listed under their most commonly-used English language titles, except for those films which have never been released in an English language variant, in which case the film is listed under its most commonly-used Italian language title. Alternative titles, including foreign language variants, production and publicity titles (where different to the final release title) and video release titles, are also listed.

The distribution company which handled the original Italian theatrical release is listed along with the date of the first public theatrical exhibition, if known.

Running times indicated refer to the original theatrical release print, unless otherwise noted. Theatrical prints are assumed to be projected at the rate of 24 frames per second.

Technical production credits are in all cases as complete as possible, as are the cast listings. We have endeavoured to indicate the appropriate character names in the cast listings wherever such identification is possible.

Deodato has made uncredited appearances in a large number of his own films. All confirmed cameo roles have been included as the last entry of the relevant cast listings.

above: Rampant nudity in a scene from **Phenomenal and the Treasure of Tutankamen**.

PHENOMENAL AND THE TREASURE OF TUTANKAMEN

1968

Italian theatrical title: **Fenomenal e il tesoro di Tutankamen**, US video title: **Phenomenal and the Treasure of Tutankamen**, French video title: **Phenomenal et le tresor de Toutankhamon**

Italy

director: Roger Rockfeller [Ruggero Deodato]

produced by Nicola Mauro Parenti for I.C.A.R. – Italiana Cinematografica Artisti Riuniti. © I.C.A.R. s.r.l. registration number: 4.389. visa number: 50924 (20/2/68). Italian takings: L34,000,000 colour by Eastmancolor. laboratory: Telecolor. filmed on location in Paris (France) & Tunisia with interiors filmed at Dear Studios (Rome)

cast: Nicola Mauro Parenti (Count Guy Norton, 'Phenomenal'). Lucretia Love (Mike Shevlove). Gordon Mitchell (Gregory Falkoff). John Karlsen (Professor Micklewitz). Carla Romanelli (Anna Giomet). Cyrus Elias (Julien). Charles Miller (Gresaunee). Mario Cecchi (Dorian). Agostino De Simone (Lord Baxter). Teresa Petrangeli. Spartaco Battisti. Bernardo Bruno. Mario De Rosa. Pieraldo Ferrante (Inspector Beauvais). Enrico Marciani (Georges). Sergio Mariotti. Maurizio Merli (Pino). Enrico Pagano. Gianni Pulone (journalist). Giuseppe Terranova (Alfred).

screenplay: Ruggero Deodato & Aldo Iginio Capone; from an idea by Aldo Iginio Capone. director of photography: Roberto Reale. music: Bruno Nicolai; published by Nazionalmusic (Milan). editor: Luciano Cavalieri. art director & costume designer: Giacomo Albano. assistant art director: Pino Aldovrandi. production manager: Armando Novelli. unit manager: Claudio Sinibaldi. assistant director: Paolo Poeti. continuity: Marina Chierici. cameraman: Luigi Catalini. production secretary: Attilio Viti. special effects: Dino Galliano. make up: Amedeo Alessi. Miss Lucretia Love's hairstyles by Tony Varani. Miss Lucretia Love's wardrobe by Albano (Rome). Nicola Mauro Parenti's wardrobe by Nino Peter Master. seamstress: Wanda Caprioli. still photographer: Mauro Paravano. assistant editor: Anna Bolli. costumes: Tigano & Lo Faro. set dressing: Set – Cinears – Alfredo D'Angelo. sound: Goffredo Salvatori. sound effects: Marinelli. Italian version: Renato Caldonazzo. synchronization by C.D.S. recording: C.D.C. Westrex Recording System.

right: Lucretia Love plays an insurance investigator called in to help solve the mystery surrounding the theft of the Mask of Tutankamen and its apparent return by the mysterious gentleman thief 'Phenomenal'. *below:* The man himself.

Italian theatrical distributor: ICAR – Italiana Cinematografica Artisti Riuniti (1st public showing on 4 March 1968). running time: 95 minutes. length: 2,644 metres.

Although Deodato has spoken in interviews of having shot footage of both President De Gaulle (in a cavalcade) and Rex Harrison (as a passer-by on the Champs Elysées), it is unlikely either is visible in release prints.

The mask of Tutankamen is stolen from the Louvre museum. The perpetrator of the crime is Falkoff, head of a criminal gang specialising in sensational thefts. A mysterious man, disguised with a black stocking, successfully retrieves the mask and returns it to the director of the museum, Auguste Dorian. The name of the perpetrator of the crime swiftly passes from mouth to mouth: it is Phenomenal, the gentleman thief who, animated by a great sense of justice, intervenes to resolve the abuse of power. However, in reality the mask handed over to the museum is a forgery, and the true identity of Phenomenal is that of the director of the museum. Insurance investigator Mike Shevlove is called in, and eventually succeeds in solving the case, but without finding out who the mysterious Phenomenal is.

Phenomenal and the Treasure of Tutankamen is the first feature film that Deodato signed as a director and, taking into account his previous work, disappointed many who were waiting to see him prove himself in this role. Deodato approached the world of dark comic art, drawing forth a superhero who is almost a parody; dressed with a black stocking without even holes for eyes! Another point of reference is the James Bond (007) series, partly for the abundance of technological gadgets and partly for the exotic settings (the film begins in Paris then moves to Tunisia).

Unfortunately Deodato chose to portray the events from an ironic and almost distanced viewpoint, a strategy which is not taken to its conclusion. The film is occasionally rather boring and in general extremely muddled. What's more, it completely lacks any degree of morbidity or pulpiness; essential components for this genre.

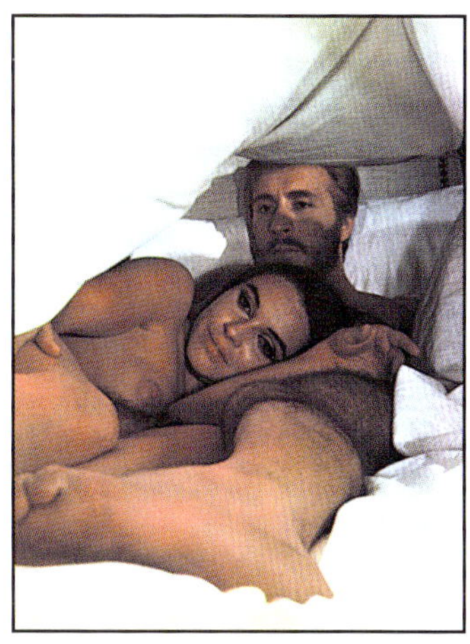

left: Japanese video cover for **Phenomenal and the Treasure of Tutankamen**.
above: Who is the mysterious masked man? Could it be...
below: Phenomenal at work.

this page: All stills are from **Phenomenal and the Treasure of Tutankamen**.

The film was inspired by adult-oriented comics and the action is presented in a context which, though possibly not intentionally, reminds one of the **Pink Panther** movies.

Phenomenal... was a colossal flop and it made very little money, recovering only part of its investment in the international market.

If he had not provided most of the capital for the film, it is doubtful whether Parenti would have landed the title role. Interestingly the cast of **Phenomenal...** also featured Lucretia Love, who enjoyed a degree of importance in the world of Italian genre cinema (**Blindman**, **The Killer Reserved Nine Seats**, **The Arena** etc.); she had been Parenti's official fiancée for many years... ***(Gian Luca Castoldi)***

GUNGALA, LA PANTERA NUDA

1968
Italian theatrical title: **Gungala, la pantera nuda**
French theatrical title: **Gungala, la panthère nue**
(translation: **Gungala, the Naked Pantheress**)
Italy
director: Roger Rockfeller [Ruggero Deodato]

produced [uncredited] by Franco Marras for Summa Cinematografica.
registration number: 4.213. visa number: 51696 (29/5/68). takings: L301,000,000
colour by Telecolor (Rome). negative: Kodakolor
filmed on location in Kenya with interiors at De Paolis studios (Rome)

cast: Kitty Swan [Kersten Svanhold] (Gungala). Micaela Cendali Pignatelli (Julie). Angelo Infanti (Morton). Tiffany Anderson (black servant) <with the participation of> Jeff Tangen <as> (Chandler). Alberto Terrani (the Arab) <also appearing> Giancarlo Sisti. M. Piero Buzzi. Luigi Scavrani. Luigi Bracale. Consalvo Dell'Arti (Sir Frederick). Fernando Piazza.

story & screenplay: Romano Ferrara. dialogue: Guido Leoni. director of photography: Claudio Raguna. incidental music: Sandro Brugnolini & Luigi Malatesta. music publisher: Bixio-Sam (Milan). editor: Adriana Novelli. art director & costume designer: Oscar Capponi. 1st assistant director: Salvatore Basile. 2nd assistant director: Oddo Bracci. continuity: Patrizia Zulini. cameraman: Giovanni Ciarlo. production manager: Luciano Cattania. 1st unit manager: Alessandro Gori. 2nd unit manager: Nino La Grassa. production secretary: Felice Santosuosso. assistant cameraman: Giuliano Grasselli. set decorator: Massimo Galloppi. stunt co-ordinator: Giulio Maculani. make-up: Cesare Cambi. 2nd make-up: Alfio Meniconi. hair stylist: Marcella De Marzi. assistant editors: Carla Zamponi & Marisa Letti. sound: Enzo Silvestri. boom operator: Giulio Viggiani. dubbing by S.A.S. (Rome). sound recording: Fono Roma. properties: Rancati. plants & flowers: Ceccotti. the song "Gungala" sung by Pat Starke; available on Cinevox-Record Milano S p A.

Italian theatrical distributor: Medusa Distribuzione (1st public showing on 31 May 1968). running time: 88 minutes. length: 2,417 metres.
French theatrical distributor: S.N.A.

Gungala, la pantera nuda begins with some documentary-style imagery accompanied by a spoken commentary in the spirit of a 'mondo' movie.

An insurance company, alerted by a rich English family, organises an expedition to find the heir to an industrial empire who was given up for lost in Africa (following an aeroplane disaster in which her parents were killed). The Europeans find Gungala and one of the explorers falls in love with her.

Gungala... is a feminine version of a Tarzan film, with all the familiar trappings, such as black extras who speak endlessly with a typical slave's accent... Gungala, ridiculously nicknamed *"the daughter of the bird of fire"*, encompasses all the stereotypes of the Tarzan theme: she speaks with the animals, has a great sense of justice, punishes the abusers of power and is in effect the sheriff of the jungle.

The initial scenes – with Gungala running naked in the jungle or swimming in the sea – are very effective. Very soon however we are assailed by white Europeans painted in black to represent the native people, exteriors clearly reconstructed in the studio, and Arabs who want to create a "Big Africa" and who are "fanatics by nature".

This is a sequel to **Gungala la vergine della giungla**, directed by Romano Ferrara in the same year. Both films star the beautiful Kitty Swan, short-lived genre film star, who ostentatiously shows off her hairy armpits. Deodato's

GUÌNGALA
LA PANTERA NUDA

LITTLE TONY
VACANZE SULLA COSTA SMERALDA
547 AXE
SILVIA DIONISIO - FERRUCCIO AMENDOLA
FRANCESCO MULE'
ALDO PUGLISI - LUCIO FLAUTO
DANA GHIA - TAMARA BARONI
E FEMI BENUSSI E CON TONI UCCI
REGIA: RUGGERO DEODATO
MUSICHE: WILLY BREZZA
DISTRIBUZIONE: FIDA CINEMATOGRAFICA
UN FILM PRODOTTO DA EDMONDO AMATI PER LA FIDA CINEMATOGRAFICA
SUPERPANORAMIC
EASTMANCOLOR
PRIMA EDIZIONE ITALIANA ANNO MCMLXVIII

film had more success than its predecessor. The director was initially supposed to have been Ferrara again, but the production team, unhappy with what had been shot, called in Deodato and entrusted him with the film. It was then decided to temporarily transfer to Africa for two weeks, where scenes were added and the roles of the two male protagonists were exchanged; the "baddie" became Jeff Tangen who left the role of the hero to Angelo Infanti.
(Gian Luca Castoldi)

MAN ONLY CRIES FOR LOVE

1968
Italian theatrical title: **Donne... botte e bersaglieri**, export title: **Man Only Cries for Love**, Italian pre-release title: **Un uomo piange solo per amore**, (translation: **Women... Bottles & Sharpshooters**)
Italy
director: Ruggero Deodato

produced by Edmondo Amati for Fida Cinematografica. visa number: 51857 (25/6/68). Italian takings: L207,000,000
colour by Eastmancolor
filmed on location in Sardinia

cast: Little Tony (Tony). Ferruccio Amendola (Fabrizio). Ira Hagen (Marina). Marisa Merlini (Mrs Jole). Renzo Montagnani (Luigi). Fiorenzo Fiorentini (porter). Ugo Fangareggi (Ottavio). Pinuccio Ardia (Alfredo, a soldier). Carla Romanelli (Carla). Janet Agren (Rika). Mirella Panfili [Mirella Panphili] (Bruna). Ettore Geri (Teodoro). Alberto Sorrentino (hairdresser's assistant). Barbara Nelli (Silvana). Enrico Montesano (Pecorelli). Franco Giacobini (marshal). Carlo Pisacane (old solider). Beatrice Bensi [Fiammetta Baralla] (Angela). Cesare Gelli (Ambrogio). Luigi Leoni (the director). Enrico Marciani. Luigi Minopoli. Ivan Scratuglia <and with> Bobby Solo (himself).

story & screenplay: Mario Amendola & Bruno Corbucci. director of photography: Riccardo Pallottini. music: Willy Brezza. editor: Vincenzo Tomassi. art director: Giorgio Giovannini. production manager: Tommaso Sagone. assistant director: Giuseppe Pollini. unit manager: Mario Caporali. production secretary: Marcello Buonomore. continuity: Renato Rizzuto. cameramen: Sergio Martinelli & Remo Grisanti. assistant cameraman: Carlo Tafani. sound: Fiorenzo Magli. hairdresser: Lucia La Porta. assistant editor: Rita Antonelli.
songs "With Those Eyes of an Angel" by D. Powell & A. Ciacci, "I Wanna Leave" by J.D. Loudermilk; "I Love Mary" by J.T. Kongas; "Un uomo piange solo per amore", "Gimme Little Sing", "I'm Coming Home", "Mille come me", "Tante prossime volte" & "Col cuore in gola" by anonymous, "A Whiter Shade of Pale" by Keith Reid & Gary Brooker – all songs performed by Little Tony.

Italian theatrical distributor: Fida Cinematografica (1st public showing on 27 July 1968). running time: 98 minutes. length: 2,865 metres.

Man Only Cries for Love is a late example of that typically Italian genre known as "Cantarello". This is the Latin equivalent of the "Beach Movie" popularised by Frankie Avalon and Annette Funicello, which were in fashion between the end of the Fifties and the first half of the Sixties. In Italy, the films of this genre revolved around a famous singer of the period, often accompanied by some of his colleagues. Here the protagonist is the famous Little Tony (a winner of the San Remo song contest) who, reluctantly carrying out his military service, tries to gain the right to a leave of absence, performing with his band during a party organised in the barracks. The concert ends in a fight, with all the guys competing for permission to leave.

In addition to Little Tony, the film features some other excellent character actors who went on to become important figures in Italian cinema in the coming years; from the brilliant comic Enrico Montesano to that great professional of low-brow comedy, Renzo Montagnani. It is also worth pointing out one of the first notable roles for Janet Agren (later to appear in **City of the Living Dead, Panic, Eaten Alive!** etc.). **Man Only Cries for Love** is the first of the two musicals which Deodato made with producer Edmondo Amati. It was remarkably successful. Deodato brought some visual flourishes to the film, which is at times reminiscent of Richard Lester's Beatles films **A Hard Day's Night** and **Help!** The movie's star, Little Tony (famous at the time as an Elvis Presley clone), demonstrates his talents by performing a cover version of the Procol Harum standard *A Whiter Shade of Pale*.
(Gian Luca Castoldi)

VACANZE SULLA COSTA SMERALDA

1968
Italian theatrical title: **Vacanze sulla Costa Smeralda**, (translation: **Holidays on the Costa Smeralda**)
Italy
director: Ruggero Deodato

produced by Edmondo Amati for Fida Cinematografica. registration number: 4.384. visa number: 52813 (28/11/68). Italian takings: L176,800,000
colour by Eastmancolor. negative: Kodak.
filmed on location on the Costa Smeralda (Italy)

cast: Little Tony (Tony Martin). Silvia Dionisio (Gianna, Grassu's daughter). Ferruccio Amendola (Nando Nardini). Francesco Mulè (Antonio Grassu). Aldo Puglisi (Tiberio, Gianna's fiancé). Lucio Flauto (Pippo Sabaudo). Tamara Baroni (Barbara). Dana Ghia (Pippo's wife). Carole Lebel (Grassu's secretary). Giacomo Furia (the accountant). Giuseppe Terranova (Eolo). Alberto Sorrentino (a waiter). Mirella Panphili. Angelo Pagano <and with> Femi Benussi (Marisa). Toni Ucci (Schiavone)

story & screenplay: Bruno Corbucci & Mario Amendola. director of photography: Riccardo Pallottini. music: Willy Brezza; music published by Prima. editor: Vincenzo Tomassi. art director & set dresser: Giorgio Postiglione. costume designer Giovanna Deodato. assistant set dresser: Vittorio Troiani. production manager: Maurizio Amati. assistant director: Renato Rizzuto. unit manager: Salvatore Scarfone. production secretary: Armando Pierini. continuity: Paolo Poeti. cameraman: Sergio Martinelli. assistant cameraman: Gianni Bonivento. special effects: Ascani. make-up: Franco Di Girolamo. assistant make-up: Maria Grazia Nardi. hairdresser: Anna Cristofani. still photography: Lucio D'Aloisiopro. assistant editor: Rita Antonelli. sound: Fiorenzo Magli. boom operator: Edwyn Forest. synchronization: Elettronica Calpini. dubbing: S.A.S.
songs "Era un giorno qualunque", "Prega, prega", "Cuore matto", "Gentle on My Mind" & "In 30 secondi" all performed by Little Tony.

Italian theatrical distributor: Fida Cinematografica (1st public showing on 6 December 1968). running time: 90 minutes. length: 2,651 metres.

In Costa Smeralda, Sardinia, two hotel owners are in fierce competition. One of the two decides to commit suicide and throws himself into the sea. As he reaches the bottom he finds some treasure, and his life is turned upside down.

Deodato's second film with Amati is clearly inferior to the first one, perhaps due to the fact that during shooting the screenplay was re-written because it was thought inadequate, and also because the setting in Sardinia was chosen mainly for funding reasons. Deodato met his future wife on the set – the cult actress Silvia Dionisio, here making her film debut.
(Gian Luca Castoldi)

above, below and opposite:
A selection of artwork for films directed by Ruggero Deodato and released in 1968.

below: Mariangela Giordano with Lino Toffolo and Paolo Villaggio in **I quattro del Pater Noster**.

all other images this page and opposite: **Zenabel**. Deodato made excellent use of the stunning locations at Bracciano in the Italian countryside.

I QUATTRO DEL PATER NOSTER

1969
Italian theatrical title: **I quattro del Pater Noster**
Italy
director: Ruggero Deodato

produced by Franco Cittadini & Stenio Fiorentini for S.P.E.D. Film.
registration number: 4.451. visa number: 53592 (3/4/69)
prints & processing: Istituto Luce.
negative: Eastmancolor.

cast: Paolo Villaggio (Eddy). Lino Toffolo (Paul). Enrico Montesano (Lazzaro) <and with> Oreste Lionello (Mambo) <with> Rosemarie Dexter. Mariangelo Giordano. Silvia Donati. Enzo Fiermonte. Salvatore Borgese. Gaetano Scala. Paolo Magalotti. Fortunato Arena. Imbro' Gaetano [Gaetano Imbrò].

story: Augusto Finocchi & Luciano Ferri. screenplay: Augusto Finocchi, Luciano Ferri & Maurizio Costanzo. director of photography: Riccardo Pallottini. incidental music composed & conducted by Luis Enriquez Bacalov. music recording & publisher: General Music. editor: Albert Gallitti. set designer: Cesare Monello. production supervisor: Livio Maffei. production manager: Angelo Cittadini. unit managers: Enzo Mazzucchi, Alberto Fiorentino & Albino Morandin. stunt co-ordinator: Salvatore Borgese. costumes: Silvano Giusti. set decorator: Giuseppe Aldrovandi. make-up: Eligio Trani. hair stylist: Stefano Trani. production accountant: Guido Cittadini. assistant director: Paolo Poeti. continuity: Patrizia Zulini. cameraman: Sergio Martinelli. assistant cameraman: Carlo Tafani. special effects: Vitantonio Ricci. assistant editor: Paola Carlozzi. sound: Fiorenzo Magli. boom operator: Edwin Forrest. costume house: Anna Mode. dubbing: C.I.D. synchronization: C.D.S. set furnishings: S.E.T. – Mancini. unit publicity: Lucherini – Rossetti – Spinola.

Italian theatrical distributor: S.P.E.D. Film (1st public showing on 3 April 1969). running time: 98 minutes. length: 2,680 metres.

Three eccentric adventurers come into possession of an outlaw gang's loot. They are accused of carrying out the raid and are imprisoned for the crime. Helped by a fourth individual they escape but they are soon tracked-down by the outlaws, who want to reclaim the loot. The climax takes place in a gambling house where a furious brawl breaks out, precipitated by the four friends, who have tampered with the roulette wheel.

I quattro del Pater Noster was made in the wake of the successful 1968 release of Giuseppe Colizzi's western **I quattro dell'Ave Maria**, Deodato choosing to turn the genre into a parody with this film, which even in its title takes up the religious / comical theme. In the place of Terence Hill, Bud Spencer, Eli Wallach and Brock Peters, Deodato used four comedians from the trans-national cabaret: Paolo Villaggio from Genova, Lino Toffolo from Venice and the two Romans Oreste Lionello and Enrico Montesano. At that time they were not very well known, but all were destined to eventually become famous to some degree, both in television and cinema. The film, which was initially to have been directed by Mariano Laurenti, is a broad, simplistic comedy very much in the style of Hollywood's golden age (particularly the Marx Brothers' **Go West**). It is far removed from the style of the **Trinity** comic westerns, which were shortly to invade Italian screens.

In addition to the principal actors, the film features an early appearance by Mariangela Giordano, later to be the sexy star of numerous horror movies and the "Decamerotici" films. Another noteworthy cast member is the versatile Rosemarie [aka Rosemary] Dexter.
(Gian Luca Castoldi)

ZENABEL

1969
Italian theatrical title: **Zenabel**, Italian theatrical poster title: **Zenabel Davanti a lei tremano tutti gli uomini**,
French theatrical title: **Faut pas jouer avec les vierges**,
French theatrical re-release title: **La furie du désir**
Italy, France & the United States
director: Ruggero Deodato

executive producer: Andrea Fantasia. produced by Nicola Parenti for I.C.A.R. (Rome)/Pierson Productions (Paris)/ Gemini Pictures International (USA).
visa number: 55095 (4/12/69). Italian takings: L124,000,000
colour by Eastmancolor
filmed on location in Bracciano (Italy)

cast: Lucretia Love (Zenabel). John Ireland (don Alonso Imolne). Lionel Stander (Pancrazio). [Nicola] Mauro Parenti (Gennaro). Fiorenzo Fiorentini (Cecco). Elisa Mainardi (Zenabel's friend). Luigi Leoni (Baldassarre). Ignazio Leone (one of the three watchers). Nassir Cortbawi. Christine [Cristina] Davray. Agostino De Simone. Beatrice Bensi [Fiammetta Baralla] (another of Zenabel's friends). Carlo Pisacane. Andrea Scotti (Don Carlos). Dominique Badeau. Vera Drudy. [Giovanni] Nello Pazzafini (captain of the guards). Adriana Alben. Vincenzo Monteduro. Elide Fabiani. Mario Cecchi. Fabio Yepes de Acevedo. Dada Gallotti. Geneviève Audrey. Margherita Simoni. Anna Recchimuzzi. Alessandro Perrella. Giovanni De Grazia. Franca Licastro. Italo Guitto. Antonella Ippoliti. Liliana Fioramonti. Antonella De Paolis.

story: Antonio Racioppi & Gino [Aldo Iginio] Capone. screenplay: Antonio Racioppi, Gino Capone, Marc Marais & Ruggero Deodato. director of photography: Roberto Reale [colour by Eastmancolor]. music composer & director: Bruno Nicolai. editor: Antonietta Zita. art director: Elena Ricci. costume designer: Angela Passalacqua. production manager: Ennio De Meo. unit production manager: Armando Novelli. production inspector: Claudio Sinibaldi. unit manager: Attilio Viti. assistant director: Paolo Poeti. script girl: Marisa Agostini. continuity: Marina Chierici. cameraman: Roberto Girometti. special effects: Gino Vagniluca. make-up: Franco Di Girolamo & Sergio Angeloni. hairdresser: Ernesta Cesetti. assistant editor: Marisa Manfredi. titles: Salvadori. stills photographer: Reporters Foto. unit publicist (Italy): Rosanna Marani; (international): Jack Lauder. synchronization: Fono Roma. dubbing: C.D.C.

Italian theatrical distributor: S.P.E.D. Film (1st public showing on 12 December 1969). rated: 14. running time: 99 minutes. length: 2,600 metres.

French theatrical distributor [as **Faut pas jouer avec les vierges**]: Molière Films (released in Paris on 12 June 1974). rated: 18. running time: "90 minutes."
French theatrical distributor [as **La furie du désir**]: France-Continental (released in Paris on 3 November 1976). rated: 18. running time: "90 minutes."

The version of this re-released in France as **Faut pas jouer avec les vierges/La furie du désir** contained additional porno scenes credited to Claude Pierson [Andrée Marchand] made with his then girlfriend Cristina Davray.

Zenabel (Lucretia Love), a girl from a humble background, discovers that she is actually the daughter of a Spanish nobleman who was killed by don Alonso (John Ireland). It transpires that Alonso usurped her title and lands, so Zenabel assembles a motley group of misfits and manages to re-claim her title. She is helped in this campaign by a young Neapolitan bandit named Gennaro (Nicola Mauro Parenti). She eventually renounces everything in order to marry him.

It seems that **Zenabel** was released in two versions, as in France it appears that the film contained many erotic scenes, whereas the Italian version is completely lacking in eroticism. **Zenabel** was shot at Bracciano, in a very evocative location in the heart of the Italian countryside. The young hero is played by producer Parenti who – as he had in the earlier **Phenomenal** – gave himself another ego-massaging role. By this time, leading lady Lucretia Love had become his wife...

During the course of the production Deodato experienced difficulties with John Ireland because the latter always expected to discuss his scenes at great length. Particularly memorable was an occasion on which Lucretia Love was made to wait for hours – tied to a stake – while the whole crew waited for Ireland to arrive and conclude the scene. Once the American actor had presented himself he expected to embellish this sequence, which should have been very straightforward. The film's cast of extras included a dwarf, and, exasperated, Deodato picked up the dwarf and put him into Ireland's arms. Ireland interpreted this gesture of anger in goodness knows what way,

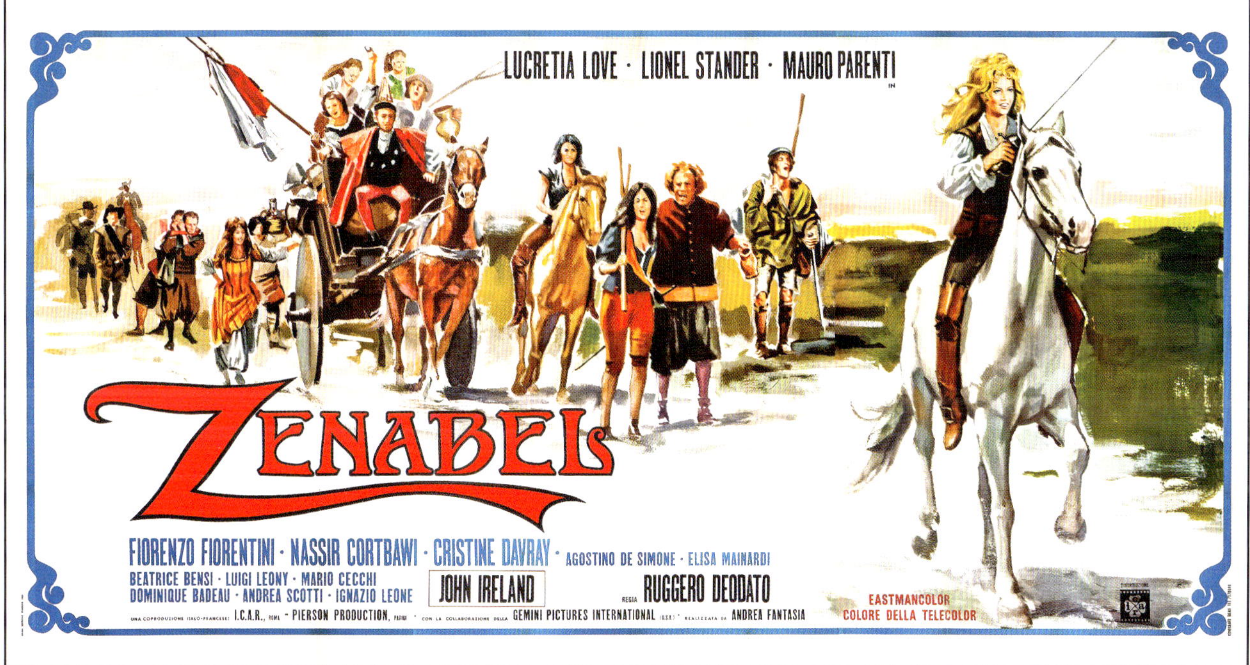

in that from this moment on he accepted the remainder of the shoot without complaint. In contrast to Ireland's peculiar behaviour, Deodato has fond memories of his collaboration with Lionel Stander who, despite being tormented by the scorching heat of the summer, willingly complied with Deodato's wishes as he was often surrounded by half-undressed girls.
(Gian Luca Castoldi)

IL TRIANGOLO ROSSO

1969 (TV)
Italy
director: Ruggero Deodato

series 2

1st episode transmitted @ 21.00 on Seconda Programma on 14 August 1969

regular cast: Jacques Sernas, Riccardo Garrone, Elio Pandolfi.

episode: **Il segreto del lago**; screenplay: Nino Marino, guest cast: Mario Colli, Marco Guglielmi, Mario Righetti.
episode: **La fuga**; screenplay: Mario Maffei, guest cast: Olga Gherardi, Armando Furlai, Giotto Tempestini.
episode: **Gli amici**; screenplay: Mario Guerra, Vittorio Vighi, guest cast: Ottavia Piccolo, Glauco Onorato, Silvia Dionisio, Roberto Chevalier.
episode: **La chiave**; screenplay: Roberto Sgroj, guest cast: Lino Banfi, Mario Feliciani, Laura Gianoli, Renzo Giovampietro, Valeria Sabel, Loredana Savelli, Nietta Zocchi.
episode: **La tromba d'oro**; screenplay: Italo Fasan, guest cast: Gisella Sofio, Andera Lala, Antonio La Rajna, Fausto Tozzi, Stefano Varriale.
episode: **L'orologio si è fermato**; screenplay: Italo Fasan, guest cast: Filippo De Gara, Augusto Mastrantoni, Gigi Reder, Piero Gerlini, Sandro Dori, Bruno Cattaneo.

Television series inspired by dramatic moments in the working lives of the traffic police. The episodes, each self-contained, were all based on true stories. Many famous faces from the world of Italian cinema appeared as guest stars in the various episodes.

Il triangolo rosso was remarkably successful, and led to Deodato being offered work for the Ministero dei Trasporti (Ministry of Transport), supervising a series of publicity spots starring Ubaldo Lai.
(Gian Luca Castoldi)

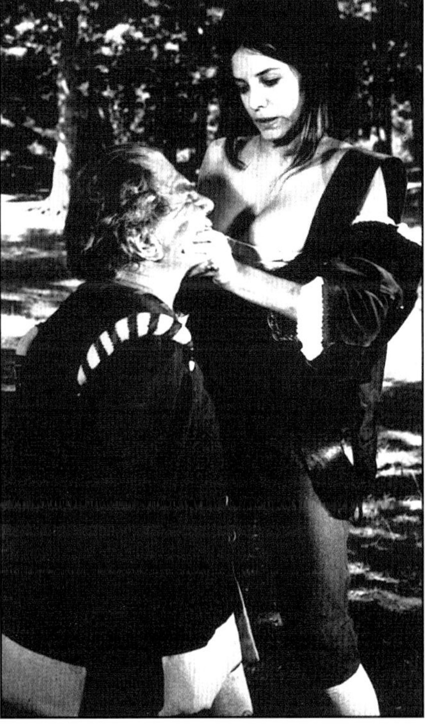

ALL'ULTIMO MINUTO

1971 (TV)
Italy
director: Ruggero Deodato

series 1

1st episode transmitted @ 22.30 on Programma Nazionale on 30 October 1971

episode: **Allarme a bordo**, cast: Eros Pagni, Franco Aloisi, Marisa Bartoli, Andrea Lala.
episode: **il buio**, cast: Martine Brochard, Luciano Spinelli, Giancarlo Bonuglia.
episode: **L'ascensore**, cast: Mario Siletti, Laura Gianoli, Gigi Reder, Bruno Cattaneo.
episode: **La scelta**, cast: Franco Volpi, Tano Cimarosa.
episode: **La prigioniera**, cast: Anna Miserocchi, Mico Cundari, Antonio La Rajna, Giovanna Mainardi.

story & screenplay: Augusto Caminito, Ruggero Deodato, Francesco Scardamaglia, Mario Guerra, Vittorio Vighi & Paolo Poeti.

all stills above and opposite: **Zenabel**

all illustrations below and opposite:
Waves of Lust. Most of the images here are taken from the British front-of-house stills set, which concentrated on Silvia Dionisio to tempt punters into the cinema. Note the painted-on 'bikini tops' used to censor the top image on the opposite page, taken from the same scene as the one shown in the still on this page below, with her female co-star Elizabeth Turner. A much more subtle form of nipple censorship can be seen in the main image on this page! The middle picture below shows the film's two male stars, Pier Luigi Conti, aka Al Cliver (left), and John Steiner (wearing the wet-suit).

ALL'ULTIMO MINUTO

1972 (TV)
Italy
director: Ruggero Deodato

series 2

1st episode transmitted @ 22.30 on Secondo Programma on 28 September 1972

episode: **Acua alla gola**. cast: Antonio Casagrande. Gino Pernice. Nietta Zocchi. Carlo Alighiero.

episode: **Il borsaiolo**. cast: Andrea Cecchi. Vittorio Anselmi. Anna Maria Dionisio.

episode: **Il rapido delle 13.30**. cast: Fausto Tozzi. Ileana Rigano. Tino Bianchi. Gianni Guerrieri.

episode: **Dramma in alto mare**. cast: Silvia Dionisio. Sofia Dionisio. Emilio Marchesini. Nino Fuscagni. Maurizio Merli.

story & screenplay: Italo Fasan & Nino Marino

ALL'ULTIMO MINUTO

1973 (TV)
Italy
director: Ruggero Deodato

series 3

1st episode transmitted @ 22.30 on Secondo Programma on 18 January 1973

episode: **Il bambino scomparso**. cast: Adrianio Asti. Mario Valdemagna. Andrea Bosic. Claudia Caminito.

episode: **L'ultima cifra**. cast: Laura Carli. Corrado Gaipa. Gisella Sofio. Massimo Daporto.

episode: **Scala reale**. cast: Alessio Orano. Annabella Incontrera. Massimo Serato.

With a few obvious incidental differences, **All'ultimo minuto** is basically an Italian version of **The Twilight Zone**; each episode in the series is a fast-paced thirty minute tele-film with a twist ending.

The title sequence was filmed with a fixed camera which framed a road filled with a flood of people walking hurriedly whilst a voice-over explained that the life of every person can suddenly and unexpectedly change because of an unforseen event.

The visual style of the series was in general more cinematographic than televisual and Deodato stands out for his innovative work over the course of three consecutive series. **All'ultimo minuto** was consistently popular throughout its run, and was well appreciated by the Italian television viewing public.
(Gian Luca Castoldi)

IL SEGRETO DI CRISTINA

1974 (TV)
Italy
director: Ruggero Deodato

cast: Monica Fiorentini. Andrea Checci
script: Tina Lagostena Bassi.

Il segreto di Cristina was the pilot episode for a television series which was never made. The work was offered to Deodato following the great success enjoyed by **All'ultimo minuto**.

The story deals with relationships between parents and their children, and their mutual lack of understanding.

WAVES OF LUST

1975
Italian theatrical title: **Ondata di piacere**
(translation: **Waves of Pleasure**)
UK theatrical/UK video title: **Waves of Lust**
Italy
directed by Ruggero Deodato

an Alberto Marras & Vincenzo Salviani production for T.D.L. Cinematografica S.r.l.
registration number: 6.045. visa number: 66947 [31/7/75].
colour by Telecolor S.p.A. (Rome).
interiors/exteriors filmed at Cefalù with studio interiors at Safa-Palatino (Rome)

story: Gianlorenzo Battaglia & Lamberto Bava. screenplay: Franco Bottari & Fabio Pittorru. dialogue: Fabio Pittorru. photography: Mario Capriotti. music: Marcello Giombini; published by Nazionalmusic (Milan). editor: Mario Gargiulo. production designer: Franco Bottari. production manager: Alberto Marras. the underwater scenes were shot with the assistance of Enzo Bottesini. underwater cameraman: Dante Di Palma. wardrobe: Giovanna Deodato. production secretary: Nicola Princigalli. assistant director: Vito Bruschini. cameraman: Gianlorenzo Battaglia. assistant cameraman: Guido Tosi. make-up: Massimo Giustini. hairstylist: Vittoria Silvi. assistant set designer: Mauro Passi. assistant editor: Carlo Broglio. sound: Luigi Salvatori. boom operator: Salvatore Grifi. costumes by Cinecostumi S.r.l. wigs: Carboni – Rocchetti. photographic lab: Leo Massa. sound recording [English language version]: Doppiaggio Internazionale.
The interiors and exteriors were filmed at Cefalù with the help and assistance of the 'Azienda Autonoma di Soggiorno e Turismo'
The S.C.U.B.A. equipment was graciously provided by Technisub S.p.A. (Genoa). "We thank Aer-Sarda of Cagliari for having graciously allowed us to use the boat, Mal 5 for the shooting of this film"

cast: Al Cliver [Pier Luigi Conti] (Irem). Silvia Dionisio (Barbara). John Steiner (Giorgio). Elizabeth Turner (Silvia). Saverio Deodato (child on beach).

Italian theatrical distributor: Overseas Film Company (1st public showing on 4 August 1976).
running time: 88 minutes. length: 2,422 metres.
UK theatrical distributor: IFD – Intercontinental Film Distributors Ltd. (released in January 1977). rated: X.
running time: 92 minutes 56 seconds. length: 8,274 feet.
Trivia Note: 1980s release in the UK on VHS as number three in the "Private shorts" collection, running just 15 minutes 47 seconds!

Waves of Lust is based in Sicily, at Cefalu, where Aleister Crowley founded his Satanist church and lived for years.

The story concerns a Satanic character by the name of Giorgio, a ruthless and cynical industrialist, married to Silvia, his obliging victim, who accepts the betrayals, violence and abuse of her husband with a sense of masochistic resignation. This couple meet Barbara and Irem, two carefree youngsters, who they invite onto their boat. There arises between the two couples a degree of erotic tension. Giorgio's unpleasant personality rapidly becomes evident, as he never misses an opportunity to humiliate Silvia and always emphasises his social superiority with regard to his guests. Barbara rises to the challenge of Giorgio's erotic games and she rapidly exasperates him by skilfully turning his own weapons against him. Giorgio courts Barbara, but in doing so is forced to put up with the fact that this gives Silvia the right to seduce Irem. Silvia grows dissatisfied with her husband, the dissatisfaction soon warping into hatred. Before long Giorgio realises that a sexual triangle has developed between his wife and the young couple, and that the three have formed an alliance against him. Giorgio becomes paranoid.

top: Fotobusta for **Waves of Lust**.
above: Typically misleading British video cover, packaged to make the film look like porno filth. This version of the film is cut...
below: Wife-swapping frolics start a chain-reaction of violence in **Waves of Lust**.

bottom right: A suspect is beaten bloody in **Live Like a Cop, Die Like a Man**.

He attacks Silvia, then throws her into the water, where helpless due to her wounds she drowns. Barbara and Irem later take advantage of Giorgio's umpteenth bout of drunkenness to throw him into the water wearing his wet-suit and oxygen cylinder, in order to simulate his death due to a diving accident. Now alone on the yacht they are free to travel anywhere they wish.

This film marked Deodato's return to the cinema after a long period spent working in television. During that period he was married to Silvia Dionisio, a true 'star' of the Italian cinema scene. The producers' idea was to make Silvia undress in one of her husband's films. In fact the film is extremely lavish in terms of the amount of nudity, with both Dionisio and the other female protagonist, Elizabeth Turner, having many nude scenes, some of which are full-frontal. Deodato has never really incorporated a great deal of eroticism into his films, but **Waves of Lust** is a perfect example of Seventies Italian erotic cinema; well shot, and graced with a scenario constructed with remarkable assurance. The film benefits from good characterisations and Deodato is extremely capable when it comes to directing the erotic scenes, where he demonstrates an uncommon mastery of the very mechanism of erotic cinema. He skilfully builds towards the climax, increasing the tension so as to provide the maximum degree of excitement for the attentive spectator.

(Gian Luca Castoldi)

LIVE LIKE A COP, DIE LIKE A MAN

1976
Italian theatrical title: **Uomini si nasce, poliziotti si muore**, UK theatrical title: **Live Like a Cop, Die Like a Man**, West German theatrical title: **Eiskalte Typen auf heißen Öfen**, UK video title: **The Terminators**, Spanish title: **Hombre se nace, policia se muere**
Dutch video title: **Het recht in eigenhand**
Italy
directed by Ruggero Deodato

produced by Alberto Marras & Vincenzo Salviani for C.P.C. [Centro Produzioni Cinematografiche] Città di Milano S.r.l./T.D.L. Cinematografica S.r.l.
registration number: 6.610. visa number: 68033 [10/3/76].
filmed on location in Rome with interiors filmed at Rizzoli Palatino Studios.
colour by Telecolor. in Eastmancolor.

cast: Marc Porel (Fred). Ray Lovelock (Tony). Adolfo Celi (the captain). Franco Citti ([Italian language version]: Ruggero Ruggerini; [English language version]: Rudy Ruginski). Silvia Dionisio (Norma). Marino Masè (Rick Conti). Renato Salvatori (Roberto Pasquini, 'Bibi'). Sergio Ammirata (the sergeant). Bruno Corazzari (Morandi, the informer). Daniele Dulbino (corrupt police inspector). Flavia Fabiani [Sofia Dionisio] (Lina Pasquini). Tom [Tommaso] Felleghy (the major). Margarita Horowitz (Mona, a hostage woman). Gina Mascetti (Maricca). Marcello Monti (third kidnapper). Claudio Nicastro (the commissioner). Gino Pagani [Pagnani] (Paul, dog trainer). Enzo Pulcrano (Mario, Pasquini's henchman). Alvaro Vitali (concierge, Pasquini's building). Gilberto Galimberti (2nd thug tortured on boat). Benito Pacifico (1st gunman). Ruggero Deodato (man walking out of bank).

story by Fernando Di Leo, Alberto Marras & Vincenzo Salviani. screenplay by Fernando Di Leo. director of photography: Guglielmo Mancori. music by Ubaldo Continiello; published by Nazionalmusic (Milan). film editor: Gianfranco Simoncelli. art director: Franco Bottari. photographer: Gianni Caramanico. assistant director: Roberto Pariante. continuity: Laura Frigo. wardrobe: Liliana Galli. cameraman: Mario Sbrenna. assistant cameramen: Aldo Bergamini & Renato Palmieri. make-up: Alma Santoli. hair styles: Vittoria Silvi. production secretary: Peppino Salviani. sound: Antonio Forrest. boom operator: Renato Alfonsi. decor assistant: Mauro Passi. tailoring: Cinecostume. cars: A.N.G.E. equipment: C.I.A.C. fabrics: D'Angelo. special effects: CI.PA. acrobatic sequences directed by O.A.C. sound effects: Marinelli. sound recording by Doppiaggio Internazionale.
The production wishes to thank Euro Sport Auto for their kind co-operation and Suzuki for kindly providing the motorcycles needed in the making of this film.
songs "Maggie" by Ray Lovelock & "Won't Take Too Long" by Fraser & Ruggero Deodato, both sung by Ray Lovelock.

Italian theatrical distributor: Interfilm (1st public showing on 11 March 1976). running time: 100 minutes. length: 2,649 metres.
UK theatrical distributor: Variety Film Distributors Ltd. (released on 30 January 1977). rated: X. running time: 95 minutes 53 seconds. length: 8,539 feet
West German theatrical distributor: Constantin (released on 3 September 1976). rated: 18. running time: 89 minutes. length: 2,442 metres.

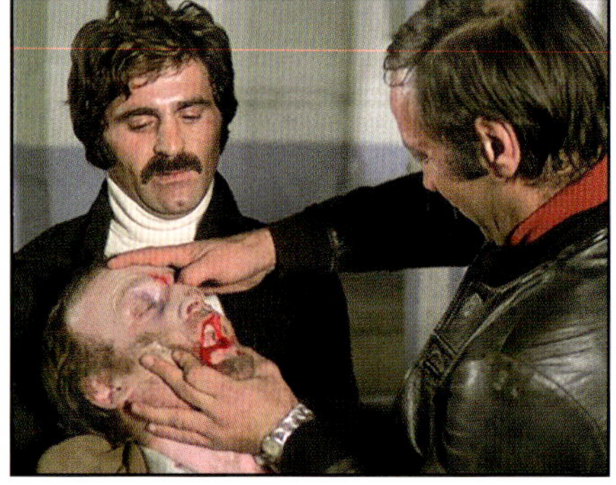

Live Like a Cop, Die Like a Man sees Deodato (working with a script from the notorious Fernando Di Leo [**Naked Violence**, **The Boss**, **Calibre Nine**, **To Be Twenty**]) dipping his toe into the murky waters of the cop thriller – popular in Italy in the mid-'70s – and coming up with an extraordinary if not entirely successful genre entry. This is not to say the film is bad, however it is not a film that offers its pleasures up easily to the casual viewer. As is so often the case with Deodato, it is not easy to divine his moral standpoint, which often makes an audience uneasy and is a rare find in such a reactionary genre.

Much of what Deodato seems to be getting at in the film is contained in the bravura ten-minute opening sequence. The rest of the film really only plays variations on these riffs and themes before fizzling out rather unsatisfactorily some 80 minutes later.

The film opens with shots of two handsome young men riding a motorcycle through the streets of a pre-Christmas Rome; Marc Porel is at the helm and Ray Lovelock is riding pillion. In case we have missed the point that this is supposed to be the time of "good will to all men", there is a shot of a man dressed as Santa Claus strolling along the street. On the soundtrack is Lovelock's song "Maggie" which is an easy-going, slightly Dylanesque number which reinforces this light, carefree tone.

Deodato cuts to a third man walking along the street putting on his motorcycle helmet. He joins his friend and the two ride off. Now we have two pairs of riders and Deodato uses cross-cutting explicitly to link them together. The second pair attempt to rob a woman of her handbag but she refuses to let go. They drag her along the street before ramming her headfirst into a lamppost. She dies instantly. Still unable to work the handbag

this page: **Live Like a Cop, Die Like a Man**:
top: British quad poster.
above: British video cover.
left: Marc Porel gives Ray Lovelock a ride.
below: Carnage on the streets of Rome.

above: Italian DVD cover for superb Italian widescreen uncut edition of **Live Like a Cop, Die Like a Man**.

lower right: **Live Like a Cop, Die Like a Man** stars Ray Lovelock, seen here in action as amoral 'special squad' cop Tony.
below: Japanese poster for the film.

free the second biker dismounts and lays into the body, delivering a series of vicious kicks to the body and stamping on the face and head. There is no reason or point to this; it is pure, blind hatred and the violence is profoundly shocking. Porel and Lovelock arrive to see the assailants fleeing. Porel heads off after them while Lovelock swiftly checks the body – his face showing no emotion whatsoever – then steals a bike and follows his friend. What follows is a stunning chase through Rome, doing for motorcycles what William Friedkin did for car chases in **The French Connection**. It is clear that much of the action was filmed guerrilla-style without permits or even forewarning the hapless shoppers. The chase is fast and dangerous, making for an exhilarating viewing experience and proving that Deodato was one of the most technically proficient directors working in Italy at the time. In case Deodato fears that this chase will have distracted us from its primary purpose – that of apprehending criminal scum – he gives us a reminder: the purse-snatchers kill the dog of a blind man crossing the road. The street is long and straight, to avoid the man and his dog is easy but they kill the dog anyway. It is gratuitous and unpleasant and Deodato can't resist showing us the dog's bloodied corpse. The man says plaintively *"Without my dog I'm helpless"*. Clearly these are bastards of the highest order, picking on society's weaker members and more important than any money it might make them is the thrill of it.

But if what the villains get up to is shocking, what their two pursuers indulge in is rather strange. Porel skids into a cafe and wrecks the place; apparently stymied by traffic Lovelock rides OVER several cars to get past. They actually seem to be enjoying the chase, in spite of its apparent danger and the fact that they are causing so much damage. Deodato reinforces this impression by re-playing Lovelock's cheerful song from the opening credits.

After a game of chicken, Lovelock and Porel succeed in herding their quarry at speed into the back of a removal van: the first rider is gruesomely impaled in the crash, the second is propelled through the cab and out into the street, injured but alive. Porel approaches the man, wakes him up and then breaks his neck. There is no arrest or trial. No recrimination or censure – this is an execution. As the police arrive we get another shock; Lovelock and Porel turn out not only to be policemen but part of a privileged "special squad".

As the film progresses our two heroes are basically portrayed as delinquents, not above torching all of the cars parked outside an illicit gambling joint purely for revenge rather than because it will do any good. In fact Deodato presents everyone as at least a little off-kilter: the captain of this special squad (played by a bored-looking Adolfo Celi) knows full well the excesses of his team and while he plays lip-service to hauling them over the coals every once in a while he couldn't really care less; and the first high-ranking policeman we meet (Daniele Dublino) turns out to be on the take. The final scene in which Celi unexpectedly turns up to save Lovelock and Porel by executing the key villain and his thugs is typical: in spite of having spent all his scenes pretending to harangue the boys for leaving piles of corpses behind them, he is really just the same.

The end titles play over a still frame of the villain's boat exploding: the boys blew it up simply because it was there and was wired to explosives, not because it would achieve anything.

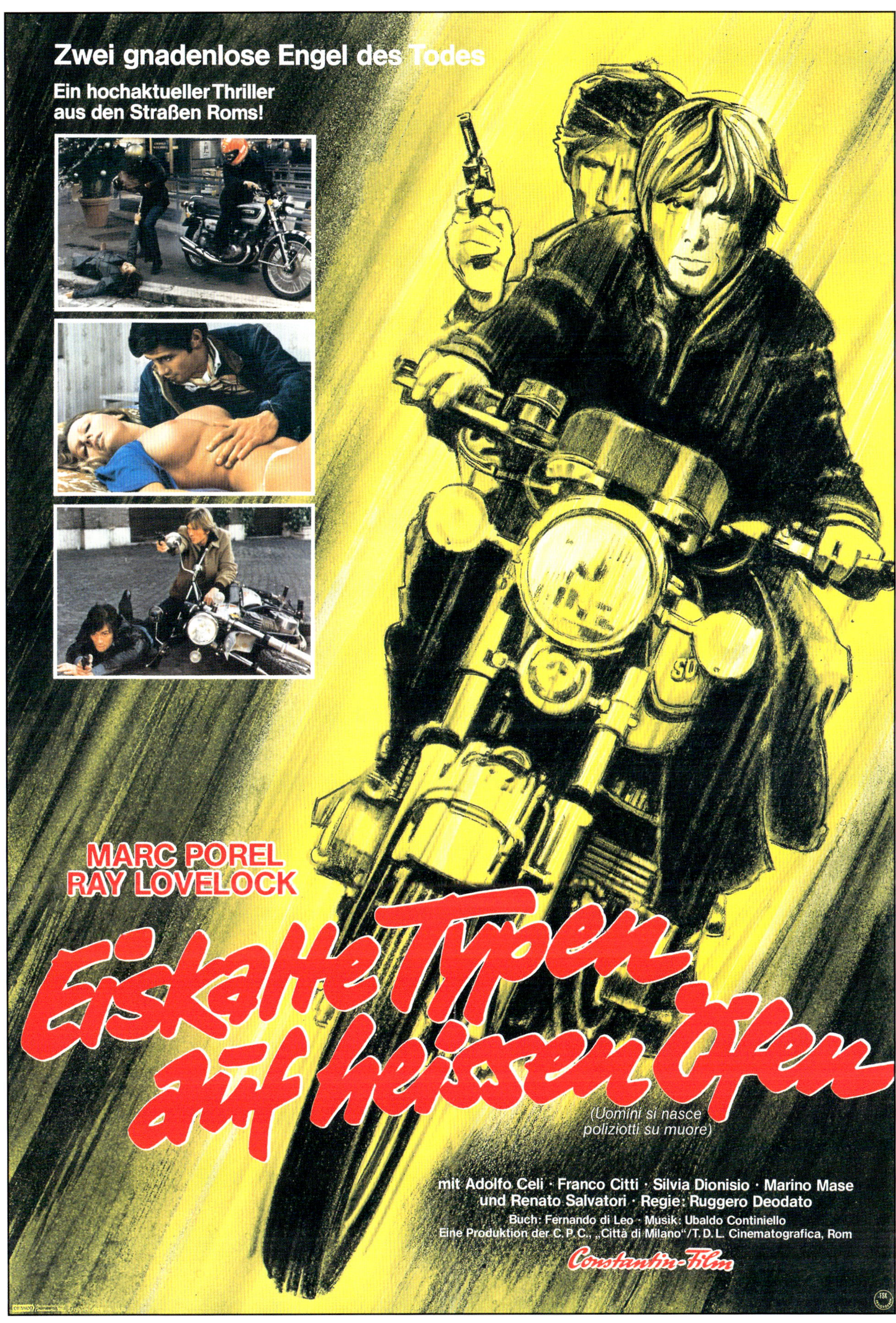

What Deodato seems to be suggesting is that violence and corruption just breed more of the same and can infect those who position themselves as society's moral arbiters just as easily as it can infect the poor and disaffected. From his nihilistic point of view, society is caught in an ever-escalating spiral of violence, depravity and death in which no-one is any better than anyone else. If many of the Seventies cop thrillers started from the position that the best way to fight crime in an increasingly violent society is for the police (and/or its citizens) to

above:
German poster for **Live Like a Cop, Die Like a Man**.

top: Original Italian theatrical poster for **Live Like a Cop, Die Like a Man**.
above: Someone's going to get hurt when Porel and Lovelock come knocking in **Live Like a Cop, Die Like a Man**.

right: Australian theatrical release poster for **Last Cannibal World**.
below: The fight for survival at all costs in **Last Cannibal World**.
bottom: US theatrical re-release for **Last Cannibal World**, under the new title **Carnivorous**, double-billed with the 1970s British subterranean cannibal classic **Death Line**, itself re-named **Raw Meat**.

adopt increasingly violent tactics, Deodato presents us with a pretty stark picture of where this will take us.

The film's sexual politics also seem to support this argument: several writers have commented on the fact that these two handsome men share an apartment. When their maid arrives to clean up the place, Porel says to Lovelock *"Let's put on the act"* and they proceed to taunt the poor woman by suggesting they have both slept with her daughter. However it seems unlikely that Deodato intends us to see the two young men as gay, rather Deodato seems to be suggesting that sex to them isn't any more enjoyable or important than bike chases or torturing suspects. Later on in the film they worm their way into the apartment of crime boss Pasquini's niece Lena (Flavia Fabiani). Porel makes a half-hearted attempt to question the woman but can't resist hitting her in the face. This appears to arouse her and seconds later the two are screwing. After a little while Lovelock comes in to take Porel's place. But there is no desire; the boys are simply taking revenge on Pasquini – sex is just another option in their attempts to enjoy fighting crime. Similarly there is the attractive special squad secretary Norma (played by Deodato's wife Silvia Dionisio) whom the boys like to try to chat up. When Porel suggests that he should make love to her, she replies that she would prefer a threesome (with Lovelock) because even between them they would manage too few orgasms! *"We girls have to work hard for the inadequate performance we get"* she says and comments that they live in a "male phallocracy". She is at least as crude as they are and for her too sex is no more important than cheap banter. **Live Like a Cop, Die Like a Man** can be taken as either a liberal or a reactionary film – depending on your point of view – but either way it's a cautionary tale of considerable power.
(Julian Grainger)

LAST CANNIBAL WORLD

1976
Italian theatrical title: **Ultimo mondo cannibale**. UK theatrical/UK video title: **Cannibal**. alternative UK theatrical title: **Last Cannibal World**. US theatrical title: **The Last Survivor**. West German theatrical title: **Mondo cannibale 2. Teil – der vogelmesch**. French theatrical title: **Le dernier monde cannibale**. US video title: **Jungle Holocaust**. Spanish title: **¡Mundo Canibal! ¡Mundo Salvaje!**. Portuguese video title: **O Último Mundo Canibal**. Greek video title: **The Cannibals**.
Italy
director: Ruggero Deodato

produced [uncredited] by Giorgio Carlo Rossi. an Erre Cinematografica production. Ruggero Deodato's film. registration number: 6.276. visa number: 69724 [3/2/77]. Italian takings L104,000,000
colour by Technicolor. negative: Kodak. in Techniscope. Filmed for three months during 1976, on location in Kuala Tahan, Malaysia.

cast: Massimo Foschi (Robert Harper). Me Me Lai (Pulan, native woman) <and> Ivan Rassimov (Ralph) <with> Sheik Razak Shikur (Charlie, the pilot). Judy Rosly (Swan). Suleiman. Shamsi.

screenplay: Tito Carpi, Gianfranco Clerici & Renzo Genta; from a treatment by Renzo Genta & G.C. [Gian Carlo] Rossi. Italian version dialogue adaptation: Attilio Tellini. lighting cameraman: Marcello Masciocchi. music by Ubaldo Continiello; published by Leonardi (Milan). film editor: Daniele Alabiso. production designer: Walter Patriarca. production manager: Giovanni Masini. assistant director: Stefano Rolla. script continuity: Lamberto Bava. make-up: Marcello Di Paolo. production accountant: Ernesto Poli. camera operator: Giovanni Ciarlo. assistant cameraman: Mauro Masciocchi. special effects: Paolo Ricci. gaffer: Tullio Marini. key grip: Alberto Emidi. props: Carlo Cascioli. 1st assistant editor: Ivana Boggian. [Italian language edition] synchronization: C.D.S. dubbing at C.V.D. [English language edition] recorded at C.D.S. (Rome). dubbing editor: Nick Alexander.

Italian theatrical distributor: Interfilm (1st public showing on 8 February 1977). rated 18. running time: 90 minutes. length: 2,529 metres.
UK theatrical distributor: Miracle Films Ltd. (released in March 1979). rated: X. running time: 88 minutes 34 seconds. length: 7,881 feet
US theatrical distributor: American International Pictures (released in March 1978). rated: R. running time: 83 minutes.
French theatrical distributor: Audifilm (released in Paris on 1 November 1978). rated: 18. running time: 90 minutes.
Spanish theatrical distributor: Pelimex S.A.

top & bottom left: Massimo Foschi, Me Me Lai and Ivan Rassimov star in **Last Cannibal World**. *above:* Original Italian press ad for the film. *below:* Leeches and snakes; more jungle hazards to contend with.

The Italian 'Third World cannibal movies' form a peculiar strain of horror cinema which has as its roots the culturally-significant 'mondo' genre, precipitated by the 1962 film from which the movement derives its name, **Mondo Cane**. Revelling in the West's fascination with 'barbaric' 'primitive' (i.e. non-white, non-Western) cultures, the early Italian mondo movies presented an unashamedly racist view of life in the jungles, deserts and savannahs of the world, the whole lurid stew spiced-up by endless sequences of animal slaughter. For food or for sport, the spectacle of predator catching prey was presented to viewers under the guise of documentary film-making. The early mondo movies were accompanied by sensationalistic, deliberately misleading narrations, with **Mondo Cane** famously informing the viewer that, in New Guinea, the "barbarians... have eaten human flesh". The stock ingredients of Italian mondo movies: the cultural clash between 'savage natives' and 'civilised whites', the dangers of wildlife, and of course plenty of gratuitous animal slaughter, were soon incorporated into a work of narrative fiction.

The cannibal cycle's first, almost unwitting, full-blooded entry, Umberto Lenzi's **Il paese del sesso selvaggio**, aka **Deep River Savages**, was released in 1972. Ivan Rassimov stars as a white man who is captured by an isolated tribe in the Thailand/Burma border region. He gradually learns the ways of the jungle and becomes completely assimilated into the tribe. The film owes much of its inspiration to the Richard Harris vehicle **A Man Called Horse** (1970), but is notable in the context of the cannibal cycle for several reasons. Most importantly, it features the screen's first sickeningly gore-drenched scene of graphic cannibalism; though there is only one such sequence in the whole film, it set the standard for all that followed.

Deep River Savages also introduced the most controversial convention of the cannibal film genre; the genuine death and mutilation of animals on screen in the context of a work of narrative fiction.

opposite: Deodato and his crew filmed for three months on location in Qualatanan & Malaysia, in the process capturing a startling vision of the stone-age lifestyle.
above: Ralph (Ivan Rassimov) and Harper (Massimo Foschi) shake off the veneer of Western civilisation and 'go native' in order to survive their jungle ordeal.
left: Hunting for humans.
below: Harper is allowed to escape after he eats the flesh of a cannibal he has killed.

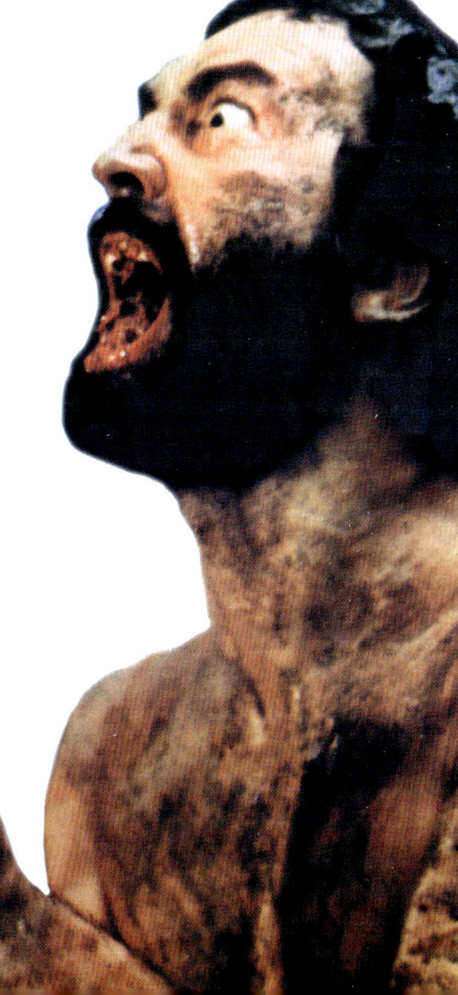

SD
MONDO CANNIBALE
SD
2. Teil – Der Vogelmensch

this page and opposite: A selection of images from the original German theatrical release lobby card set for **Last Cannibal World.**

above: Life in the Stone Age. Deodato's crew captured some beautiful images in the caves of South East Asia.

Lenzi, obviously 'inspired' by the degree of verisimilitude which such footage lends to an otherwise unremarkable, pedestrian rip-off of a superior film, incorporated many such scenes: there is a staged cobra vs. mongoose fight (both animals are held on leashes), a monkey has its head sliced in two, there is a cock-fighting scene, a small crocodile is killed and butchered, and a goat has its throat cut. However distressing such imagery may be to sanitised Western eyes, it is actually fair to say that all these scenes are justified within the context of the South East Asian rural lifestyle. Whether it is morally correct to introduce such imagery into a fictional movie is debatable; though the mondo movies had already shown sequences of staggering cruelty, these were in the context of a documentary – the reporting of life in the 'real world'. Hence, however tenuous the 'reality' presented may have been, they were presented primarily in the context of *information*. Filming such scenes with the intention of including them in a film produced primarily for *entertainment* clearly takes the process into a new arena of social responsibility. Whatever the ethical arguments, Deodato was clearly of the same opinion as Lenzi when he made **Last Cannibal World** four years later, and by following Lenzi's lead he helped to solidify the convention of animal slaughter within the cannibal genre.

Lenzi's massively influential role in the development of the cannibal genre is cemented by the third convention adopted by Deodato: a title card which attempts to convince the audience that the film which follows can legitimately claim a degree of authenticity. Lenzi's title card proclaims "...though some of the rites and ceremonies shown are perhaps gruesome and repugnant they are portrayed as they are actually carried out. Only the story is imaginary". Deodato adopted the convention, but not the sentiment, going one step further with **Last Cannibal World** by claiming a factual basis for the story itself: "This is the true account of the series of events that led to the discovery of a stone age tribe on the island of Mindanao. The ceremonies and rituals portrayed were all experienced or witnessed by the central character Robert Harper."

Deodato cast experienced stage actor Massimo Foschi in the role of Harper. He was ably assisted in the supporting roles by **Deep River Savages** stars Ivan Rassimov and Me Me

Lai, here reprising her role of sympathetic native woman who aids the white protagonist.

A light aircraft is flying over spectacular jungle terrain. Aboard the plane are oil prospector Robert Harper, his partner Ralph (Rassimov), Charlie the pilot and a young lady called Swan. There is much talk during the flight about how inhospitable and harsh the jungle is...

They are on their way to visit an oil prospecting party which has set up camp there, but upon landing they find the area abandoned. They soon discover a native weapon covered with blood. Ralph is concerned, exclaiming that the weapon indicates the people who raided the camp were "worse than natives; judging from the way this was made, they're still living in the stone age". Harper wanders off into the jungle in a daze – cue the first totally gratuitous mondo-style scene as a huge snake kills and devours a lizard. Ralph follows Harper and they both get lost. They eventually make their way back to the plane, *en route* discovering a partially-decomposed corpse. The seriousness of their predicament becomes apparent, but thanks to their impromptu wander in the bush, it is by now too dark to take-off. They decide to sit out the night in the plane. Later, Swan unwisely decides to leave the plane in order to relieve herself, and is captured by the natives. The men are all too scared to help even though they hear her screams, convincing themselves that they should stay put for the night and look for her the next day, when it is light.

Within moments of starting their search, Charlie springs a native trap and is horribly impaled. Momentarily losing his mind at the sight of his dead friend, Harper runs blindly into the jungle, pursued by Ralph. This time they really do get hopelessly lost. After witnessing a group of natives feasting on the remains of Swan, the two men find a river and decide that if they build a raft and float downstream, they will be carried towards the airstrip. Their raft overturns on some rapids and Harper is left alone in the jungle as Ralph is swept away by the current. Desperately seeking sustenance in the alien environment, Harper unwisely gorges himself on mushrooms, starts to hallucinate and soon passes out. He is awakened by a group of natives, who take him back to their huge cave dwelling-place.

In the film's most powerful sequences, Harper is stripped and humiliated by the chanting natives, then strung up in a harness and hoisted into the heights of the misty cavern. Having seen him arrive by aeroplane, the natives believe that

he has the power of flight, so they let him freefall twenty metres or so before his descent is abruptly halted by the harness and rope device to which he is attached. His painful ordeal continues until he passes out; meanwhile the natives wave their arms as if they were wings, and hoot hellishly. These scenes are brilliantly choreographed, lit and photographed, attaining an otherworldly aura which the remainder of the film fails to match.

The rest of the film details Harper's continuing ordeal at the hands of the natives who, it is soon clear, are preparing to use him as bait to catch a very large meal... He befriends a native woman called Pulan (Me Me Lai), seizes a chance to escape, and heads off into the jungle once more, taking Pulan as a hostage / guide. When she tries to escape, Harper cements their bond by raping her; in the dubious social politics of the **Last Cannibal World** Pulan becomes, from this moment on, his companion and servant. Harper is reunited with Ralph (whose mobility is impaired by a festering leg wound) whilst sheltering from a storm, and the men force Pulan to lead them back to the airstrip by guiding them through cannibal country. The film becomes bogged-down for a while here with a lot of rambling jungle-survival incidentals, though at one point, Ralph ensnares a cobra, milks its venom and applies the deadly liquid to the end of Harper's makeshift lance...

Pulan's hesitation about travelling through cannibal country is soon justified as the small party becomes surrounded by natives. Ralph is hit by a spear but escapes, whilst Pulan falls prey to the cannibals and is quickly killed. Whilst the two men continue to flee, Pulan is beheaded, sliced open and gutted. Hot coals are placed into her gaping chest cavity and the film's most gruelling sequence ends with her flesh being devoured. By the time the cannibals catch up with the two men, Ralph is weakening fast from his fresh wound and can no longer defend himself, so Harper is forced to fight.

opposite middle & bottom right: More nipple censorship in Spanish publicity material.
opposite bottom left: Harper catches Pulan and rapes her after she attempts to escape.

top left: French theatrical poster.
above: Human meat, fresh off the bone.
below from the top: Cobra venom turns Harper's stake into a deadly weapon; Me Me Lai plays the sympathetic cannibal woman Pulan, who forms an intimate bond with Harper whilst he is held captive by her tribe, and later becomes his companion; This alligator is about to become dinner in one of the film's graphic and very real scenes of animal butchery.

He kills his opponent with the poisoned lance. His assimilation into the savage ways of the jungle is then completed in devastating fashion, as he disembowels his foe, pulls out an internal organ, and dementedly eats it in front of the intimidated cannibals. Following this show of strength, Harper is allowed to continue, carrying his barely conscious friend, as the cannibals look on from a respectful distance. Harper finds the plane and manages to escape his ordeal, but Ralph keels over and dies soon after take-off.

Last Cannibal World is slightly over-long, and hampered by Ubaldo Continiello's dreary score. However, Deodato coaxed fine performances from the leading men, the transformation of Foschi's character from civilised man to savage being particularly commendable. More than twenty years later, Deodato's involving tale of survival against the odds still packs a punch, and although it is now considered to be a minor genre landmark, the film was to be forever eclipsed barely three years later. Deodato applied all the lessons he had learned from this experience and honed them to razor-sharp intensity, pulling the rug from under his audience and asking questions of himself which yielded no easy answers in the form of his fiercely intelligent and dangerously enigmatic classic of confrontational exploitation cinema, **Cannibal Holocaust**...
(Harvey Fenton)

LAST FEELINGS

1977
Italian theatrical title: **L'ultimo sapore dell'aria**
UK theatrical/UK video title: **Last Feelings**
French title: **Le dernier souffle**
Italy
directed by Ruggero Deodato

Giorgo Carlo Rossi presents a Tritone Cinematografica production. registration number: 6.485. visa number: 71522 [4/2/78]. Italian takings: L26,500,000 Eastmancolor. processing laboratory: Technicolor S.p.A. negative: Kodak. in Cinescope.
filmed on location in Amsterdam (Holland) and Asti, Rome & Varazze (Italy) with interiors at Dear International Studios (Rome, Italy)

cast: Carlo Lupo (Diego Micheli). Vittoria Galeazzi (Claudia). Luigi Diberti (Marco). Jacques Sernas (sporting director) <and with> Angela Goodwin (Maria Micheli, Diego's mother) <and> Fiorenzo Fiorentini (Anselmo). Alfio Androver (Giovanni). Emilio Delle Piane (sports doctor). Luigi Pagnani Fusconi. Richard Raynsford. Anna Maria [Deddi] Savagnone (school teacher). Gianni Solaro (hospital doctor). Maurizio Rossi (Lori).

screenplay by Roberto Gandus & Tito Carpi; based on an original story by Ruggero Deodato & Roberto Gandus. director of photography: Claudio Cirillo. music: Ubaldo Continiello; published by Leonardi (Milan). film editor: Daniele Alabiso. production designer: Carmelo Patrono. production manager: Giovanni Masini. technical consultant: Prof. Roberto Pangaro. production co-ordinator: Libero Balduini. assistant director: Lamberto Bava. script continuity: Rosanna Rocchi. make-up artist: Goffredo Calisse. assistant to the editor: Ivana Boggian. 1st assistant editor: Rosanna Landi. 2nd assistant editor: Alfredo Menchini. unit manager: Vito Di Bari. production secretaries: Angelo Scacco & Franco Rossi. production accountant: Ernesto Poli. camera operator: Oddone Bernardini. assistant cameraman: Maurizio Zampagni. action stills: Paolo Maria Cavicchioli & Alessandro Carlotto. gaffer: Bruno Angeletti. key grip: Luigi Ietto. cinematographic equipment: Cinenoleggio S.p.A.; Elma s.r.l. set furnishings: Cinearredamenti Mobilificio Umbro (Rome). drapes: Alfredo D'Angelo. sound recordist: Davide Magara. boom operator: Gianni Ruggiero. [Italian language version] synchronization: N.C. dubbing: C.D. [English language version] recorded at N.C. Studios for Cinitalia (Rome). dubbing editor: Nick Alexander.
song "Feelings" composed & performed by Morris Alpert.

Italian theatrical distributor: Cidif (1st public showing on 24 February 1978). running time: 105 minutes. length: 2,647 metres.
UK theatrical distributor: G.T.O. Films (released in 28 September 1980). rated: A. running time: 98 minutes 41 seconds

Diego Michele (Carlo Lupo) is a lad with big problems both at home, where he lives with his mother and stepfather, and at school, where some of his classmates are pressurising him to become involved in criminal activities. Seeing as even his mother does not understand him, Diego decides to run away from home and to make ends meet he takes on work with mechanic Anselmo (Fiorenzo Fiorentini). After only a few days he accidentally causes some damage to a car which is in for repair, and he runs away from Anselmo's. He meets Marco (Luigi Diberti), the coach of a swimming team, who takes him on as an assistant warden at the local pool. Diego's passion for swimming pushes him to train at night, when the swimming pool is closed. It is during one of these night-time sessions that Marco sees him and recognises the boy's exceptional potential. The president of the sports club (Jacques Sernas) hears about Diego's swimming prowess, and allows him to join the team where he soon becomes the leader, provoking the envy of the other athletes. The boy takes part in the Italian junior championships and wins, but immediately afterwards he falls ill. Tests diagnose a terminal illness. From this point on the film concentrates on Diego's battle to conquer his illness, alternating between scenes in the hospital showing his treatment at critical moments, and plenty of shots of Diego training in the style of **Rocky** when he reacts positively to the treatment. However, the boy inevitably finds that as time goes by he has gradually less energy, and he becomes aware of his inevitable death. The doctors advise Diego against continuing his competitive activity, but the boy nevertheless insists, and obtains permission from Marco to participate in the last grand event in his life, the European Championships in Amsterdam. In preparation for this, Marco takes Diego to his house in the country where he puts him through a rigorous training program. Whilst there Diego is re-united with Marco's sister Claudia (Vittoria Galeazzi) and the two fall in love. Diego travels to Amsterdam confident in his ability to take on the challenge of the great race. He begins in spectacular fashion, in the first few lengths wiping the floor with the opposition, but gradually his illness makes itself felt and slows down his swimming. The crowd, aware of his health problems, begins to cheer the boy on whilst his swimming becomes ever more laboured. One by one the other competitors overtake him but Diego does not give up – he continues to swim, floundering until he completes the race in last place to an ovation from the spectators. He is embraced by Claudia, and collapses exhausted.

Deodato is proud of this film, which was a terrible commercial failure in Italy (in terms of Italian television screenings on the other hand, it has enjoyed a modest degree of success), whilst it went down very well abroad, particularly in Japan which was the nation which commissioned him to make the film after having seen **Last Cannibal World**.

Shot with impressive attention to detail, **Last Feelings** is a hybrid of the Italian 'tear-jerker' genre, ushered in by Raimondo Del Balzo's **L'ultima neve di primavera**, and **Rocky** by John Avildsen.

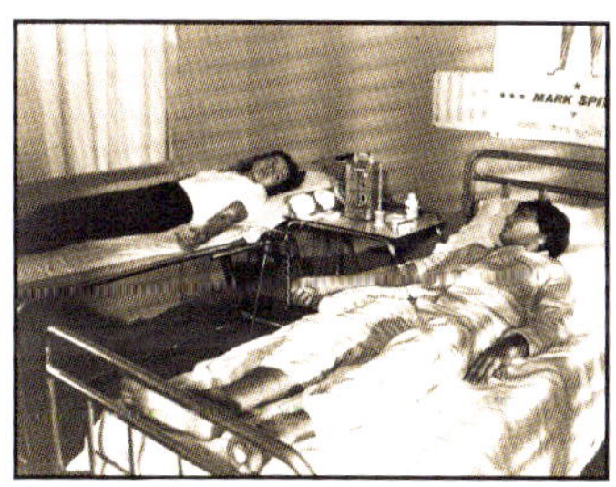

all illustrations above: **Last Feelings**.
top: Diego, champion swimmer.
middle: Diego and Claudia enjoy some quality time together.
bottom: When illness strikes down Diego, Claudia does everything in her power to help him make a full recovery.

all illustrations on the opposite page: **Last Cannibal World**.
top: Spanish lobby card
bottom left: A variety of video covers from: USA (VHS, as **Jungle Holocaust**); UK (pre-certification VHS, as **Cannibal**); Portugal (VHS, as **O Último Mundo Canibal**); Italy (DVD, as **Ultimo mondo cannibale**); USA (DVD, as **Jungle Holocaust**)
bottom middle: A montage image of cannibals in action, taken from the extensive Spanish publicity materials for the film.
bottom right: Charlie the pilot is killed by a vicious cannibal trap.

Deodato's film simply and effectively combines the central theme of each of its precursors: firstly, the concept of the adolescent (or child) who has been through a difficult and tormented upbringing, and who is tragically diagnosed as having a terminal illness at the precise point when he has regained the joy of living; secondly, social and personal redemption by means of sport and its rites (in this case the furious training sessions emphasised by an overwhelming musical score).

The character of the trainer Marco is curious, clearly homosexual, though one finds little or no enlightenment in the discovery of this fact. Strange then that Deodato should leave a trail of clues throughout the film regarding this aspect of his personality. Marco's tragic family situation is skimmed over too much; it is a precariously closed unit which does not concede anything to the boy.

Deodato shot some beautiful footage during the swimming races, with a singular realism which refers directly back to actual television coverage of swimming events.

(Gian Luca Castoldi)

below: British video cover for **Last Feelings**. *all other illustrations this page & opposite:* **Concorde Affair**. The film was released by Dutch video company EVC in both Holland *(above)* and the UK *(opposite)*.

CONCORDE AFFAIR

1979

Italian theatrical/Italian video title: **Concorde Affair '79**
French theatrical & UK video title: **SOS Concorde**
West German theatrical title: **Das Concorde-Inferno**
alternative UK video title: **Concorde Affair**
Polish theatrical title: **Afera "Concorde"**
Danish video title: **Concorde 820 forsvinder**
Italy
director: Roger Deodato [Ruggero Deodato]

produced by Mino Loy & Luciano Martino for Dania Film/National Cinematografica. registration number: 6.624. visa number: 73237 [16/3/79]. Italian takings: L309,000,000 colour by L.V. – Luciano Vittori. in Eastmancolor. scope. filmed on location on the island of Martinique, Newark (New Jersey, USA), London, Rome and Paris with interiors filmed at De Paolis INCIR Studios (Rome)

cast: James Franciscus (Moses Brody). Mimsy Farmer (Jean Beneyton) <with> Venantino Venantini (Forsythe). Mag Fleming (Nicole Brody). Edmund Purdom (Danker). "Francisco" Charles (George). Francesco Carnelutti (co-pilot, 2nd Concorde). Ottaviano Dell'Acqua (John, Forsythe's henchman). Aldo Barberito (priest, 2nd Concorde). Roberto Santi (navigator, 2nd Concorde). Maria D'Incoronato (woman who looks at sunset). Renzo Marignano (Martin, Milland's advisor). Renato Cortesi. Giovanni Battista Felici. Maria D'Alessandro. Cosimo Milone. Alessandra Stordy (stewardess, 2nd Concorde). Enrico Papa (Charlie, man who panics). Walter Toschi. Monica Scattini (woman in Moses's office). Renata Zamengo (woman with little girl) <and with> Mario Maranzana ('Papa', man who suffers heart attack) <and with> Van Johnson (Captain Scott, 2nd Concorde) <and with> Joseph Cotten (Milland, president of multi-national). Robert Kerman (Kelman, Chief Operator at London Control). Goffredo Unger (Bill, radio operator at London Control). Ruggero Deodato (man in restaurant).

story: Alberto Fioretti. adaptation: Renzo Genta. screenplay: Ernesto Gastaldi & Renzo Genta. director of photography: Federico Zanni. underwater photography: Lorenzo Battaglia. music by Stelvio Cipriani, music ©N.C. - Flipper. film editor: Eugenio Alabiso. production design: Mimmo [Bartolomeo] Scavia. costumes: Adriana Spadaro. production manager: Giovanni Masini. assistant director: Goffredo Unger. unit manager: Marcello Tagliaferri. assistant camera: Mario Pastorini. continuity: Maria Luisa Rosen. make-up: Stefano Trani. sound engineers: Roberto Petrozzi & Remo Ugolinelli. boom operator: Giulio Viggiani. stills: Carlo Alberto Cocchi & Garibaldi Giorgio Schwartze. 2nd unit director of photography: Claudio Cirillo. 2nd unit camera: Oddone Barnardini. special effects: Angelo Fattoracci & Fabio Traversari. assistant editor: Teresa Negozio. chief grips: Alberto Emidi & Quinto Proietti. chief electrician: Roberto Belli. props: Rodolfo Ruzza. wardrobe: Mario Russo Tailors; GP 11 Tailors. footwear: L.C.P. sound recording & post-synchronization: N.C. Studios. sound mixer: Bruno Moreal. sound effects: A. Ciorba & Co. the production wishes to thank for their kind cooperation: Newark Flight Region Control, (Newark, New Jersey, USA); the authorities and populace of the island of Martinique (France); the Historical Museum of Military Aeronautics (Vigna Di Valle, Italy); Technisub s.p.a. for diving equipment. song "Nydia" by Charles Denis Frantz, arrangement by Marius Cultier.

Italian theatrical distributor: Medusa Distribuzione (1st public showing on 23 March 1979). running time: 100 minutes. length: 2,620 metres.
French theatrical distributor: UGC/CFDC (released in Paris on 9 May 1979). running time: 95 minutes.
West German theatrical distributor: Avis-Film & Ascot Filmverleih (released on 26 April 1979). rated: 12. running time: 94 minutes. length: 2,583 metres.

Following on from **Last Feelings**, **Concorde Affair** is another curious attempt by Deodato to establish his mainstream credentials. Released as direct competition to the genuine Airport series entry of the same year (**Airport '79: The Concorde**), there was only so much that Deodato could achieve here with this typically Italian pastiche, the project being hamstrung from conception by a lacklustre and uninvolving scenario.

Deodato complained that with extra funds he could have made **Concorde Affair** into something really special, but it is difficult to sympathise with this viewpoint, if only because the timing of this film was all wrong. At the end of the Seventies, the passenger-plane-disaster-movie was a dying breed which was flinging itself headlong into the netherworld of farce; the overblown 1970 progenitor **Airport** spawned a brace of sequels, but is perhaps most noteworthy in retrospect for being responsible for the two **Airplane!** spoofs, the first of which was released in 1980, to huge financial success. Clearly the early Seventies audience for air-bound drama had gained a sense of humour, and let's face it, Deodato only really knows how to play it straight.

Concorde Affair is in fact suffocatingly serious-minded in intent, despite having nothing of interest to say. The plot concerns a reporter, played by James Franciscus, who is thrust into the middle of a complex web of intrigue involving a big business conglomerate who are terrified that this new-fangled Concorde thing is going to disrupt their extremely profitable South American passenger airline business. In order to deter public interest in Concorde, they arrange

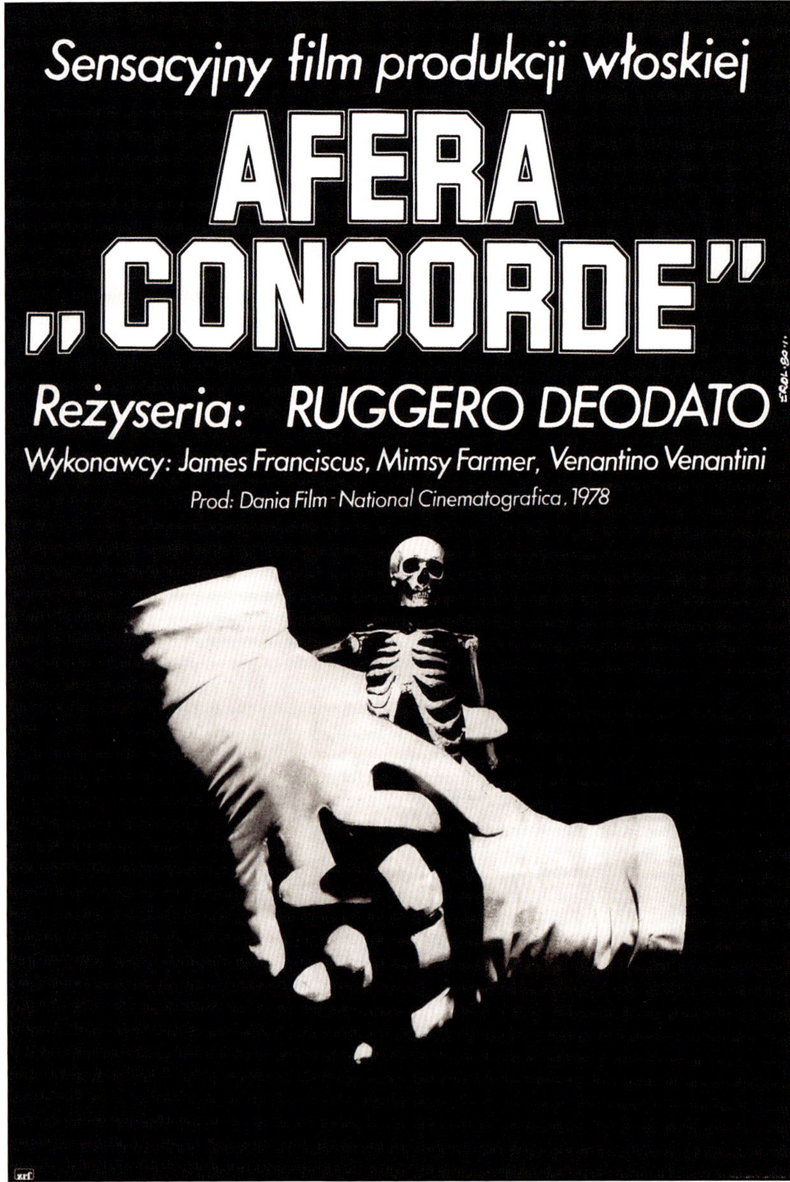

top left: Striking monochrome Polish theatrical poster for **Concorde Affair**.
above: Panic on the plane!

top right: Detail from Japanese artwork for **Cannibal Holocaust**; Deodato's horrifying epic is one of the most commercially successful films ever released in Japan.
opposite top: Jack Anders intrudes on the final moments of a mortally-burned Yacùmo woman's life.
opposite middle: Lurid, misleading German theatrical poster, under the title **Nackt und zerfleischt: Cannibal Massaker**.
opposite bottom: Jack Anders *(left)*, Alan Yates *(centre)* and Faye Daniels *(right)* are interviewed shortly before they set off on their ill-fated mission to shoot sensational footage of life and death in 'The Green Inferno'. The cocky film-makers declare *"for us the difficult doesn't exist and the impossible takes just a little more time."*

for the plane to have a series of 'accidents'. After a test flight crashes into the ocean as planned, they attempt to complete their coup by downing a fully-subscribed passenger flight. Franciscus saves the day by enlisting the help of test-flight survivor Mimsy Farmer, who explains the sequence of events leading up to the crash, thus enabling a last-minute rescue plan to be hatched. In charge of the team at air traffic control is a man whose face who was soon to become familiar to Deodato-watchers as he went on to play a pivotal role in **Cannibal Holocaust**... American Robert Kerman, at the time better known as prolific East-coast porno star Robert Bolla, impresses in his few minutes of screen time. Kerman is one of the few noteworthy points of interest in a generally workmanlike production, which is further hindered by some laughable model effects, the worst of which are all saved for the underwater scenes. These super-cheap compromises are especially glaring when contrasted with the competent lensing, exotic locations and a solid cast full of seasoned Italian B-movie pros.

Lessons learned, Deodato honed his ambitions and mere months later the restrictions of a minimal budget were turned to his advantage in the jungles of South America where he forged the movie which would forevermore define his position in the world of film-making...
(Harvey Fenton)

CANNIBAL HOLOCAUST

1980
Italian/French theatrical & UK/US video title: **Cannibal Holocaust**, Spanish theatrical title: **Holocausto Canibal**, German theatrical title: **Nackt und zerfleischt Cannibal Massaker**, Danish video title: **Kannibal Massakren**.
Italy
director: Ruggero Deodato

Franco Palaggi & Franco Di Nunzio present a Ruggero Deodato film. an F.D. Cinematografica production. registration number: 6.719. visa number: 74702 [6/2/80]. Italian takings: L360,000,000
colour by LV – Luciano Vittori. in Eastmancolor. filmed in June/July 1979 on location in Leticia (Colombia) and New York with interiors filmed at De Paolis – INCIR studios (Rome)

cast: Robert Kerman (Professor Harold Monroe, NYU anthropologist). Francesca Ciardi (Faye Daniels). Perry Pirkanen (Jack Anders, blond cameraman). Luca Giorgio Barbareschi (Mark Tomaso, 2nd cameraman). Salvatore Basile (Chaco). Ricardo Fuentes (Miguel). Gabriel Yorke (Alan Yates, the director). Paolo Paoloni. Pio Di Savoia. Luigina Rocchi. Lucia Costantini (woman stoned for adultery by the river). Ruggero Deodato (man sitting on lawn outside New York State University).

story & screenplay: Gianfranco Clerici. director of photography: Sergio D'Offizi. music composed & conducted by Riz Ortolani; recorded at RCA studios; music ©United Artists (Italy) Edizioni Musicali s.r.l. film editor: Vincenzo Tomassi. production designer: Massimo Antonello Geleng. in charge of production: Giovanni Masini. assistant directors: Salvatore Basile & Lamberto Bava. continuity: Rosanna Rocchi. cameraman: Roberto Forges Davanzati. assistant cameraman: Enrico Maggi. make-up: Massimo Giustini. assistant make-up: Nicola Catalani. props: Rodolfo Ruzza. wardrobe: Lucia Costantini. production secretary: Vito Di Bari. key grip: Ennio Brizzolari. chief electrician: Luigi Pasqualini. stills: Paolo Maria Cavicchioli. assistant editor: Rita Antonelli. editing room assistant: Armando Pace. sound engineer: Raul Montesanti. boom operator: Umberto Montesanti. sound studios: Cinefonico Palatino. mixage: Bruno Longobardo. sound effects: Aldo Gasparri.

Italian theatrical distributor: PIC Distribuzione (first public showing on 7 February 1980). rated: 18. running time: 95 minutes. length: 2,588 metres.
West German theatrical distributor: Jugendfilm (released on 16 January 1981). rated: 18. running time: 92 minutes. length: 2,522 metres.
French theatrical distributor: Eurogroup Film & Femina Distribution (released in Paris on 22 April 1981). rated: 18. running time: 86 minutes.
Spanish theatrical distributor: ACE – Alianza Cinematografica Española. rated: S.

Although credited for quota reasons, Lamberto Bava did not work on this film.

The defining moment in Ruggero Deodato's film-making career came on 7 February 1980, when **Cannibal Holocaust** received its world première screening in Italy. The public reaction to this perplexing and genuinely transgressive movie set a pattern which persists to this day. While some see a powerful visionary work which critiques the role of journalists and documentary film-makers whose work brings them into contact with non-Western cultures, others see only cruel exploitation, **Cannibal Holocaust** being the barbarous product of film-makers who had lost all sense of reason in their quest to make a film designed to *"shock, scandalize the spectator and upset his stomach". (Marc Toullec, Mad Movies)*. To its supporters, the movie is the very pinnacle of Italian horror film making, a technical *tour de force*, frequently hailed as *"a masterpiece of cinematographic realism"*. To its detractors, Deodato's cynical meditation on man's capacity for evil remains, quite simply, the very definition of obscenity. Regardless of opinion, Deodato hit pay-dirt big time with **Cannibal Holocaust**; the film went on to become one of the most profitable Italian movies of the Eighties, securing unprecedented box-office action wherever it was screened. But Deodato was made to pay for his success...

Within weeks of its release, the film had been withdrawn from circulation in Italy, banned from further screenings in Deodato's home country after court officials had cited an ancient law, originally drafted in order to outlaw the 'sport' of bull-fighting, which prohibited the torture and killing of animals for the purpose of entertainment. Prints were destroyed, and Deodato was forced to defend himself in court. The legal injunction remained in place for three years, during which time Deodato did not make any more movies (he had completed the filming of **House on the Edge of the Park** before **Cannibal Holocaust** had been screened to the public). For a while Deodato's film-making career was in the balance, but following several trials he finally cleared his name and the film, in a slightly truncated version, was allowed to be screened again in Italy.

Despite being under no illusions about the power of the film he had made, Deodato can be forgiven for not foreseeing the violent protestations of his detractors. After all, if the incidents portrayed are considered individually, **Cannibal Holocaust** shows nothing that had not been seen before in Italian movie theatres. As discussed earlier, in the review of **Last Cannibal World**, animal mutilation had by this time – unfortunately – become common place in Italian exploitation movies due to the perennial success of the mondo genre, and Deodato's incorporation of this element into a work of narrative fiction had caused him no legal problems with his first excursion into cannibal country. What's more, Umberto Lenzi's positively

right: This is the only surviving colour still of the piranha bait sequence, which Deodato left out of the film's final edit.
below: Professor Monroe (Robert Kerman) gains the trust of these Yamamomo women by stripping and bathing with them. They soon lead him to a clearing where the Yates team's remains have been arranged to form a bizarre totemic shrine.

opposite: Shortly after being gang-raped by the white men, this native woman is found ritually impaled. Alan Yates (Gabriel Yorke) patronisingly agonises over what could have driven the Yamamomo to do such a thing as Mark Tomaso (Luca Giorgio Barbareschi) captures yet more sensational footage on his trusty Bolex. This grotesque image was used in publicity materials all over the world. Shown opposite are a Danish video cover and a Japanese theatrical poster.
below: Faye Daniels (Francesca Ciardi) is stripped and raped before being killed and eaten by the Yamamomo.

demented **Cannibal Ferox** (1981) was in free circulation even as Deodato's superior film languished in legal limbo, this despite the fact that **Ferox** easily surpasses **Holocaust** in terms of the sheer number of violent acts shown (at some point or another during this film, pretty much every part of the human anatomy is either hacked-off, impaled, sliced open or yanked-out. In close-up. Slowly.), and is also arguably the more morally reprehensible of the two due to its unapologetically gleeful, misanthropic attitude. Ultimately the most compeling explanations for this conundrum revolve around the *context* in which individual transgressions are presented, and the *effectiveness* of the presentation...

Cannibal Holocaust is the bastard son of the mondo genre. It seeks to critique the form and lambast the methods of its proponents. It questions the integrity of all involved in an industry which sells images of genuine pain, humiliation, torture and death, packaged for the consumer under the guise of 'public interest' programming. Ultimately, a documentary must turn a neat profit, and nothing sells better than rampant sensationalism. The mondo film-makers knew this, and as the films became ever more excessive, concerned parties began to ask questions about the methods which were used to obtain the footage. Were the film-makers really just innocent spectators, recording incidents in the

real world as and when they happened? Or were they perhaps partly responsible for what they filmed, catalysts who precipitated events so that their camera lenses could capture sacred moments of life and death simply to fulfil the voracious demands of the commercial media machine?

These ideas were nothing new. In 1965, Paolo Cavara (who in 1962 had co-directed **Mondo Cane**), put himself and his contemporaries under the microscope in **L'occhio selvaggio** (aka **The Wild Eye**), but Deodato set about tackling these issues with a degree of veracity which threw the subject back in his face: the most pertinent argument pitched against **Cannibal Holocaust** is that it is guilty of the transgressions which it seeks to condemn.

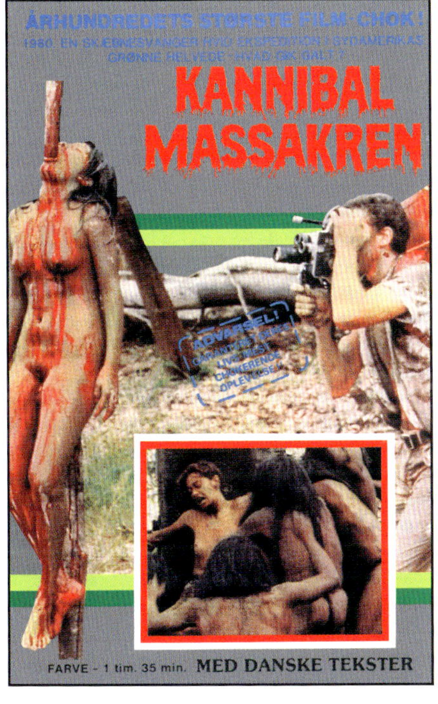

top: The Dutch 'Cult Epics' release was arguably the ultimate version of the film on VHS: a pristine print, uncut, letterboxed at 1.85:1 and in stereo. There have been many subsequent DVD editions across the globe, demonstrating the film's enduring appeal.
middle: The Yacùmo chief shows Professor Monroe's party evidence of the damage inflicted by the Yates team.
bottom: A young Yacùmo man carries out the "ritual punishment for adultery".

This is the film's greatest weakness and also the reason why it will always retain its power to disturb and stimulate; it is a paradox.

Establishing its familiarity with the language of the mondo genre from the very start, **Cannibal Holocaust** opens with aerial shots of the South American jungle, accompanied by Riz Ortolani's beautiful orchestral theme; the parallels with the opening moments of the Castiglioni brothers' **Magia nuda** (aka **Mondo Magic**) (1975) are instantly apparent. The title sequence is terminated by the appearance of an on-screen warning: *"For the sake of authenticity some sequences have been retained in their entirety"*. Clearly, after only a couple of entries, the cannibal genre had already developed conventions of its own, but as we shall see later this warning was taken to heart by many viewers, leading to allegations of 'Snuff' from the gullible (and those who *want* to believe...), which stubbornly persist to this very day.

Following the title sequence, we are instantly transported to the USA, where a TV news reporter recounts the known details surrounding the mysterious disappearance of a documentary film crew which has gone missing in South America. Instead of seeing an airborne vista of lush jungle vegetation, we are looking down at the 'concrete jungle' of Manhattan from the top of a skyscraper, establishing the theme of the clash between Western and Third World cultures.

The missing film-makers are introduced. *"Alan Yates, the director famous for his documentaries on Vietnam and Africa"* (Gabriel Yorke, in his only film role), *"Faye Daniels, his girlfriend and script-girl"* (Francesca Ciardi, later seen in Mauro Bolognini's **Mosca addio** (1987) and Roger Vadim's **Safari** (1991)), *"and inseparable friends Jack Anders and Mark Tomaso"* (the latter played by Luca Barbareschi, still active in the Italian film industry, most recently writing, directing and starring in the acclaimed **Ardena** (1997)).

Two months have passed since contact was last made with the conceited, over-confident crew. 'NYU's noted anthropologist' Professor Monroe is assigned the task of leading an expedition to establish their fate. Monroe is played by prolific Seventies porn star 'Robert Bolla', appearing here under his real name of Kerman. In a bizarre career decision he briefly escaped the porn ghetto, only to appear in *three* cannibal movies – he can also be seen in **Cannibal Ferox** and **Mangiati vivi!** (aka **Eaten Alive!**) (1980).

Establishing scenes in Colombia show Portuguese-speaking soldiers hunting some natives who are indulging in a spot of cannibalism. They capture one of the men in anticipation of Monroe's arrival, reasoning that *"A Yacùmo prisoner is like a ticket into the Green Inferno"*. The man was in possession of a lighter which Monroe confirms belonged to Faye Daniels. Monroe's guide Chaco explains that a tattoo borne by the prisoner indicates that he is the son of a shaman, and that the Yacùmo are not really cannibals. The conclusion is that they were probably indulging in a religious ceremony meant to chase evil spirits out of the jungle. *"White men spirits."*

The search party heads into the jungle, *en route* witnessing a savage, ritualistic punishment for adultery. Out of context this scene appears to be insanely gratuitous, but it serves to introduce a continuing theme in the movie – that in the Green Inferno, sexual transgressions are punishable by death. They soon reach the Yacùmo village, where they are greeted with fear and suspicion. After demonstrating their good intentions however, they are guided on the next stage of their journey, deeper still into the jungle, towards the ultimate goal of the Yates party – to meet the feared Yamamomo, also known as the Tree People. The Yamamomo are perpetually at war with the Shamatari, and when Monroe's team stumble across a skirmish between the two tribes, they intervene, establishing relations with the Yamamomo by shooting several Shamatari warriors. This unethical action is the first flaw in the film's tenuous attempt to present itself as a savage morality play, though in the daze induced by the film's latter half, it is easily forgotten. Regardless, Monroe gains the trust of the Yamamomo and is eventually led to a clearing where the skeletal remains of the Yates party have been arranged in a fetishistic totem. Through further psychological manipulation, he secures the still-sealed cans of film shot by the renegade film-makers and heads back to the USA, hoping that the cans will hold the key to the mystery of the team's demise.

The remainder of **Cannibal Holocaust** basically consists of the Yates footage, shown reel-by-reel, interrupted only by brief asides as Monroe realises with growing horror exactly what went on in the jungle a few months before. This film-within-a-film approach is the movie's trump-card; it lends the powerful second half an unprecedented aura of *cinéma-vérité* (Deodato's work with Rossellini paying dividends here). It is also the movie's stumbling block; in order to show the fictional film-makers committing unforgivable atrocities against indigenous wildlife, Deodato's cast and crew actually carried out the actions which the narrative condemns.

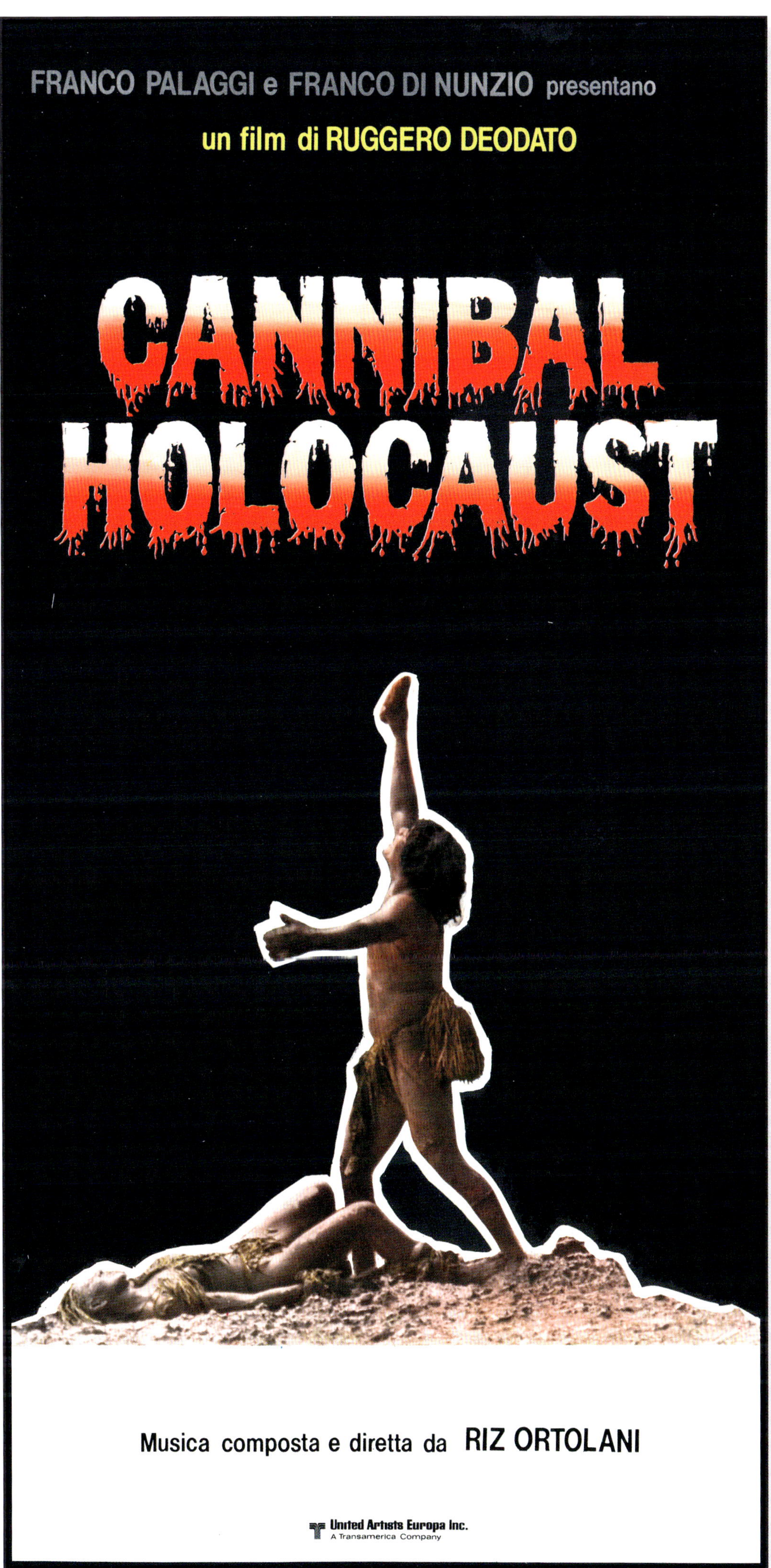
FRANCO PALAGGI e FRANCO DI NUNZIO presentano
un film di RUGGERO DEODATO
CANNIBAL HOLOCAUST
Musica composta e diretta da RIZ ORTOLANI
United Artists Europa Inc.
A Transamerica Company

above: **Perry Pirkanen, who plays Yates's trusty cameraman Jack Anders, in a rare behind-the-scenes photograph taken whilst Deodato's crew was filming the scene in which the Yacùmo village is burned to the ground.**
below: **Anders hacks off Felipe's leg in a vain bid to save their guide after a snake has bitten his foot.**

bove: The Yamamomo strip Jack Anders's lifeless body before hacking him to pieces and devouring him. This rare out-take shot shows the elaborate special make-up effects ppliances – the eyeball resting on Pirkanen's cheek and the prosthetic penis necessary to simulate his castration. In the film's final edit these details are barely noticeable.
elow: A Shamatari warrior. Also known as 'the swamp people', this tribe is perpetually at war with the Yamamomo.

above: The Yates team's two photographers, Jack Anders and Mark Tomaso, rape a terrified Yamamomo woman in the mud. Alan Yates commits the atrocity to film, then hands the camera to Tomaso and rapes the woman himself while Anders holds his violently protesting girlfriend Faye Daniels at bay.
below: A Yacùmo man stands over his bound wife, making peace with the Gods by holding his sacrificial dildo aloft before commencing the ritualistic punishment for adultery.

above: The dubious fictional patriarchal politics of the Yacùmo are used as a justification for the film's first scene of gratuitous misogynist violence. As Professor Monroe's team look on from a safe vantage point, the adulterous Yacùmo woman is violated by her husband who, we are told, has been forced by tribal lore into committing this act.
below: The unfortunate woman's ordeal is finally brought to an end as she is bludgeoned to death.

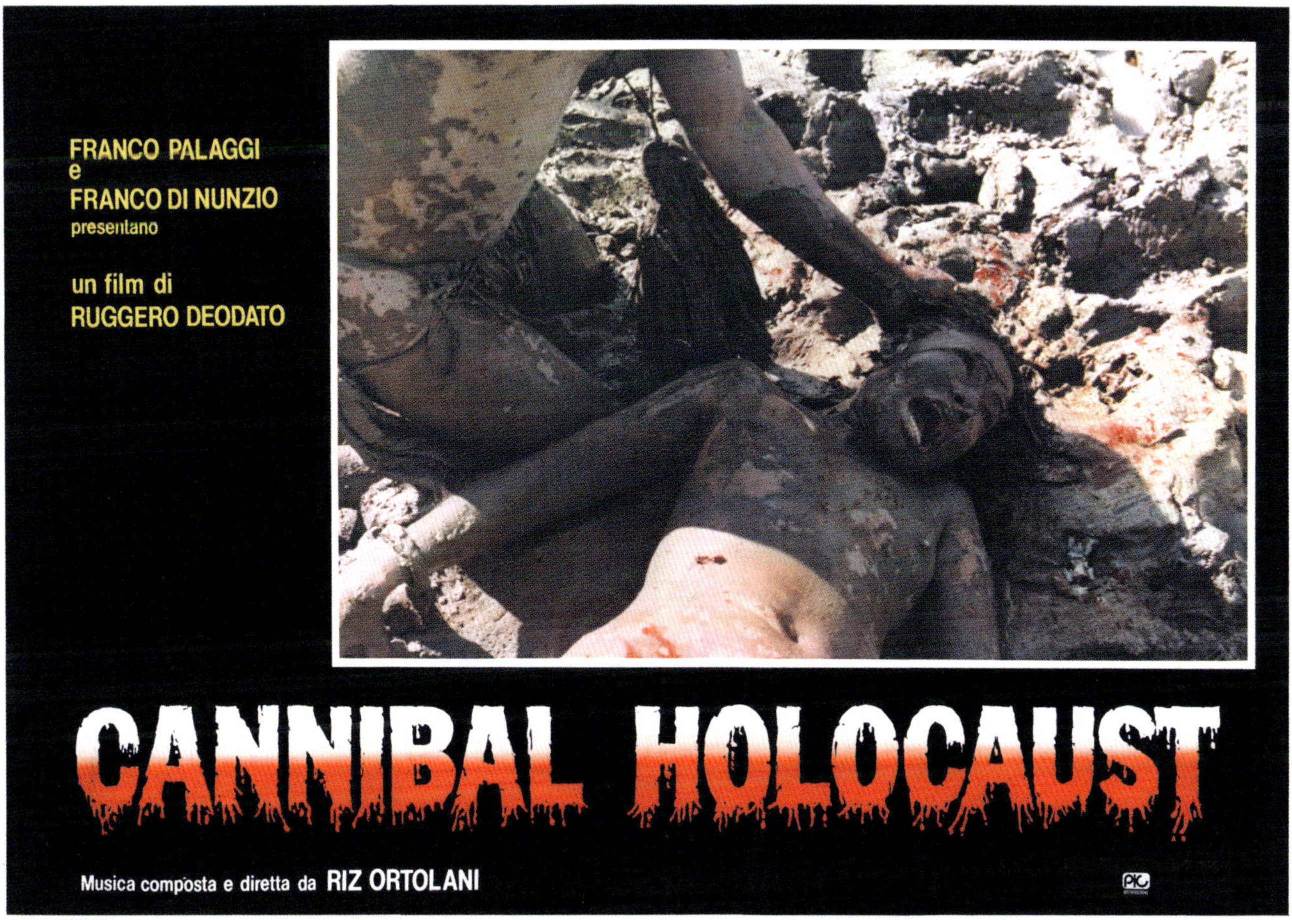

FRANCO PALAGGI
e
FRANCO DI NUNZIO
presentano

un film di
RUGGERO DEODATO

CANNIBAL HOLOCAUST

Musica composta e diretta da RIZ ORTOLANI

PIC

Above: At home with the Yamamomo, also known as the Tree People. The body of a criminal, executed for a crime unknown to Monroe and Chaco, is lowered from the trees before being butchered and cooked.
Below: Jack Anders's head is held aloft. The Yamamomo's revenge is swift, brutal and deadly.

above: Professor Monroe (Robert Kerman), seen seated in the foreground next to his guide Chaco (Salvatore Basile), undertakes the ritualistic exchange necessary in order to secure the undeveloped cans of film shot by the Yates crew. The Yamamomo chief accepts their gift of a cassette recorder. But first they must partake in a cannibal feast. They are offered the freshly-removed internal organs of the Yamamomo criminal who had been executed in front of their eyes upon their arrival at the village.
below: The aftermath of the Yamamomo's human hunt.

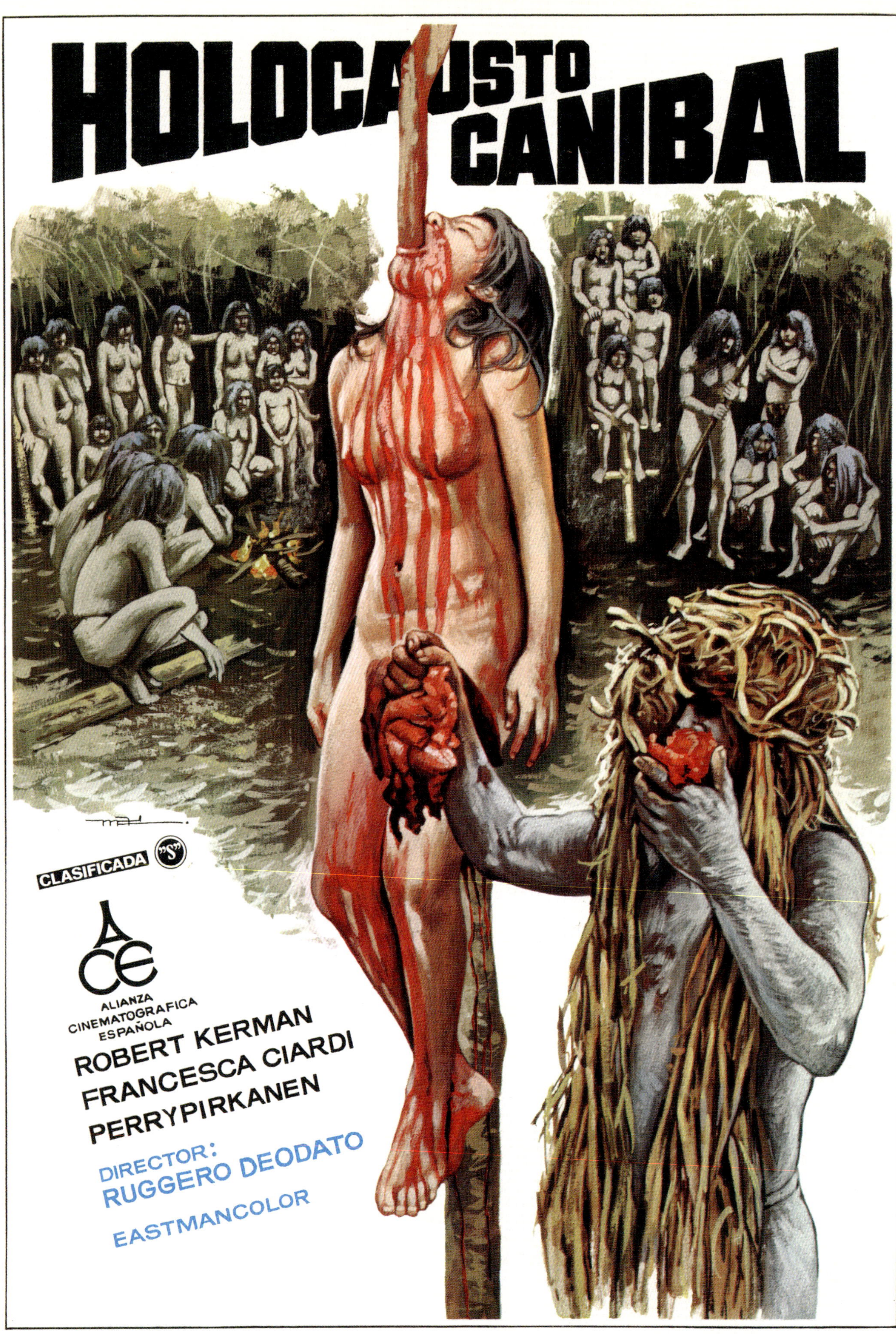
HOLOCAUSTO
CANIBAL
CLASIFICADA "S"
ALIANZA
CINEMATOGRAFICA
ESPAÑOLA
ROBERT KERMAN
FRANCESCA CIARDI
PERRYPIRKANEN
DIRECTOR:
RUGGERO DEODATO
EASTMANCOLOR

opposite: Spanish poster.

left: Original French press ad, based upon a flash-frame image of the Yamamomo moving in for the kill at the film's climax *(above)*.

below from the top: The Yacùmo run from a burning hut. They are terrorised by the Yates team, who intend to use this footage in their finished film to represent a raid by the Yamamomo ; Yates filming the mayhem ; More natives flee the inferno ; Yates, aroused by his monstrous actions, fucks Faye in full view of the frightened, bewildered villagers.

Monroe is shown the Yates footage at the offices of the TV company which financed the expedition. They plan to broadcast the film under the title of "The Green Inferno", excitedly anticipating massive ratings. Before seeing the unedited footage though, a female TV executive introduces Monroe to Yates's 'style' by showing him extracts from a film he made for them a year before, entitled "The Last Road to Hell". Appropriating genuine archival film of firing-squad executions, Deodato slyly ups the ante considerably at this point; if genuine animal mutilation footage helps lend the stench of authenticity to the cleverly staged, though faked, scenes of human carnage soon to erupt across the screen, the incorporation of actual human death scenes, in a tangentially contextualised scenario such as this, serves to confuse the issue even more. Driving the point home, Deodato concludes this aside by having the TV executive comment, *"Just to give you an idea how Alan and the others worked, everything you just saw was a put-on. Alan paid the soldiers to do a bit of acting"*. Precisely the allegations which were levelled against Gualtiero Jacopetti and Franco Prosperi when **Africa addio** was released in 1966. Subtlety is not **Cannibal Holocaust**'s strong point, in fact it wallows in rhetoric, but the positioning of this segment immediately before the infamous turtle disembowelment scene is unfortunate to say the least...

A detailed recounting of the events which lead to the film crew being hunted down, tortured, mutilated and eaten by the Yamamomo is superfluous, because from this point on the film's narrative degenerates into a remorseless procession of ever-more barbaric actions by the film-makers. It is sufficient to know that they humiliate the Yacùmo, kill their livestock, burn their village to the ground and callously intrude firstly upon the death agonies of a seriously burned villager, then (in **Cannibal Holocaust**'s most gratuitous scene – in that it serves no perceivable purpose within the structure of the film whatsoever) they film a ritualistic forced abortion and the clubbing to death of the former mother-to-be.

Before heading into Yamamomo territory, "The Green Inferno" is interrupted on a couple of occasions by asides featuring Monroe engaged in earnest, moralistic soul-searching as he attempts to persuade the executives to abandon their plans to screen the film. Monroe counters arguments that the footage is *"exceptional... Let's be realistic. Who knows anything about the Yacùmo? Today people want sensationalism. The more you rape their senses, the happier they are!"*, by asking the executives to imagine that the Yacùmo had invaded their homes and destroyed their belongings. This has no effect. One reel later, his anxiety has mutated into anger. *"This so-called documentary footage is offensive, it is dishonest, and above all it is inhuman"*. The lady executive still doesn't get it. *"But it's just a rough cut... this is the most sensational documentary to come along in years!"* (Deodato continually reminds the viewer that what they are seeing is amazing...)

Yates speaks directly to the camera. He explains that they are pushing on, trying to make contact with the Yamamomo. Or Yanomamo, as he calls them. I'd like to think we should trust Professor Monroe's pronunciation, he being a noted NYU anthropologist, and I'd also like to think that Yates's mis-pronunciation of the word was in the script, a way of showing that he did not even know the basic facts about the people he was exploiting so violently. But it's probably just an error on the part of one of the actors. Anyway, I've stuck with Monroe's favoured version...

The film stops, and starts again. The vegetation is notably different. Several days have passed, and they have still seen no sign of the Yamamomo. Suddenly they capture a native girl. A Yamamomo girl. Triumphantly, inexplicably, the men attack her, taking it in turns, rolling around in the mud as one holds the girl down, another rapes her, the third filming the action. Faye objects

right: Carefree Yamamomo women run to the river in order to bathe.
below: The Yacùmo are initially anxious when they see Professor Monroe's other guide, Miguel, holding a gun. Memories of the Yates team come flooding back to them as they huddle together in fear.
centre: A young native woman has her unborn child forcibly aborted in **Cannibal Holocaust**'s most outlandishly gratuitous moment of unpleasantness. The central actress in this scene was actually pregnant, and a doll was used to simulate the aborted foetus.
bottom: A very special dinner is prepared by the Yacùmo women.

strongly, displaying a callous breed of concern as she screams into the camera, *"What do you want to use it for?! a porno film?!"* (thinks: you're wasting our precious film...), and attempts to physi-cally prevent Yates – her boyfriend – from raping the girl (thinks: don't you dare fuck another woman...) Barely noticed, a Yamamomo warrior watches the rape, crouched in the long grass, only metres away.

We cut directly to a riverside clearing, where a young Yamamomo woman is vertically impaled, suspended several feet from the ground. The ten-foot pole exits via her mouth. Yates is overjoyed and must be told to look concerned for the camera. He talks about *"the almost profound respect these primitives have for virginity..."* It is not clear whether Yates is correct, and this scene

is meant to represent swift 'punishment' handed out by the Yamamomo. The implication of this being that, according to Yamamomo lore, rape victims deserve to be executed. As she was one of their own, the inevitable conclusion is that the perpetrators of the crime will soon meet the same fate. The alternative explanation is that the woman was impaled by the Yates team themselves and that it is simply the most blatantly calculated piece of 'rigging' they have so far conceived in order to achieve 'spectacular' footage. Either way, they deserve to die, and Deodato wastes no more time with the trivialities of narrative, settling in for ten solid minutes of apocalyptic violence.

Yates's head hits the ground, facing into the lens of the still-running camera. His eyes close, the film stops, and in the screening room everyone agrees with Monroe's assessment at last. The projectionist is ordered to destroy the film, and in a final, unwise touch we are reminded of the film's message once again as Monroe leaves the building pondering *"I wonder who the real cannibals are?"* Monroe crosses the busy road and the camera pans up for a final shot of towering skyscrapers...

Much has been made of the technical accomplishments of the "Green Inferno" segment of **Cannibal Holocaust**. By using techniques such as shaky hand-held camerawork, deliberately scratched and fogged frames, crash zooms and incorrectly-exposed sequences, Deodato plays the second-half of the film for maximum visceral effect but in the process the movie as a whole loses narrative cohesion. Ironically, it degenerates into little more than a relentless barrage of horrific set-pieces; in fact by the end **Cannibal Holocaust** structurally imitates the form which it seeks to critique – the mondo movie.

above: Warriors of the Shamatari tribe, also known as "The Swamp People", carry away a fallen Yamamomo following a deadly skirmish with their sworn enemies.
below: Cover of the famously-banned UK video release of **Cannibal Holocaust**: one of the first, and still one of the most infamous of the 'video nasties'. The print which 'GO Video' used was cut by more than 6 minutes.
bottom left: In one of the film's controversial scenes of animal butchery, Anders and Felipe catch a turtle and haul it ashore where *(bottom right)* they hack off its head and limbs before devouring it.

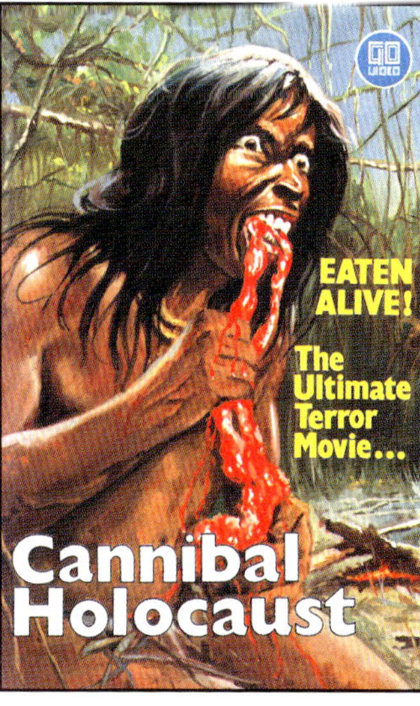

below from the top:
Preparing to burn the Yacùmo village to the ground. Yates operates the camera whilst Anders (backed up by Tomaso) wields a gun in order to control the terrified natives. Only a few days later they are dead: Anders is stripped and hacked to pieces *(middle)*. Yates unwisely decides to stay in the vicinity of the massacre, filming the hideous deaths of Anders and Daniels. It is not long before he pays for his indiscretion with his own life. When he is attacked, his camera keeps running as he falls to the ground, in the process capturing his own horrifying death in close-up. *(bottom)* In a fitting touch of irony, the last thing which his dying eyes see is the same camera lens which he and his crew have used to capture the images of death and destruction for which they were all responsible.

In order to study the ethics of the mondo movie, Deodato himself trod the fine line between recording events, inciting them and actually staging them for the benefit of the camera. While he might defend the animal butchery on show by saying the animals were eaten anyway, this ignores the fact that arguably the most shocking scene of all occurs as the Yates crew prepare to stage the burning of the Yacùmo village: Deodato filmed Mark (i.e. Luca Barbareschi) shooting a piglet which was tied to a post, as Yates screams excitedly *"In the jungle it's the daily violence of the strong over-coming the weak!"* The piglet squeals, mortally-wounded, lying on its side in the mud. Soon the village is on fire. The smiling, adrenalised film-crew obsessively films the carnage, Ortolani's haunting score dramatises the imagery. Someone screams *"It's beautiful!"*. The piglet is forgotten. Until we cut back to the safety of a New York park and Monroe says to the lady TV executive. *"You know that pig that was killed? That was food for those people..."* This comment catapults the veracity of this segment to another level. It is just one example of the tangled mess of accusation and integrity which binds the structure of the film to the fabric of the world in which it resides, revered and reviled in equal measure.

Cannibal Holocaust is a challenging, marginal film. It is difficult to watch it without 'taking sides' in a battle in which it demands that the viewer must become engaged. It is also very easy to attack the film on the grounds that it is nothing more than a mutilation extravaganza; a relentless procession of extreme imagery which serves no purpose, but this (gut) reaction is simplistic, as careful consideration of its themes can yield valuable insights. Personally, I am left in an impossibly ambivalent state when considering the moral questions which it raises; I no more want to 'defend' it than I wish to 'attack' it for the embarrassed ethical corner into which it paints itself. It's Deodato's film. His best. It's also his responsibility, and his alone.
(Harvey Fenton)

HOUSE ON THE EDGE OF THE PARK

1980
Italian theatrical title: **La casa sperduta nel parco**, US theatrical & UK/US video title: **House on the Edge of the Park**, German theatrical title: **Der Schlitzer**, French video title: **La maison au fond du parc**, Spanish title: **Trampa para un violador**, Italian shooting title: **La casa ai confini del parco**, alternative title: **The Ripper on the Edge**, Dutch video cover title: **The House at the Edge of the Park**, Danish video titles: **Farlig indbydelse**.
Italy
director: Ruggero Deodato

Franco Palaggi and Franco Di Nunzio present an F.D. Cinematografica production.
registration number: 6.857. visa number: 74874 [2/4/80]. filmed in September 1979 (19 days) on location in Rome and New York (USA) with interiors at De Paolis – INCIR studios (Rome). colour by LV – Luciano Vittori.

cast: David A. Hess (Alex). Annie Belle [Annie Brilland] (Lisa). Cristian [Christian] Borromeo (Tom). Giovanni Lombardo Radice (Ricky). Marie Claude Joseph (Glenda [also referred to as 'Roots' – a term of racial abuse]). Gabriele Di Giulio (Howard). Brigitte Petronio (Cindy). Karoline Mardeck (Tom's sister) <and with a special appearance by> Lorraine De Selle (Gloria).

story & screenplay: Gianfranco Clerici & Vincenzo Mannino. directors of photography: Sergio D'Offizi. music composed & directed by Riz Ortolani, ©CAM Edizioni Musicali Roma. film editor: Vincenzo Tomassi. production design & costumes: Massimo Antonello Geleng. in charge of production: Giovanni Masini. unit manager: Vito Di Bari. continuity: Claudia Florio. cameraman: Enrico Lucidi. assistant cameraman: Enrico Maggi. key grip: Sergio Profili. chief electrician: Enrico D'Offizi. wardrobe mistress: Lucia Costantini. make-up: Raoul Ranieri. hairstyles: Nerea Rosmenit. props: Rodolfo Ruzza. stills: Paolo Maria Cavicchioli. assistant editor: Rita Antonelli. cutting room assistant: Armando Pace. sound engineer: Alfonso Montesanti. sound studios: Cinefonico Palatino. mixage: Bruno Longobardo. songs "Sweetly" by Benjamin & Riz Ortolani, sung by Diana Corsini; "Much More" by Benjamin & Riz Ortolani, sung by Charlie Cannon, Rosamaria D'Andrea & Patrizia Neri – all recorded on CAM Records.

Italian theatrical distributor: Adige Film 76 (1st public showing on 6 November 1980). rated: 18. running time: 94 minutes. length: 2,482 metres.
US theatrical distributor: Bedford Entertainment/Trio Entertainment (released in February 1985). rating: none. running time: 91 minutes.
West German theatrical distributor: United Artists (released on 17 April 1981). rated: 18. running time: 88 minutes. length: 2,410 metres.

Submitted to the British Board of Film Classification in April 1981 by Target International Films Ltd. with a running time of 89 minutes 55 seconds. (length: 8,002 feet). The film was rejected outright.

The casting of David A. Hess in a lead thug role is a signal that Ruggero Deodato's **La casa sperduta nel parco/House on the Edge of the Park**, like many Italian exploitation films, at least partially a do-over of an American hit… in this case, Wes Craven's **The Last House on the Left** (1972). There's a character in a P.G. Wodehouse novel who writes mystery novels under the pseudonym 'Adela Bristow' on the assumption ill-spoken patrons will barge into bookshops and demand 'gimme an Agatha Christie' and hard-of-hearing clerks will sell them an Adela Bristow instead… and, more importantly, the customer won't care. With only a slight degree of irony, the Italian film industry cheerfully adopted this model. A few patrons for Deodato's **Concorde Affair** (1979) might have assumed they were buying tickets for **Airport '79: The Concorde** (1979), the official **Airport** series entry that year – but it was hoped that once they settled in their seats, what they got wasn't too much of a let-down. At about the same time Italian filmmakers turned out **Zombi 2** (1979), **Cacciatore 2** (1980) and **Alien 2 – Sulla Terra** (1980) – spurious but entertaining mock-sequels to **Dawn of the Dead** (1978), **The Deer Hunter** (1978) and **Alien** (1979) – so it's almost a surprise the film wasn't called **L'ultima casa sulla sinestra 2**. Lucio Fulci might not have matched the zeitgeist-riding George Romero movie, but he staged a zombie-shark fight and Antonio Margheriti's **Deer Hunter** riff owed more to **Apocalypse Now** (1979) but never mind. Note that distributors of these films outside Italy tended to downplay any passing off, perhaps to avoid legal hassle, and titled these films **Zombie/Zombie Flesh Eaters**, **The Last Hunter** and **Alien Terror**. At that, they were lucky – Universal and Warners managed successful lawsuits against **Abby** (1975) and **L'ultimo squalo/Great White** (1981), imitative cash-ins on **The Exorcist** and **Jaws**.

As with many Italian exploitation films too easily dismissed as ripoffs of American movies, **House on the Edge of the Park** plays games with audience expectations, deviating from the template of the imitable hit as much as it sticks to it. Aldo Lado's **L'ultimo treno della notte/Late Night Trains** (1975), positioned as a **Last House** sequel in some markets, is a virtual remake Craven's film, itself a remake of Ingmar Bergman's **Jungfrukällan/The Virgin Spring** (1960), albeit with a glossier look (which Deodato carries over) and some plot streamlining. **House on the Edge of the Park**

above: David A. Hess is the focal point of **House on the Edge of the Park**. His terrifying performance in the role of Alex is a potent reminder of his similarly powerful screen presence in Wes Craven's notorious 1972 rape/revenge grindhouse classic **The Last House on the Left**.
top: Giovanni Lombardo Radice was also a familiar face in exploitation movies. Most of his roles were of Italian origin and filmed in a flurry of activity in the early 1980s. Here he stars as Alex's impressionable sidekick Ricky, initially oblivious to the fact that his hosts *[clockwise from left:* Gloria (Lorraine De Selle), Glenda (Marie Claude Joseph), Tom (Christian Borromeo) & Howard (Gabriele Di Giulio)*]* are humiliating him.
opposite bottom right: Glenda and Lisa (Annie Belle) are forced by Alex to kiss each other.

Cutting-edge artwork from Germany *(right)*, UK *(top)* and Denmark *(below)*.

features Hess as Alex, who isn't just a version of Krug, his character from **Last House**, but an embodiment of Hess's screen image. The character name Alex evokes the home-invading droog of **A Clockwork Orange** (1971), but it seems more relevant that the actor's full name is David Alexander Hess. Hess had already played a variation on Krug in Pasquale Festa Campanile's **Autostop rosso sangue**/**Hitch-Hike** (1977), an on-the-road triangle drama with Franco Nero and Corinne Cléry. By the time he signed up with Deodato, he seems to have started finding typecasting onerous. If anything, he is more uncontrolled and maniacal in **House on the Edge of the Park** than in his other Krug-type roles – relishing Alex's repulsive come-on catch-phrase ('Hello lady …') and at one point opening his mouth wider than the special effects rubber head of Garrett Morris in **The Stuff** (1985). However, as with the about-face 'who are the real cannibals?' theme of **Cannibal Holocaust**, the film presents us with an obvious monster only to set up reversals that force us to reassess our presumptions. As with **Cannibal Holocaust**, the bluntness doesn't always work – Deodato wobbles a bit whenever he wants to humanise horrible people – and it's not easy to determine exactly who the film wants us to hate most.

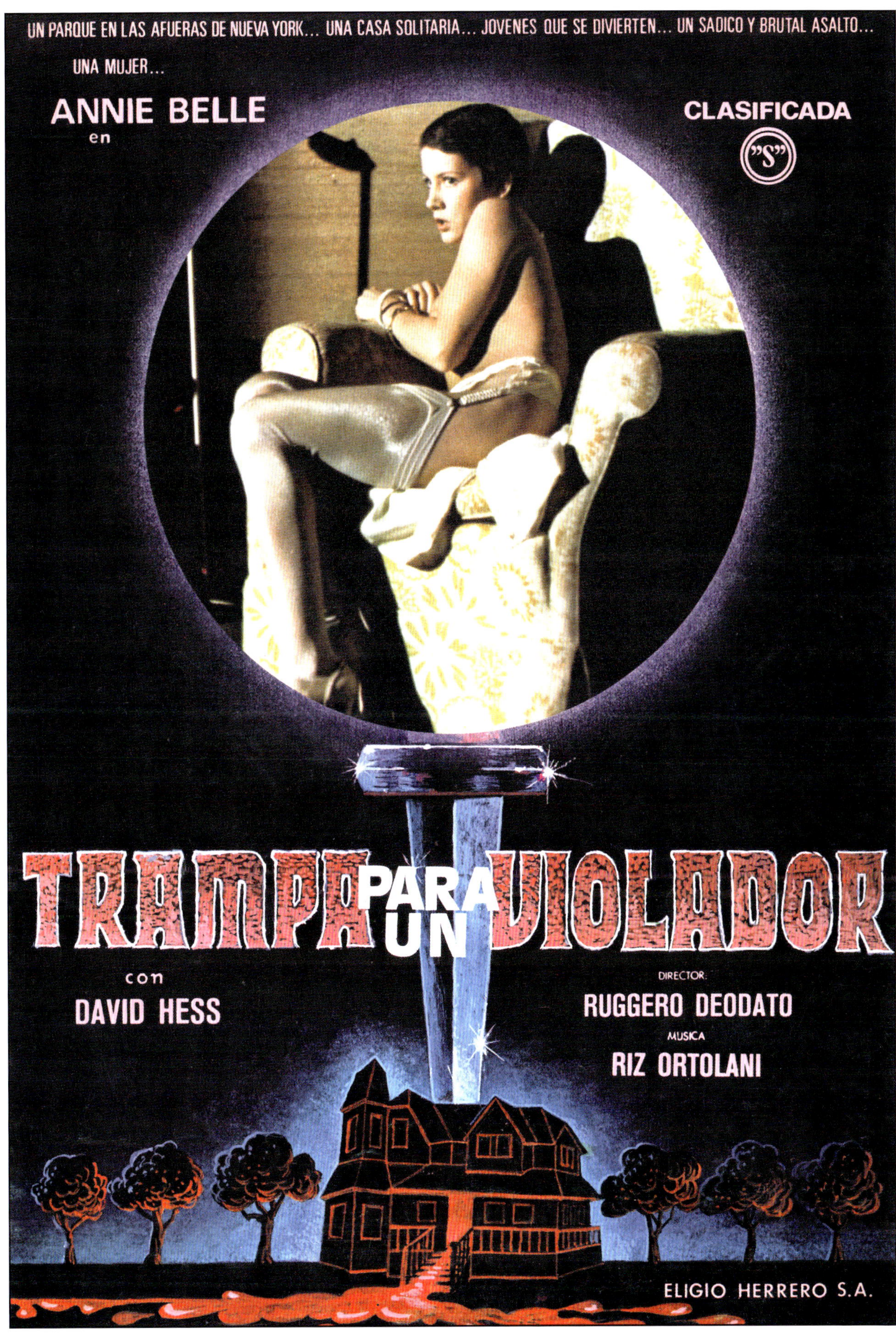

above: Annie Belle features prominently in the Spanish poster for the film. *opposite bottom left:* David Hess takes control of his victims' plush middle-class abode in **House on the Edge of the Park**.

In a prologue, Alex barges into a woman's car – apparently in Central Park, New York – and rapes and throttles her (the actress, Karoline Mardeck, was Hess's wife). This initially seems a random bit of character-establishing nastiness but – spoiler! – the crime turns out to be the motor for the whole plot. It's not established whether the atrocity is a one-off or the sort of thing Alex does every Friday and Saturday night to women he's set eyes on in a disco. Hess certainly plays

above: **The Last House on the Left** was such a huge success that its influence was still being felt when **House on the Edge of the Park** was made in 1980. The presence of Hess in the cast inevitably led to Deodato's film being promoted by association with its eight-years-old precursor.
The Variety/Cannes advertising even used a graphic of Hess wielding a knife which was lifted directly from one of the most infamous scenes in **The Last House on the Left**!

the role as if he were a serial rapist/killer, but the Gianfranco Clerici-Vincenzo Mannino script implies that this is the first and only time he's gone this far. Alex sports a slightly-too-tight Travolta disco outfit to suggest that he's basically every 1970s guy's fantasy of himself as irresistible stud taken to grotesque, horrific extremes. He has an impressionable tagalong sidekick, mechanic Ricky (Giavanni Lombardo Radice) – a teaming reminiscent of Tony Musante and Martin Sheen in Larry Peerce's **The Incident** (1967), an ur-text of the tormented-by-hoods/exposé-of-every-day-hypocrisy suspense-horror melodrama. After prowling night-time stock footage of New York City, preppie Tom (Christian Borromeo) and his chic girlfriend Lisa (Annie Belle) roll into the garage where Alex and Ricky work, just as the duo are ready to go out on the town. In return for a small repair, Tom invites the unlikely pair to his isolated villa in New Jersey (which doesn't seem to be anywhere near a park, the way the Cunningham house wasn't last or on the left) for an evening of implied decadent entertainment. Being idiots as well as horny, the greasy mechanics go along with it.

Given the film's reputation as one of the nastiest of the video nasties – the current UK release is *still* censored – it's a surprise that the evening takes so long to descend into the expected ultra-violence. After the credits, the narrative unfolds in something close to real time. For a while, it owes as much to **Who's Afraid of Virginia Woolf?** (1968) as **The Last House on the Left**… indeed, not only does Deodato play out the games playwright Edward Albee put on the agenda for a disastrous social evening (Get the Guests and Humiliate the Host) but delivers on the third game (Hump the Hostess) Albee proposes but never gets round to. Tom, who sports a natty blazer and a Shane Briant circa 1972 haircut, owns a mod bourgeois fantasy home with glass sliding doors and a swimming pool – obviously located on a stage at Incir De Paolis in Rome rather than anywhere near the Garden State. As in **Hitch-Hike**, Hess is a crude, ugly American surrounded by effete, decadent Europeans – he's almost like a *daikaiju* blundering through a cardboard city, trampling extras underfoot. Also present are Howard (Gabriele Di Giulio), a macho male model type ('the only one with balls'), and his girlfriend Gloria (Lorraine De Selle, with the same character name she has in **Cannibal Ferox**, 1981) – who is marginally the most sympathetic of the crowd. Plus black, bald, strikingly odd Glenda (Marie Claude Joseph, in her only known film role), labelled a 'Grace Jones' type in some notices – though she turns out disappointingly to be a passive, neutral character. While Alex leers at the women, coming on to them equally – and not wondering why they're putting up with him – Ricky is jollied into being a clown, performing a clumsy disco strip while drunk then cheated out of all his cash in a rigged card game. It's this demonstration of the corruption of superficially polite, monied people that spurs Alex to pull out his straight razor and abuse the hosts.

Howard gets beaten up and shoved in the pool – which Alex pisses in as the floundering victim tries to climb out and is repeatedly kicked back into the water – then tied to a table with electric flex and ignored for much of the evening. Tom has his face repeatedly battered against a glass table and has to watch as ornaments get broken, though notably Alex only smashes china figures apparently on display for that purpose (given a later plot twist, this might even be the case) and is gingerly respectful of the rest of the set dressing (which might have had to go back to the prop store at De Paolis) even as he comes up with ways to break the people in the house. Alex takes Lisa upstairs for Hump the Hostess, paying her back for **Emmanuelle**-style soapy shower teasing earlier, and encourages Ricky to rape Gloria, which he is unable to do until she gives him encouragement, presumably as part

Up close and personal... **House on the Edge of the Park** features a relentless parade of personal abuse. *(left):* Ricky gropes Gloria. *(below):* Alex attacks Cindy and *(bottom right)* he eventually even turns on Ricky.

opposite top right: The Dutch VHS video cover features one of the many moments during which Alex threatens his captives with a straight razor. In this particular case the unlucky recipient of his attentions is Gloria.

of a plan to cut him loose from the alpha thug. One aspect of 1970s movie rape culture seldom remarked on is that, at least earlier in the decade, it was assumed that rape could be a political act – there were, let's face it, actual people in the counterculture who seriously said this. Italian films especially were prone to indulging this she-deserves-it-because-she's-posh-and-looked-down-her-long-nose-at-the-sweaty-peasant-and-besides-she-enjoyed-it-anyway tosh (cf: Sergio Leone's **Giù la testa**/**A Fistful of Dynamite**, 1971, Lina Wertmüller's **Travolti da un insolito destino nell'azzuro mare d'agosto**/**Swept Away**, 1974). Alex seems to imagine he's in one of those films and Deodato strings the character along – Belle's blank, unreadable performance is surprisingly effective – even as he films Hess' gurning antics through a lens of disgust. Glenda is generally pawed, but left out of the worst of the abuse. An American film would have addressed the racial angle, and perhaps had the lower-class white home invader ask the black woman what she's doing with these awful rich people. An equivalent character (Judy Pace) hangs out with a rich white family in **Frogs** (1972) only to realise she's classed with 'the help' rather than really included among the guests when the horror starts.

Just as the cruelty is flagging, another guest arrives. Blonde, young-looking, virginal innocent Cindy (Brigitte Petronio) is subjected to a lengthy, hard-to-watch Sadean torture as Alex strips her and then repeatedly slices her breasts, thighs and stomach with his cutthroat razor. This is the scene everyone remembers from the film. It functions like the unfaked animal cruelty in **Cannibal Holocaust** to push the limits of what devotees of

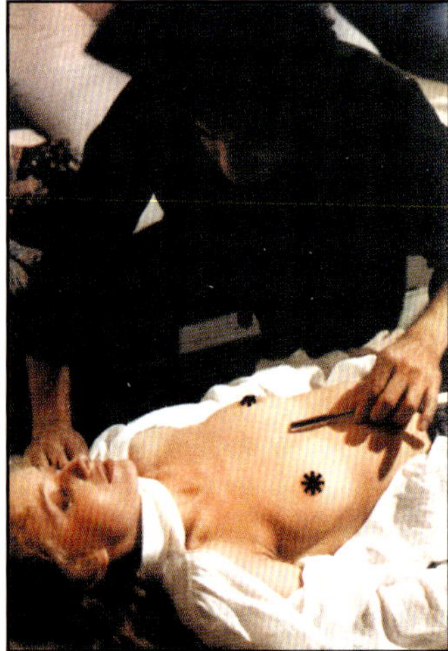

top: Alex uses his razor to threaten and *(above)* to torture his captors. In the film's most appalling scene, innocent interloper Cindy's naked body is gently caressed by the razor before Alex proceeds to repeatedly slash her breasts. But don't you just love those prudish Spanish censor stars...
above right: Alex ties-up Howard (*"the only one with any balls!"*) whilst Ricky offers his excited encouragement.
bottom right: The tables are turned during the climax of **House on the Edge of the Park**.

extreme horror are willing to watch. It's sadistic, misogynist and prurient – and unnecessary in the sense that the whole character could be removed from the film without affecting the plot. With the twists that take over the narrative in the film's closing minutes, poor scarred-for-life Cindy is forgotten as if Petronio had worked her scheduled days and hurried off to her next gig (she was in Fellini's **La città delle donne/City of Women** that year) before pick-up shots could be done to specify her fate. Nevertheless, the abuse of Cindy sticks in the minds of anyone who sees **House on the Edge of the Park**, a film which boasts a surprisingly low body count for a nasty (only two deaths). In *Nightmare Movies*, I described the razor caress scene as 'an achievement, certainly, if not a particularly pleasurable one.' My feelings haven't changed over the years. What happens to Cindy is the major reason I've not rewatched the film as often as I have other Italian horrors of the same vintage. Your mileage may vary.

Broadly, **The Last House on the Left** is a rape/revenge film. So, as it turns out, is **House on the Edge of the Park**, though it has been posing as something else, a confrontation of bourgeois hypocrisy and underclass criminality. The thematic meat of the party scenes has been chewed over quite often in horror – a recent example is Paul Andrew Williams' **Cherry Tree Lane** (2010), a handy reminder that rape and murder aren't as bad as being middle-class and repressed – though, in this instance, the cartoonishness of Hess' caveman act takes the edge off the analysis. Poor Ricky is thoroughly abused by his own best friend well before the posh people make a fool of him and attempts to make him the feeling character in the film – somewhere between Junior in **Last House** and the gormless Matthew in **I Spit on Your Grave** (1978) – are token. Radice, a performer who matches Hess in demented glee, plays no one's idea of a sensitive soul and most viewers tend to feel Ricky gets off easy when the film shifts to the revenge part of the equation. Just as it seems Alex is about to execute everyone in the house, the battered Tom reaches into a drawer and pulls out a gun. He tells Alex that the girl in the pre-credits sequence was his sister and this whole evening has been a trap designed so that he can shoot her murderer in self-defence. Simply gunning Alex down wouldn't register as a fit punishment for his screen villainy, so he has to be brutalised first. As in **Cannibal Ferox**, where Radice plays the alpha bastard role, the macho villain has to be unmanned during his execution so there's a close-up of a bullet squib going off in Alex's crotch as his dick is shot off. He's also shoved in the pool – it's not quite clear, but I think Howard pays Alex back by shooting him in the rectum, a particularly unpleasant fatal wound explicated in **Things to Do in Denver When You're Dead** (1995).

Though Lisa at least is in on the revenge scheme and takes a shot at Alex as he flounders in the pool, the women play only minor roles in the disposal of Alex – and it's Gloria who argues for not murdering Ricky, muting the film's cynical depiction of the New Jersey haut bourgeoisie. A few lines about how surprisingly difficult it was to get to the drawer with the gun don't quite defuse the audience's qualms about the practicality of Tom's plot. Did he *have* to get his nose smashed flat and subject his friends to all manner of possibly lethal abuses before turning the tables? There are hints that Tom and Lisa

have now got a taste for this kind of vigilante bloodletting – and maybe a masochist relish for the punishment they've taken along the way – and will set up more evenings like this, suggesting that they are at least as much classist serial killers as righteous avengers. The ending of **House on the Edge of the Park** isn't quite as memorable as the finish of **Cannibal Holocaust** (little is, to be fair) but it trucks in the same brand of all-purpose indictment of everyone involved in this nasty little story and the nasty wider society that has indulged neanderthal creeps like Alex and sadist crackpots like Tom, not to mention everyone who buys a ticket to the horror show or rents or buys the feelbad film on VHS, DVD, Blu-Ray and media as yet uninvented. The unique strangeness of **House on the Edge of the Park** might come from unresolved tensions between script, director and cast (not to mention composer Riz Ortolani, who provides a memorable easy listening/nursery jazz score that includes a creepy wail of a song 'Sweetly') as much as actual intent – but it deserves its place as its auteur's second most significant contribution to the outrageous, defiantly disreputable, inventive, notorious late flowering of the Italian exploitation industry. A sequel, **The House on the Edge of the Park, Part II**, is listed on the IMDb, but that seems to be wishful thinking rather than an active project.
(Kim Newman)

THE ATLANTIS INTERCEPTORS

1983
Italian theatrical/Italian video title: **I predatori di Atlantide**, German theatrical title: **Atlantis Inferno**, French theatrical title: **Atlantis Interceptors**, UK video title: **The Atlantis Interceptors**, US video title: **Raiders of Atlantis**
Italy
directed by Roger Franklin [Ruggero Deodato]

a Regency Cinematografica production. a Regency Productions presentation
registration number: 7.205. visa number: 79327 [10/11/83].
colour by Telecolor.
filmed in April & May 1983 on location in the Philippines and in Florida (U.S.A.) with interiors at RPA Elios studios (Rome)

cast: Christopher Connelly (Mike Ross). Marie Fields [Gioia Maria Scola] (Dr. Cathy Rollins). Tony King (Washington, 'Mohammad'). Mike Miller (Nemnez, ex-con). Ivan Rassimov (Bill Cook). John Blade [Giancarlo Prati] (Frank, a technician). Bruce Baron (Crystal Skull) <and with> George Hilton (Professor Peter Saunders). Mike Monti [Mike Monty] (George). Michael [Michele] Soavi (James, a technician). Audrey Perkins. Morris Fard [Maurizio Fardi] (Larry Stoddard). Benny Lewis [Lewis Eduardo Ciannelli] (The Commander). John Vasallo. James Demby. Gudrun Schemissner. Ruggero Deodato (helicopter pad technician).

associate producer: Alex Tiu. original story & screenplay: Vincent [Vincenzo] Mannino & Robert Gold [Dardano Sacchetti]. director of photography: Robert D'Ettorre Piazzoli. music composed & conducted by Oliver Onions [Guido & Maurizio DeAngelis]; published by Cabum Publishers. film editor: Vincent Thomas [Vincenzo Tomassi]. art director: Benny Amalfitano. costume designer: Judy Serano. stunt co-ordinator: Rock Stuntman Team. assistant director: Mary Anthony. script continuity: Georgia Sullivan. unit manager: Ted Dobson. assistant unit manager: Tom Ward. camera operator: Robert Forges [Davanzati]. assistant cameramen: Fred Vicar, Vince Aronica. action stills: Frank Vitali. special effects: Gene Reds [Gianetto De Rossi]. set dresser: Joe Peters. gaffer: Lewis Patters. key grip: Alfred Donovan. props: Sandy Brown. wardrobe: Lucille Bennett. wardrobe assistant: Cindy Martins. 1st production assistant: Geraldine Picar. 2nd production assistant: Pat Gauvan Dizon. make-up artist: Maurizio Trani. hair stylist: Mary Morris. 1st assistant editor: Peter Thomas. camera & lighting equipment: Arco 2. costume house: Art and Fashion Costumes. wigs: Rocchetti & Carboni. footwear: Arditi Footwear. set furnishings: Sorman Bros. sound effects by Cineaudio Effects. foley: Al [Alvaro] Gramigna. transportation: Cinema Service. special optical effects: V.G. miniatures: Al Passeri. sound supervisor: Dean

top: Crystal Skull (Bruce Baron), leader of the renegade biker gang in **The Atlantis Interceptors**, flanked by two of his cronies. *above:* There is a lot of fighting in this film. *below:* Mike Ross (Christopher Connelly) and Nemnez (Mike Miller), armed and ready. Connelly was a big star in Italy at the time due to his leading role in the hugely successful television series **Martin Eden**.

Peterson. boom man: Janet Bock. sound mixer: Benny [Bruno] Moreal. [English language version] dialogue editor: Michael Billingsley. post-synchronization director: Nick Alexander.
The Production thanks AGIP SpA and Philippine Airlines for their co-operation.
song "Black Inferno" performed by The Inferno Group.

Italian theatrical distributor: Regencyregional independents (1st public showing on 25 November 1983). running time: 92 minutes. length: 2,524 metres.
West German theatrical distributor: Jugendfilm (released on 25 November 1983). running time: 92 minutes. length: 2,516 metres.
French theatrical distributor: Visa Film Distribution (released in Paris on 15 October 1986). running time: 92 minutes.

The early eighties witnessed an explosion of Italian-made adventure movies designed to capitalise on the worldwide success of **Mad Max** (1979) and especially its riotous sequel **The Road Warrior** (aka **Mad Max 2**) (1981). Deodato made **The Atlantis Interceptors** in 1983, the peak year for such productions. He was in good company, joining the likes of Sergio Martino (**2019: After the Fall of New York**), Aristide Massaccesi (**Endgame**) and Lucio Fulci (**Rome 2033: The Fighter Centurions**). The stock ingredients for such films were some sort of Post-Apocalypse scenario and colourful gangs of violent renegades riding custom motorbikes.

When a secret Atlantic mission to re-float a stricken nuclear submarine is inexplicably disrupted by blackened skies and towering waves, the domed island of Atlantis rises from beneath the waves, and a motorcycle gang called 'The Interceptors' lays waste to an American coastal town. The Interceptors, led by the ruthless 'Crystal Skull', are opposed by a motley crew of survivors from the wrecked military recovery vessel. Amongst them is Dr. Cathy Rollins, an expert in pre-Colombian dialects, who has managed to decipher the symbols on recently-recovered Atlantean artefacts. The Interceptors kidnap Cathy and take her back to Atlantis, where their leaders hope to use her to re-discover the lost secrets of their world, thus enabling them to dominate the Earth once again. Cathy's friends, led by Mike (Christopher Connelly) and his sidekick Washington (Tony King) commandeer a helicopter and fly to Atlantis to save her...

After the action-packed, scene-setting first half, shot mainly in urban Florida, the rest of the film takes place in the exotic environment of the Philippines, chosen to represent the luxurious perfection of the mythical Atlantis. The change of scenery is merely cosmetic however, as the film doggedly continues to follow its established routine of minimal dialogue and maximum action right up until the utterly silly final scenes, which see Mike and Washington saving the day and escaping just in the nick of time by flying their helicopter through the rapidly diminishing gap in Atlantis's closing dome, before the mighty island sinks below the waves once more.

The Atlantis Interceptors is a fast-paced, lightweight action movie, made by a professional cast and crew, only slightly hampered by less than adequate resources. Misfires include all the water-bound effects work – real toy-boat-in-a-bath-tub stuff. Highlights include some very dangerous-looking stunts involving moving vehicles, most hazardous of all being several cross-over incidents (chopper to bus and vice versa). Michele Soavi has a decent supporting role as a radar operator who is kidnapped by the Interceptors, then turns up later on Atlantis, presumably brainwashed, and proceeds to shoot his former allies with a rifle. Look out also for a couple of Deodato's favourite gags – e.g. a spiked booby-trap (see **Last Cannibal World**), and a hanged corpse whose freely-swinging legs knock against a playing jukebox, causing the record to skip. This gag was re-used several years later in **Dial: Help**.
(Harvey Fenton)

CUT AND RUN

1985
Italian theatrical/Italian video title: **Inferno in diretta**, US theatrical/UK video title: **Cut and Run**, French theatrical title: **Amazonia, la jungle blanche**, shooting title: **Hell, Live**, pre-shooting title: **Marimba**
Italy
director: Ruggero Deodato

produced by Alessandro Fracassi for Racing Pictures, S.r.L. a film by Ruggero Deodato.
registration number: 7.337. visa number: 80582 [24/4/85].
colour by Telecolor S.P.A.
shooting from 25 June 1984 in Venezuela and Miami & Dade County (Florida, USA).

cast: Lisa Blount (Frances Hudson). Leonard Mann [Leonardo Manzella] (Mark Ludman). Willie Aames (Tommy Allo). Richard Lynch (Colonel Brian Horne, 'El Fantasma'). Richard Bright (Bob Allo). Michael Berryman (Quecho). Eriq Lasalle (Fargas, informant). Gabriele Tinti (Manuel) <with> Valentina Forte <in the role of> (Ana) <with the participation of> John Steiner (Vlado) <special appearance by> Karen Black (Karin, network supervisor) <with> Barbara Magnolfi (Rita, drugs courier). Luca Barbareschi (Bud, Bob's contact in Rio Negro). Penny Brown (Lucy, Karin's assistant). Carlos De Carvalho (Tony Martina, pilot). Edward Farrelly. Ottaviano Dell' Acqua (Bob's helicopter pilot). Roffredo Gaetani. Ruggero Deodato (other guy in TV footage of Colonel Horne at Jonestown)

story & script by Cesare Frugoni & Dardano Sacchetti. director of photography: Alberto Spagnoli. music composed by Claudio Simonetti. music publisher (copyright): Bixio C.E.M.S.A. S.p.A. film editor: Mario Morra. production manager: Maurizio Anticoli. art director: Claudio Cinini. costumes: Francesca Panicali. continuity: Rita Agostini. assistant director: Marina Mattoli. cameraman: Emilio Loffredo. assistant cameraman: Sergio Melaranci. make-up: Maurizio Trani & Alberto Blasi. assistant editors: Massimo Quaglia. other editing assistants: Nadia Boggian & Mario D'Ambrosio. chief electrician: Fernando Massaccesi. chief grip: Franco Micheli. equipment: Carlo Cascioli. special effects grip: Paolo Ricci. dialogue coach: Frank Von Kuegelgen. sound: Piero Fondi. sound editor: Michael Billingsley. mixage: Danilo Morono. synch lab: C.D.S. S.r.L. titles & special effects: Penta Studio S.r.L. sound effects: Gjst Movie S.N.C.

Italian theatrical distributor: C.D.E. – Compagnia Distribuzione Europea (1st public showing on 8 August 1985). rated: 14. running time: 90 minutes. length: 2,476 metres.
US theatrical distributor: New World Pictures (released in May 1986). rated: R. running time: 87 minutes.
French theatrical distributor: Eurogroup (released in Paris on 21 August 1985). rated: 13. running time: 90 minutes.

Due to film as **Marimba** in August 1980 under the direction of Wes Craven and starring Tim McIntyre, Dirk Benedict and Chris Mitchum.

Cut and Run was released in 1985 following a long and turbulent production. Plans for the film were laid as early as 1980, when Racing Pictures optioned a script by Wes Craven entitled **Marimba**. Filming commenced over four years later, on 25 June 1984, by which time the shooting title had been changed to **Inferno in diretta** (which translates literally as **Hell, Live**), and Deodato had been called in as Craven's replacement following a disagreement between the producers and the American, at this time on

opposite: **The Atlantis Interceptors**.
top: Deodato with some of the colourful members of the evil 'Interceptors' gang.
middle: Norwegian video cover.
bottom: Deodato directs a scene featuring Crystal Skull and members of his gang.
this page: **Cut and Run**.
below: Quecho (Michael Berryman).
bottom right: American video cover.
bottom left: Quecho's final surprise visit.

the cusp of massive international acclaim with his seminal horror movie **A Nightmare on Elm Street**. Deodato claims to have been involved in a comprehensive re-working of Craven's script prior to the commencement of shooting, so the extent to which Craven's vision remains intact in the finished film is debatable. Regardless of these murky background details, **Cut and Run** is a fine action movie which marked a definite return to form for Deodato. Several lean years had followed the potentially career-wrecking apocalyptic 1980 double-whammy of **Cannibal Holocaust** and **House on the Edge of the Park**, but the success of **Cut and Run** made Deodato 'respectable' again in the eyes of the movie business.

Somewhere in South America, a riverside drugs-producing operation is attacked by a group of merciless Indios under the command of mute assassin Quecho (Michael Berryman). Armed with blow-pipes and machetes, the Indios ruthlessly kill everyone in sight, saving the worst treatment for two women, who are raped after having their spread-eagled legs pinned to the floorboards by long, thin daggers which are driven through their knees. The operation is

watched from a safe distance by a white man, Colonel Horne (Richard Lynch), who with a barely perceptible nod gives Quecho the signal to finish off the women. The killer decapitates them with single blows from his machete. Deodato gives notice of his intentions with this show-stopping pre-credits sequence; **Cut and Run** is a brutal, action-packed journey into the hell of the South American drugs barons.

The title sequence follows the progress of a Colombian woman through Miami International Airport. She clears customs with ease, apparently carrying a baby in her arms. A car is waiting for her outside the terminal, and it quickly becomes apparent that the 'baby' was actually a doll packed with high-grade cocaine. The woman is driven back to the drug-runners' low-rent accommodation in the city, at which point we meet reporter Frances Hudson (Lisa Blount) and cameraman Mark Ludman (Leonardo Manzella), who are staking-out the smugglers' apartment, hoping to be able to film their arrest by the DEA (the action to be broadcast live on cable news). Entering the apartment, they find a bloodbath. The woman's spread-eagled legs are pinned to the floor by long, thin daggers... Later, Fran speaks to her informant, who hints at connections to the Jim Jones sect...

Following her informant's lead, Fran studies old footage of Jim Jones and his sect, filmed by a news team during the run-up to the infamous Jonestown massacre. In a minor cinematic coup, Deodato seamlessly integrates a shot of Richard Lynch into genuine Jonestown newsreel footage,

opposite top left: Italian fotobuste showing *(top):* Ana (Valentina Forte) and Frances Hudson (Lisa Blount) menaced by snakes, and *(below):* a female member of the drug-producing operation is raped by Indios in the film's pre-credits sequence.
opposite top right: The Indios use traditional weapons to overwhelm the drug-producers.
opposite middle: Ana suffers sexual abuse at the hands of Vlado's men.
opposite bottom: More action from the film's explosive opening sequence.
this page top: Frances makes a surprise discovery, many weeks later, at the scene of the film's opening massacre.
above: Quecho (Michael Berryman) runs riot.
left: The pilot, Tony Martina (Carlos De Carvalho) is killed by Quecho's raiding party upon landing at Vlado's encampment.
below: **Cut and Run** developed from a script called **Marimba**, announced at Cannes 1980. Wes Craven was slated to direct.

taking the inspired idea into the realm of sheer audacity by featuring *himself* in the same scene, seated just behind Colonel Horne! Fran decides to head into the jungle, intending to interview the supposedly dead Horne, his place in the drugs conspiracy confirmed by his appearance in a photograph which Fran took from the female smuggler's handbag. She persuades her employers at Cable Video News to fund her excursion after showing them the photograph, which just happens to feature Tommy Allo, long-lost son of Cable Video News boss, Bob Allo (Richard Bright). Desperate to be reunited with his son, Allo equips Fran and Mark with live broadcast equipment so he can keep track of their progress.

The two reporters arrive at their destination, Vlado's camp, just as Horne's hit-squad, led once more by the ruthless Quecho, are carrying out their most devastating raid yet. By a miracle they survive, and the next day they are literally beaming back pictures from Hell, Live... (Hence the film's Italian title.) The only other person

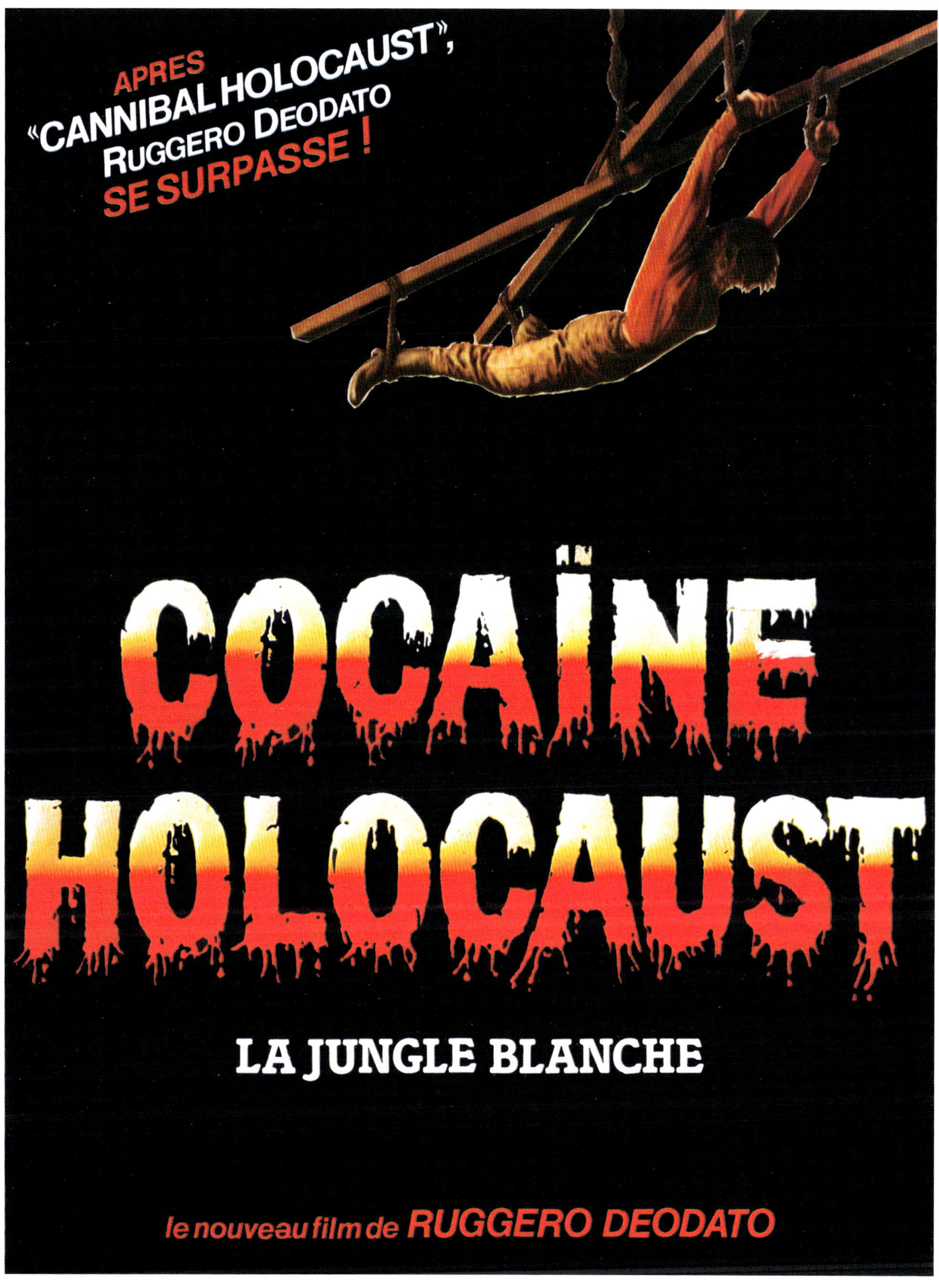

still alive at the camp is Ana (Valentina Forte), who they soon discover is more than willing to help them in any way she can, having suffered sexual abuse at the hands of Vlado and his men. She informs them that Tommy Allo also escaped the carnage and agrees to guide them towards Horne's encampment, where the mystery of the violent drugs-feud is revealed to be a result of Horne's determination to carry on in the footsteps of his mentor Jim Jones. He wants to control the world's cocaine market, claiming that he plans to destroy the weak by helping to corrupt them with cocaine, in the process freeing humanity of its self-indulgence, purifying it once and for all...

Thanks to Fran's infrequent but informative live broadcasts, Bob Allo helps to co-ordinate an operation by the South American authorities to destroy Horne's operation and in the process is at last reunited with his son.

The sappy, happy ending aside, **Cut and Run** is a highly enjoyable, low-budget action

above and opposite bottom left:
Two variants of the French poster under different release titles.
opposite top:
During the film's brutal pre-credits sequence, Quecho finishes off two brutalised women by decapitating them with his machete.
bottom right:
The film's most gruesome sequence. Vlado (John Steiner) begs Tommy Allo (Willie Aames) to shoot him before he is torn apart by a nightmarish Indio death trap.

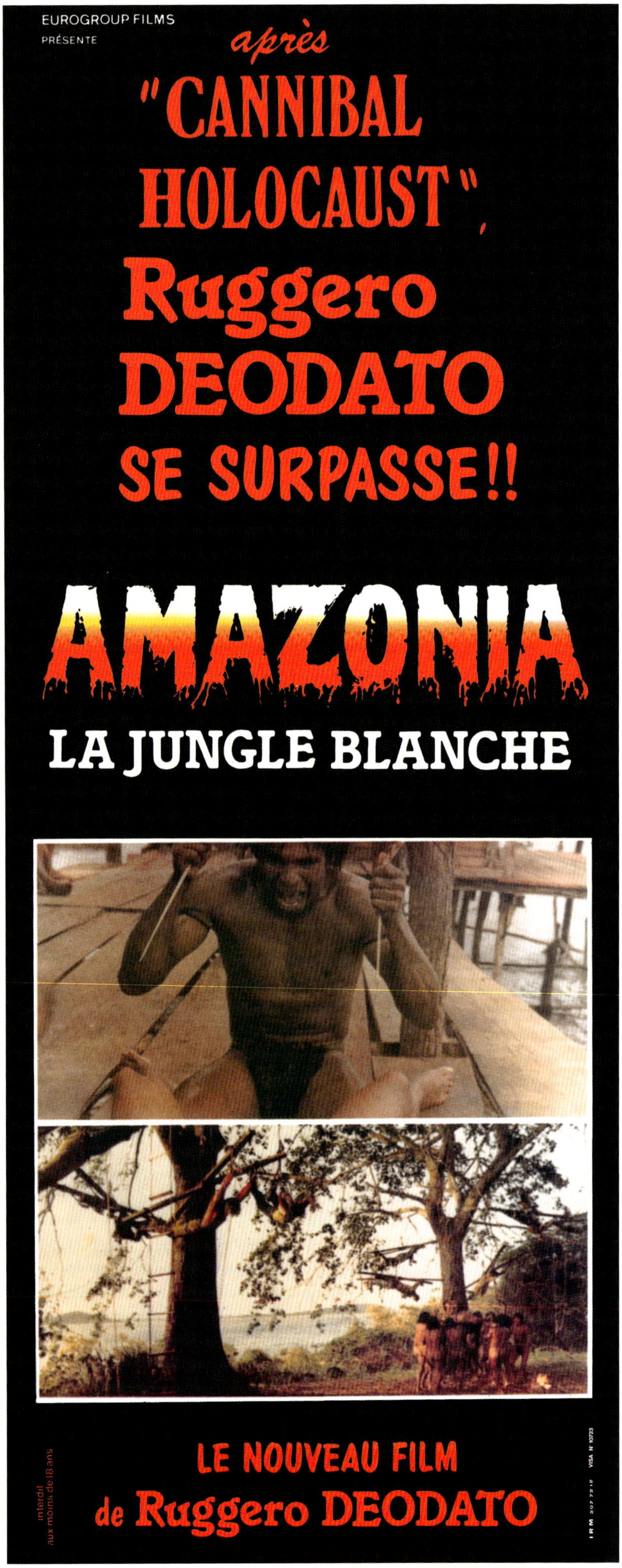

EUROGROUP FILMS
PRÉSENTE

après
"CANNIBAL HOLOCAUST",
Ruggero DEODATO
SE SURPASSE!!

AMAZONIA
LA JUNGLE BLANCHE

LE NOUVEAU FILM
de Ruggero DEODATO

interdit aux moins de 18 ans

VISA N° 10723

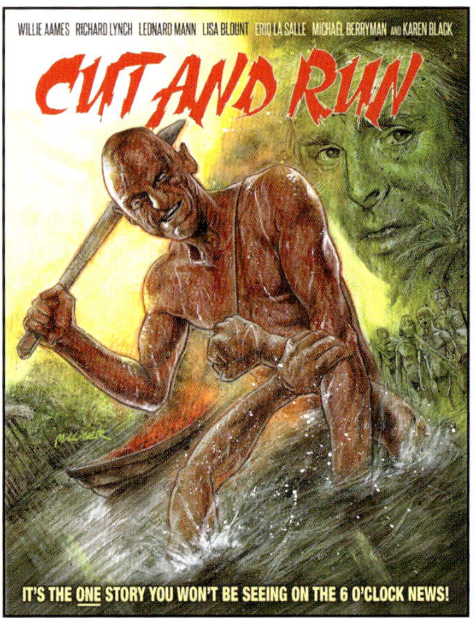

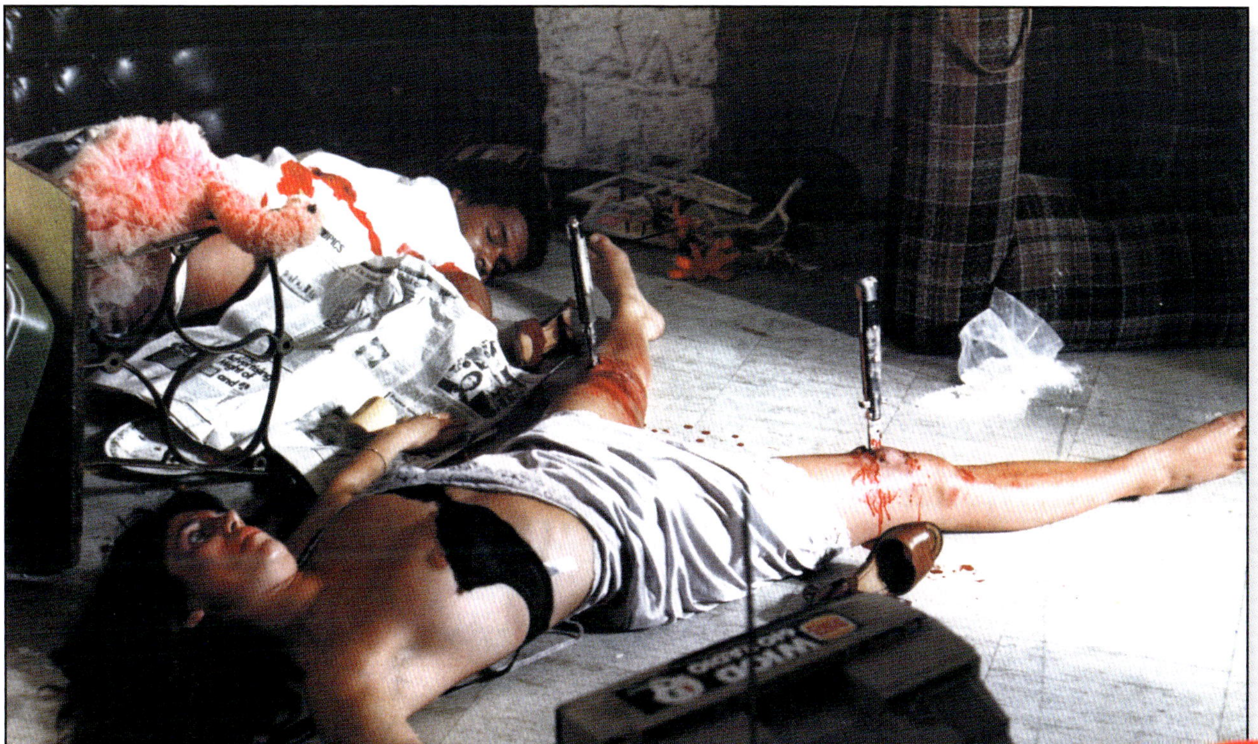

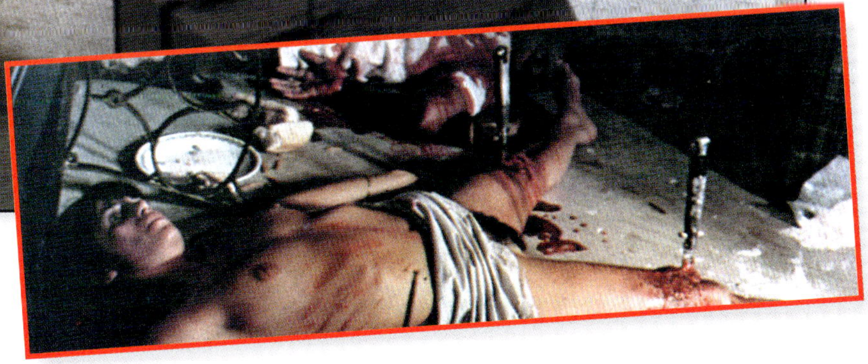

movie; the definitive latter-day highlight of Deodato's turbulent directing career. The film benefits enormously from yet another infectious score by the prolific ex-Goblin Claudio Simonetti, and some absolutely stunning South American locations (Deodato insisted on shooting in Venezuela rather than the original intended location of Colombia).

The performances are mostly of the 'solidly professional' (i.e. adequate) variety, with a welcome sprinkling of hysteria being added to the mix by over-enthusiastic native South American extras, but Lynch and Steiner are outstanding as Horne and Vlado respectively.

Lynch momentarily strives for greatness in his Kurtz-like monologue, delivered to a bewildered Fran, who is unaware that he has been wounded, possibly mortally, and has already decided to order his own execution. "There are no answers. Only actions. For by our actions we are judged pure or unholy", he says, serene in the knowledge that his destiny is in his own hands...

But the final word must be reserved for genre veteran John Steiner, who effortlessly brings the role of Vlado to snarling, spitting life. Vlado is the single most dislikeable character in the whole film, Steiner relishing drop-dead lines such as "You can thank God you're white!" (to Tommy Allo, after the no-judge-no-jury execution of his fellow escapee), and "Fuck her! Fuck her till she screams!" (referring to Ana, offered to a visitor as a 'recreational gift'.) Fittingly, in a film chock-full of 'natural justice' platitudes, Vlado dies ensnared in the finest gore effect to feature in a Deodato film since **Cannibal Holocaust**; his tree-bound bisection is so horrible that the viewer *almost* feels pity for him. Bravo Ruggero! ***(Harvey Fenton)***

top left: Ana (Valentina Forte), Frances Hudson (Lisa Blount) and Mark Ludman (Leonardo Manzella) head into the jungle.
top right: Quecho kills one of the guards at Vlado's encampment.
above: Fran and Mark enter the drug-runners' apartment to find a bloodbath. In common with many of the film's strongest scenes, Deodato filmed two versions. The main image shows the damage as seen in the version of the film intended for the USA and Britain, with nudity covered-up and relatively restrained blood-letting. The inset image shows the lady's corpse as seen in the film's full-blooded cut, intended for more liberal territories. Despite being the 'soft' version, the distributors cut the original British video release by 1 min 43 secs!
opposite: More **Cut and Run** chaos!

Images from **BodyCount**.
right: Carol (Luisa Maneri) recoils upon finding the bodies of Tony (Stefano Madia) and Tracy (Nancy Brilli).
below: Sharon (Elena Pompei).
bottom right: Danish video cover for **BodyCount** under the title **Shaman**.

below: More images from **BodyCount**.
from the top: Tracy's dead, and Tony's going to die soon ; Cissy (Cynthia Thompson) – soon to be another victim ; Charlie the Sheriff (Charles Napier) ; Tony is killed.

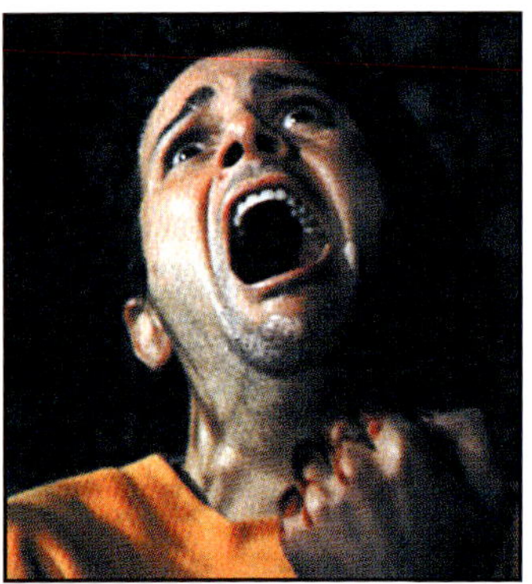

BODYCOUNT

1986
Italian theatrical title: **Camping del terrore**, Italian shooting title: **Camping delle morte**, UK video title: **BodyCount**, Danish video title: **Shaman**.
Italy
director: Ruggero Deodato

produced by Alessandro Fracassi for Racing Pictures. a film by Ruggero Deodato. visa number: 82421 [20/3/87]. colour by L.V. Luciano Vittori S.p.A. in Panavision. filmed in October/November 1985 in Abruzzo (Italy).

cast: Bruce Penhall (Dave Calloway). Mimsy Farmer (Julia Ritchie). David Hess (Robert Ritchie) <with> Luisa Maneri (Carol). Nicola Farron (Ben Ritchie). Andrew [J.] Lederer (Sidney). Stefano Madia (Tony). John Steiner (Doctor Olsen). Nancy Brilli (Tracy). Cynthia Thompson (Cissy). Valentina Forte (Pamela Hicks). Ivan Rassimov (Deputy Sheriff Ted). Elena Pompei (Sharon) <and with> Charles Napier <as> (Charlie, the Sheriff) <with> Sven Kruger (Scott). Lorenzo Grabau. Stefano Galantucci. Clelia Fradella (Rose Olsen). Fabio Vox.

story: Alex Capone [Alessandro Capone]. script by Alex Capone, David Parker, Jr. [Dardano Sacchetti], Sheila Goldberg & Luca D'Alisera. director of photography: Emilio Loffredo. music by Claudio Simonetti. film editor: Eugenio Alabiso. assistant director: Alberto Acciarito. continuity: Ludmila Blat. location manager: Mario Olivieri. cameraman: Sandro Rubeo. assistant cameraman: Andrea Fastella. gaffer: Marcello Ciferri. key grip: Rocco Fernando Fusco. make-up: Mario Di Salvio. 1st assistant make-up: Cinzia Di Salvio. special effects: Roberto Pace. props: Claudio Villa. 1st assistant editor: Nadia Boggian. 2nd assistant editor: Erminia Marani. titles & special effects: Penta Studio S.r.l. sound effects: Gjst Movie Snc. lens & camera: Panaflex-Panavision, supplied by Arco 2 S.r.l. sound: Raffaele De Luca. boom man: Giuliano Piermarioli. mixage: Danilo Moroni. sound editor: Raphael Guzman. synch lab: C.D.S. S.r.l. score engineered by Jeff Neiman & Jerry Riopelle.
songs "She Can Steal Your Heart Away" written & performed by Randy Nicholas; "Holding On" written & performed by Jerry Riopelle; "Push and Shove" written by Joel Goldsmith, Jerry Riopelle & Lauren Daniel, performed by Lauren Daniel; "Make Me Crazy" written by Jeff Mandel & Joel Goldsmith, performed by Doug Senecal. all songs published by Jacaranda Music Inc.

Italian theatrical distributor: Titanus Distribuzione (1st public showing on 14 May 1987). running time: 87 minutes. length: 2,362 metres.

This late entry in the **Friday the 13th**-inspired teenagers-get-slashed-in-the-woods genre is really very poor. Deodato directs on auto-pilot, and obviously does not care for the subject matter or the daft, insulting script.

BodyCount's only real point of interest is the fine, typically bombastic score by frequent Argento-collaborator Claudio Simonetti.

A solid cast of exploitation movie veterans are pitifully wasted as this boring, nonsensical tale of a vengeful Shaman spirit wreaking havoc in a run-down mountainside holiday resort staggers ineptly from one telegraphed death scene to the next. The trouble with teen-slashers is that all the best parts go to... teenagers. Hence, **BodyCount** underuses the mighty talents of actors like Charles Napier, Italian sleaze veterans John Steiner and Ivan Rassimov, and a grizzled-looking David Hess, who is reduced to mumbling lines like *"the old Indian Shaman is out there somewhere!"* whilst shuffling, wild-eyed around the woods. Mimsy Farmer bravely attempts to inject some pathos into her role, but it's all for nought as the constant onslaught of talentless, stupid American teenagers spouting idiotic dialogue condemns the film to failure from the start.

The obnoxiousness level reaches staggering depths early on as we are assailed by the sight of

typical mid-80s fashion-victim bimbo 'Tracy' energetically doing her 'exercises' before inevitably running to the showers... in one of the film's few enjoyable moments, the wretched girl is promptly despatched with a knife through the back of her head, the blade emerging Fulci-style through her mouth.

And so it goes... another victim, another gore effect, another moment of vicarious physical trauma to entertain the massed ranks of slasher fanatics. It's a sad form, the slasher movie. The ultimate example of the filmic repeat-offender, doomed never to learn its lesson. Luckily for us however, Deodato never went back for more... ***(Harvey Fenton)***

THE LONE RUNNER

1986

US theatrical & Italian/UK/US video title: **The Lone Runner**, Dutch video title: **FlashFighter**, shooting title: **Un pugno di diamanti** [A Fistful of Diamonds], alternative title: **Lo scrigno dei mille diamanti** [The Casket of a Thousand Diamonds]

Italian title: no theatrical release

Italy

director: Roger Deodato [Ruggero Deodato]

an Ovidio G. Assonitis production

©1986. Brouwersgracht Investments B.V.

colour: Technicolor. filmed in Fujicolor. in Dolby stereo. filmed in April/May 1986 [five weeks] on location in Morocco

cast: Miles O'Keeffe (Garrett, the Lone Runner). Savina Gersak (Analisa Summerking). Donal Hodson (Mr Summerking). Ronald Lacey (Misha). John Steiner (Skorm). Michael J. Aronin (Emerick). Al [Haruhiko] Yamanouchi (Nimbus, Skorm's henchman). Richard Raymond (Emerick's assistant).

producer: Ovidio G. Assonitis. associate producer: Peter Graf [Romeo Assonitis]. written by Chris Trainor & Steven Luotto. director of photography: Robert Bennet [Roberto Forges Davanzati]. music composed & conducted by Charles Cooper [Carlo Maria Cordio]; music published by Triple Time Music. editor: Eugene Miller [Eugenio Alabiso]. art director: Bob Glaser. script continuity: Amelia Scott. special effects supervisor: Burt Spiegel. production secretary: Colin Diamond. 1st assistant: Jerry Vaughan. 2nd assistant: Andrew Miller. camera operators: Jan Amler & Philip Berk. focus puller: Paul Brodie. gaffer: Luis Peters. best boy: Bob Barry. creative make-up: Howard Lating. creative hair dresser: Michael White. wardrobe supervisor: Gwen Carlisle. wardrobe assistant: Francis Gibson. set dressing: Garry Marlow. property master: Al Simon. swordmaster: Steve Massey. still photography: John Currie. assistant film editor: Donna Tracy. titles & opticals: Video Gamma. sound mixer: Carl Schaefer. post synchronisation director: Leslie J. Lane. re-recording mixer: Eddie Paskin. sound editor: Robert Madsen. Dolby stereo consultant: Federico Savina.

US theatrical distributor: TransWorld Entertainment (released in January 1988). rated: PG. running time: 89 minutes.

The producer, Assonitis, told Deodato that this film was being made for television. He was surprised to see cinema posters on a subsequent visit to Los Angeles.

The Lone Runner is a rambling and repetitive wasteland adventure fable set in an unspecified desert region in which most of the people are English-speaking Caucasians. This is a lawless land, patrolled by a multitude of tribes, some of whom are good and some of whom are bad, we're informed. The Malacoots, led by Skorm and his henchman Nimbus are *really* bad, and their arch-enemy is Garrett, aka *the Lone Runner* who, as played by Miles O'Keeffe, is a variant on the "man with no name" character (except that he's got a name of course... never mind.)

We are introduced to Garrett during the title sequence, in which he saves a girl called Analisa from the unwelcome attentions of the Malacoots. Flash forward ten years and Analisa, now a fully-grown woman, is in trouble again – kidnapped and held hostage by a petty crook named Masud. When a nasty piece of work called Emerick becomes involved, the stakes are raised considerably, the greedy lone shark intending ultimately to get his hands on a fortune in diamonds (hence the alternative title, **The Casket of a Thousand Diamonds**). To help him realise this ambition he enlists the help of the Malacoots.

From this point on the film rapidly starts its descent into a sorry parade of mind-numbingly pointless kung-fu action set-pieces which can basically be summed up thus: Analisa escapes, Analisa is re-captured, Analisa is rescued by Garrett, Analisa is re-captured, Garrett tries to save Analisa but fails, then he tries again and succeeds, but she is recaptured again. No, really....

top left: a shot from **BodyCount**.

main picture this page: Miles O'Keeffe in a publicity still for **The Lone Runner**. O'Keeffe also made the dreadful **Iron Warrior** for the same producer (Ovidio G. Assonitis). O'Keeffe's other past roles included playing Tarzan opposite Bo Derek's Jane in **Tarzan, the Apeman** (1981), and he featured as the titular character in Aristide Massaccesi's 'Ator' movies **Ator, the Fighting Eagle** (1982) and **Ator the Invincible** (1983).

below: Skorm (John Steiner) threatens Analisa (Savina Gersak) in **The Lone Runner**.

above from the top: Danish video cover for **The Lone Runner**; Promotional artwork; Skorm calls the shots.
top right: The Barbarian Brothers are forced to enter into gladiatorial combat against one another in **The Barbarians**.

and this just goes on and on and on, each escape and capture punctuated by a similarly relentless comic-relief running-gag about an unfortunate trader who always comes off worse whenever he tries to make a deal. It's amazing the way that Garrett and the trader keep on bumping into each other in the apparently vast, inhospitable outback... We are first introduced to the rogue trader in perhaps the film's most insane moment, during which we see Garrett perform a miracle as he uses one of his trademark explosive arrows to blow a hole in the desert floor at a dried-out oasis. The explosion causes a water fountain to spring up from the sand!

Former Tarzan O'Keeffe, so wooden as the muscle-bound hero of the **Ator** movies, is actually fairly well-suited to this role; his lack of thespian skills is no handicap when playing such a one-dimensional character, but really everyone here is simply going through the motions. The comic relief is painfully misjudged (it's *not* funny...) and Carlo Maria Cordio's music is the final insult; a really bad, up-beat synth pastiche of a spaghetti western score. **The Lone Runner** is one of Deodato's poorest films and is best forgotten.
(Harvey Fenton)

THE BARBARIANS

1987
US theatrical & UK/US video title: **The Barbarians**, Italian theatrical title: **The Barbarians & Co.**, West German theatrical title: **Die Barbaren**, French theatrical title: **Les barbarians**, Danish video title: **Barbarene**, shooting title: **I barbari**
the United States & Italy
director: Ruggero Deodato

visa number: 82545 [23/4/87].
The Cannon Group Inc. presents a Golan-Globus production. A Cannon film. [uncredited production company] Cannon Italia
©1987. Cannon Films, Inc. and Cannon International.
colour by Telecolor S.p.A. in Dolby stereo.
shooting from 4 August 1986 on location in Abruzzo with interiors filmed at Incir De Paolis Studios in Rome (Italy)

cast: The Barbarian Brothers: Peter Paul (Kutchek) & David Paul (Gore). Richard Lynch (Kadar). Eva La Rue (Ismene). Virginia Bryant (Canary). Sheeba Alahani (China). Michael Berryman (The Dirtmaster). Franco Pistoni (Ibar). Raffaella Baracchi (Allura). Pasquale Bellazecca (Kutchek as a young boy). Luigi Bellazecca (Gore as a young boy). Wilma Marzilli (fat woman). Paolo Risi (Clown). Giovanni Cianfriglia (Ghedo, the strongman). Angelo Ragusa (Dead Bone, one of Kadar's men). Nanni Bernini (Sligot, one of Kadar's men). Lucio Rosato (One Ear, one of Kadar's men). George Eastman [Luigi Montefiore] (Jacko). Franco Daddi (Bluto). Benito Stefanelli (Greyshaft). Tiziana Di Gennaro (Kara). Renzo Pevarello (Bones). L. Caroli (Nose). Paolo Risi (Pin, the dwarf).

screenplay: James R. Silke. director of photography: Lorenzo Battaglia. music: Pino Donaggio, conducted by Natale Massara; recorded at Trafalgar Recording Studios. film editor: Eugenio Alabiso. executive producer: John Thompson. producers: Menahem Golan & Yoram Globus. production supervisor: Claudio Grassetti. production manager: Luciano Balducci. production design: Giuseppe Mangano. unit manager: Carlo Carpentieri. 1st assistant director: Roberto Palmerini. continuity: Fabrizia Iacona. dialogue coach: Ricky Sacco. stunt coordinator: Benito Stefanelli. choreographer: Pino Pennese. accountants: Alfonso Farano & Silvia Caperna. production assistants: Massimo Iacobis, Bruno Mancinelli & Paola Fogagnolo. cameraman: Guido Tosi. focus puller: Stefano Falivene. clapper loader: Federico Martucci. set dresser: Giancarlo Capuani. assistant production designer: Atos Mastrogirolami. assistant set dresser: Pasquale Avvisato. prop master: Sebastiano De Caro. head painter: Giancarlo Sensidoni. construction chief: Romano Chessari. make-up & visual effects: Francesco & Gaetano Paolocci. costumes: Francesca Panicali. costumes for the Barbarian Brothers: Michela Gisotti. assistant costume designer: Stefania Del Guerra. seamstresses: Anna Rasetti & Giacoma Manes. chief make-up artist: Rosario Prestopino. assistant make-up artists: Franco Casagni & Amedeo Alessi. chief hairdresser: Vitaliana Patacca. assistant hairdressers: Gerardo Lepre & Marcello Longhi. gaffer: Domenico Caiuli. electricians: Lorenzo Broglio, Enrico Morgia & Massimo Montarsi. generator operator: Giovanni Favella. key grip: Franco Micheli. grips: Bruno Ietto, Pietro Tiberti & Vittorio D'Ammassa. still photographer: Sergio Colombari. post production facilities: C.D.S. unit publicist: Eugene Rizzo. titles: Studio 4 (Rome). cameras: Cineroma. transportation: Romana Trasporti

Cinematografici. assistant editor: Nadia Boggian. 2nd assistant editor: Silvana Di Legge. sound mixer: Massimo Loffredi. boom operator: Ettore Mancini. sound editor: Cesare D'Amico. assistant sound editor: Liberata Zocchi. sound effects editor: Roberto Arcangeli. looping supervisor: Nick Alexander. sound engineer: Gaetano Ria. re-recording mixer: Danilo Moroni.

Italian theatrical distributor: Warner Bros. (1st public showing on 24 April 1987). running time: 89 minutes. length: 2,586 metres.
US theatrical distributor: Cannon Releasing Corporation (released in May 1987). rated R. running time: 88 minutes.
French theatrical distributor: Cannon France (released in Paris on 8 July 1987). running time: 95 minutes.

Deodato started work on his biggest-budgeted film to date after being called in to replace US-based director Slobodan Sijan after one month of pre-production on the $4 million Golan-Globus project. Deodato was the sole director of the finished film, which went on to be a minor hit in many territories around the world.

The Barbarians is built entirely around the physical presence of the astonishingly over-developed "Barbarian Brothers", identical twins Peter Paul and David Paul. Perhaps the greatest surprise in store for first-time viewers of the film is that these professional body-builders actually acquit themselves fairly well in their (admittedly unchallenging) roles. They seem to be fully aware of their self-imposed status as faintly ridiculous freaks, and play up to this fact by bringing a healthy dose of self-effacing irony and subtle physical humour to the film.

The Barbarians is a fantasy adventure film set in an unspecified time and place (*"Once Upon*

this page: **The Barbarians**.
top left: Canary (Virginia Bryant) is captured by one of Kadar's henchmen.
above from the top: Danish video cover ; The sorceress hunts for the magical ruby ; Deodato directs a scene on location.
left: Deodato with The Barbarian Brothers.

above: Scenes from **The Barbarians**.
main image: Canary (Virginia Bryant) is whipped by The Dirtmaster (Michael Berryman).
side-bar images from the top:
US one-sheet poster ;
Peter Paul and David Paul, who played the Barbarian Brothers, were described by Deodato as being "completely mad and full of steroids" ;
Kutchek and Gore, protected by sacred arms and armour, prepare to face the dragon which guards the magical ruby in the otherworldy realm which is found behind a secret waterfall...

a Time... a time of Demons, Darkness and Sorcery", the credits-sequence voice-over helpfully informs us...), in which only one tribe is guaranteed safe passage through the massive stretches of hostile no-man's land. The Ragniks are joyfully welcomed anywhere, as they possess a magical Ruby which gives the bearers the gifts of music, art and entertainment. The ruby had been traded for a mountain of gold, the wise leaders of the tribe knowing that its gifts were worth far more than material possessions.

One day, as the tribe's caravan of horse-drawn covered waggons is travelling between settlements, they are attacked by the evil Kadar (a sinister turn from Deodato regular Richard Lynch) and his men. Canary (Virginia Bryant, looking particularly vibrant here), the sacred guardian of the Ruby's magic, quickly realises that they are in serious trouble, so before they are overwhelmed she passes the stone to another member of the tribe and tells him to hide it well. Canary is taken prisoner, along with two small boys, Kutchek and Gore. Back at Kadar's city, the court witch does not take kindly to the petulant twins and has them sent to "the pit", where they are enslaved to a life of hard labour... Ten Years Later, the boys are transformed into *The Barbarian Brothers*, and whilst being forced to battle against one another in gladiatorial combat they contrive to escape their captors. Teaming up with the insanely beautiful Kara (Tiziana Di Gennaro... those eyes...), they eventually fulfil their destiny by returning the magical Ruby to their tribe.

Ultimately this is a very, very silly movie which looks fabulous thanks to sterling work by the costume department, and an outstanding cast who all appear to have been chosen for their various physical attributes – the women are all stunning, and the men are either physically remarkable (the Barbarian Brothers, Michael Berryman, several dwarfs) or memorably domineering characters (Lynch, and look out for man-mountain Luigi Montefiore, aka George Eastman, in an arm-wrestling cameo!). Clearly much of the healthy budget must have been spent on the impressive sets, but the film is lumbered with a terribly inappropriate score by the usually reliable Pino Donaggio.

The Barbarians is like a comic-book come to life. Its hard-nosed approach to violence is typical Deodato, but for once the element of humour is successfully incorporated into the mix. ***(Harvey Fenton)***

PHANTOM OF DEATH

1988
Italian theatrical title: **Un delitto poco comune**, US theatrical title & UK/US video title: **Phantom of Death**, French theatrical title: **Le tueur de la pleine lune**, German / alternative UK video title: **Off Balance**, Spanish title: **Bestia asesina**, production titles: **Squilibrio** / **The House on Percival Rubens Street** / **An Unusual Murder**
Italy
director: Ruggero Deodato

registration number: 7.783. visa number: 83223 [13/1/88] Pietro Innocenzi/Tandem Cinematografica S.r.l./D.M.V. Distribuzione S.r.l. present a film of Ruggero Deodato [sic]. produced by Pietro Innocenzi for Globe Films S.r.l./ Tandem Cinematografica S.r.l./D.M.V. Distribuzione S.r.l. in association with Reteitalia S.p.a. developing/printing: Luciano Vittori, S.p.a. negative: Kodak. in Panavision. in Dolby stereo. shooting from 10 August 1987 in Rome & Venice with interiors at Empire Studios (Rome)

cast: Michael York (Robert Dominici). Edwige Fenech (Hélène Martell). Donald Pleasence (Inspector Datti Downey) <with> Mapi Galan (Susanna). Fabio Sartor (David). Renato Cortesi (Mikey, Datti's assistant). Antonella Ponziani (Gloria, Dattis's daughter). Carola Stagnaro (Dr Carla Pesenti, 1st victim). Daniele Brado (Doctor Vani, pathologist) <and with> Caterina Boratto (Robert's mother). Lewis Eduardo Ciannelli (examining doctor). Renata Dal Pozzo (Corsi, Gatti's assistant). Giovanni Lombardo Radice (Giuliano, a priest). Gianni Franco. Marino Masè (expert on ageing). Achille Brugnini. Giovanni Tamberi (Andrea, Hélène's friend). Loris Loddi (Danzil, a cop). Hal Yamanouchy [Haruhiko Yamanouchi] (Kendo instructor). Diego Verdegiglio. Raffaella Baracchi (Venice prostitute). Emi Valentino [Emy Valentino]. Ruggero Deodato (man who gets on moped at station).

story by Gianfranco Clerici & Vincenzo Mannino. screenplay by Gianfranco Clerici, Vincenzo Mannino & Gigliola Battaglini. director of photography: Giorgio Di Battista. music by Pino Donaggio, conducted by Natale Massara; published by Gipsy. film editor: Daniele Alabiso. wardrobe: Giovanna Deodato. scenic designer: Paolo Innocenzi. associate producers: Gianfranco Clerici & Vincenzo Mannino. production manager: Giuliano Piermarioli. assistant director: Roberto Tatti. 1st cameraman: Gianni Maddaleni. 2nd cameraman: Fabrizio Lucci. dialogue director: Lewis Eduardo Ciannelli. script girl: Susanna Pellegrini. unit manager: Fabrizio De Martino. production assistant: Alberto Paluzzi. business manager: Massimo Esposti. accountant: Maria Pia Mancini. make-up (Michael York): Fabrizio Sforza, (Edwige Fenech): Franco Schioppa. make-up artist: Antonio Maltempo. hair stylist: Carla Indoni. assistant scenic designer: Alessandro Laurenti. assistant wardrobe mistress: Franca Vigano. head grip: Martino Valente. gaffer: Gaetano Coniglio. prop man: Antonio Murer. seamstress: Clary Mirolo. scenic [special] effects: Cataldo Galiano. transport: Cinetecnica, Sandro Loreti. cameras: Panavison; Arco 2. titles & optical effects: VideoGamma. electrical equipment: M.G.M. upholstery: Sanchini. furnishings: Rancati; Dedalo; L'Immaginoteca. costumes: Ferroni (Rome); 'Il Baule' (Venice). wigs: Rocchetti – Carboni. the clothes worn by Mr Michael York and Miss Edwige Fenech are by 'Gianni Versace' of Milan. assistant film editors: Rita Triunveri & Enrico Crescenzi. sound: Tommaso Quattrini. boom operator: Ettore Mancini. re-recording & synchronization: N.C. Studios (Rome). mixing: International Recording (Rome). sound mixer: Renato Giannelli. sound effects: Studio Sound. the producers wish to thank the following: Grundig S.p.A.; Sansonite S.p.A.; San Pellegrino S.p.A.; 'Della Valle' Footwear; 'Livien by Finesi' furs; Hotel 'Emma' (Merano); 'Centro Euclide'; Lingerie 'La Perla' (Bologna); 'Ballon' (Rome); 'L'Amore Miei' of Bologona for clothing furnished; 'Carla Dacia' of Como for clothing furnished; Centro Carta 'Vertecchi' S.p.A.

Italian theatrical distributor: DMV Distribuzione (1st public showing on 11 March 1988). running time: 92 minutes. length: 2,580 metres.
US theatrical distributor: Vidmark (released in December 1988). rating: none. running time: 91 minutes.
French theatrical distributor: Films Jacques Leitienne (released in Paris on 24 May 1989). rated: 13. running time: 100 minutes.

left: Detail from the British DVD cover for **Phantom of Death**, issued by Shameless.
below: The devastating effects of the disease rapidly become apparent.

Not long before the start of a concert by famous pianist Robert Dominici (Michael York), a doctor is barbarically killed in her office. At the end of the concert, Robert and his fiancée Susanna (Mapi Galan), have a discussion which develops into an argument and ends with them splitting-up. The woman takes refuge in the arms of an occasional lover (who practises Kendo with Robert). Eventually Susanna decides to return to her man in Perugia, and after having telephoned Robert, she sets off towards her house. Before she can reach her destination she is killed by a mysterious assassin.

Inspector Datti (Donald Pleasence) is investigating the case but knows no more than that the culprit is a young man of about thirty years of age. Robert is distraught when he hears the news of Susanna's death, and he decides to break up with Hélène Martell, with whom he has been having an affair. He travels to his mother's place in Venice, where he conducts a series of clinical tests to try to understand the nature of the illness which is wearing him out. It becomes apparent that he is affected by Progenia, an extremely rare illness which, in a short time, causes premature and devastating physical ageing. The illness not only changes him physically, but also distorts his mind. As the condition progresses his hatred of the human race also grows stronger. He commits a series of brutal homicides. Robert however stays in contact with Hélène who, madly in love with him, announces to him by telephone that she is expecting his child. Robert is further devastated by this new revelation and tries to murder Hélène. Only the intervention of Inspector Datti can put an end to this vicious spiral of death.

The welcome return of Deodato to the thriller format is embellished by the director with elements of horror thanks to the horrible transformation of York who, from the film's half way point to the end, is basically a monstrous entity in decomposition. Deodato worked with a varied and talented cast whose members included the diva of Italian thrillers (Fenech), the charismatic horror film icon Pleasence, and Michael York, well-known through his many appearances in American mega-productions, and was enhanced by excellent character actors such as Hal Yamanouchi, Marino Masè, Fabio Sartor and Giovanni Lombardo Radice.

below: The **Phantom of Death** slashes another victim's throat.

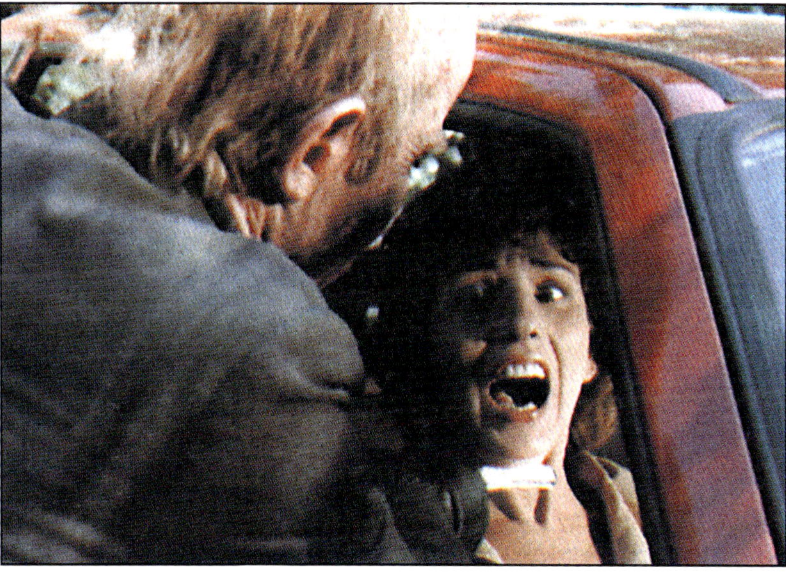

above: Poster for the French theatrical release of **Phantom of Death**.
below: Donald Pleasence as Inspector Datti in **Phantom of Death**.

The film is in essence, for the first half an hour, a thriller about an unknown killer on the loose. Then the culprit is unveiled, and from this point onwards the director concentrates more on the psychological aspects of the protagonist and his nemesis Inspector Datti. The homicides are very heavy on the splatter, in accordance with the extreme reputation of Deodato's films. The director is not very fond of this film, having claimed that the sympathy we feel for York due to the onslaught of this horrific disease serves to soften the dynamics of a thriller which requires the audience to loathe its killer. Cronenberg's **The Fly** (1986) seems to be the main reference here since it too had considerable sympathy for its doomed, decaying protagonist Seth Brundle (Jeff Goldblum). Despite Deodato's doubts, Fenech (dubbing aside) seems to really have got into her role.

(Gian Luca Castoldi)

DIAL: HELP

1988
Italian theatrical title: **Minaccia d'amore**, UK / US / German video title: **Dial: Help**, French video title: **Un coup de fil peut vous couter la vie**, French television title: **Angoisse sur la ligne**, Danish video title: **Drej 0.0.0**, Italian shooting title: **Ragno gellido**
Italy
director: Ruggero Deodato

Giovanni Bertolucci & Galliano Juso present a film by Ruggero Deodato. a Metro Film S.r.l./San Francisco Film S.r.l. production with the collaboration of Reteitalia S.p.A. visa number: 84091 [24/10/88]
processing laboratory: Telecolor S.p.A. film: Kodak S.p.A. shooting from 29 April 1988 on location in Rome with interiors filmed at Incir de Paolis S.r.l. (Rome)

cast: Charlotte Lewis (Jenny Cooper). Marcello Modugno (Riccardo, Jenny's neighbour). Mattia Sbragia (Mole, keyboardist). Carola Stagnaro (Carmen, Jenny's friend). Victor Cavallo <with> Carlo Monni (the fireman) <and with> William Berger (Professor Irving Klein) <with> Giorgio Tirabassi. Jole Silvani (cleaning woman). Cesare Di Vito. Antonietta Di Vizia. Emanuela Fuin. Cyrus Elias (bar owner). Fausto Lombardi (café bartender). Monica Dorigatti (one of Caps's women). Anne Maj Montonen. Alessandra Izzo (hat check woman at nightclub). Ruggero Deodato (man in telephone booth).

story by Franco Ferrini. screenplay: Joseph Caravan, Mary Caravan & Ruggero Deodato. director of photography: Renato Tafuri. film editor: Sergio Montanari. music by Claudio Simonetti; published by BMG Ariola S.p.A., DRUMS Edizione Musicali s.n.c. art director: Antonello Geleng. set dresser: Giacomo Calò Carducci. costumes by Giovanna Deodato. US casting: Jeff Gerrard. production manager: Tullio Gentili. production accountant: Maurizio Spinelli. administration: Anna Rita Della Rocca. script continuity: Gaia Gorrini. assistant to the director: Carlo Corbucci. unit manager: Alessio Juso. production secretaries: Claudio Lo Cascio & Vito Morea. camera operator: Enrico Maggi. hair stylist: Ferdinando Merolla. make-up: Rosario Prestopino & Luigi Ciminelli. fencing coach: Goffredo Unger. chief electrician: Francesco Di Bartolomeo. special effects: Germano Natali. property men: Antonio Murer & Sebastiano De Caro. action stills: Roberto Biciocchi. titles & opticals: Penta Studio. shoes: L.C.P. S.r.l. set design: L'Immaginoteca; G.R.P. Postiglione; Votre Maison et Jardin; Dedalo; Internos; Art'è; Euromobilia. equipment: Arco Due. transport: R & P. S.A.S. sound: Massimo Loffredi. boom man: Giulio Viggiani. post synchronization: C.D.S. mixer: Franco Bassi. We wish to thank: Cinefotottica, Vittoria Colonna; Bijou Philippe, S.lle Molajani; Ballon; Brick Di R.R.; Albanese, S.lle Mascetti S.r.l.; Cadetti for their kind collaboration.

Italian theatrical distributor: Europa Cine TV (1st public showing on 10 November 1988). running time: 97 minutes. length: 2,730 metres.

For some strange reason, Deodato expresses particular fondness for **Dial: Help**, a sentiment which is not shared by most of his fans. I suspect that he may be particularly proud of the 'look' of the film, which is a high-gloss exercise in superior internal lighting schemes, fluid camera movement and precise rhythmic editing. Add a typically efficient Claudio Simonetti score (forgetting the *bad* heavy metal title ditty...) and the undeniably pleasing appeal of lead actress Charlotte Lewis, and the surface attraction of the movie is immediately apparent. Stylistically, **Dial: Help** has much in common with the dynamics of a late 80s music video, thematically it is quite simply on its own planet... It is impossible to take the film seriously as the storyline is utterly demented, but a great deal of fun can be had if it is approached in the right spirit.

Charlotte Lewis plays Jenny, an English model living in Italy who is having problems communicating with her increasingly estranged

boyfriend. One night, frustrated by her inability to get past his secretaries when calling him, she accidentally dials a wrong number. Cut to an abandoned old office – now home to a moody flock of atmospherically cooing doves – where a solitary phone rings... A cleaning lady hears the phone and shuffles towards the office, unlocking the door as she says *"It's been twenty years or more since anyone called this office..."*. She reaches for the phone, at which point the handset leaps towards her and she is strangled by the cord as a bank of reel-to-reel tapedecks spring into life, playing back a bedlam of distressed voices. At the other end of the line, a bemused Jenny gives up trying to communicate and puts down the phone...

From this moment on, Jenny is haunted by the spirit of the line she has called. She is soon receiving weird calls, and it is not long before she must contend with a series of bizarre telephone-precipitated 'accidents' in which: mirrors explode in nightclubs; her fish are sonically massacred (their tank is right next to the phone); someone is pelted to death by a hail of coins which are violently ejected from a pay-phone; her friends and even casual acquaintances are being

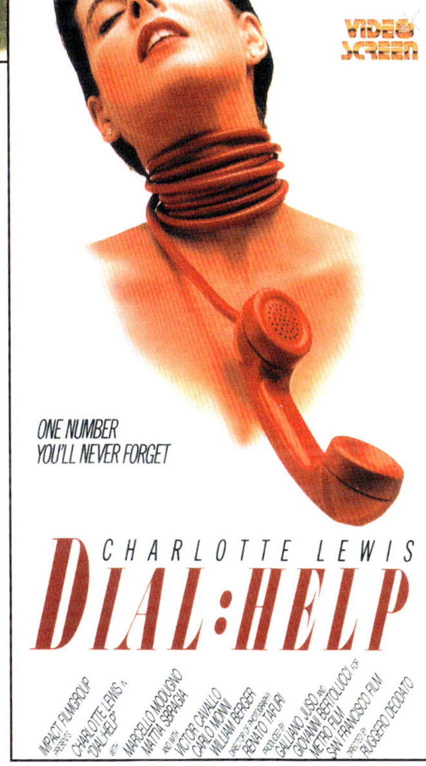

above left: A hypnotised Jenny (Charlotte Lewis) takes a near-fatal bath wearing her best undies in **Dial: Help**
above from the top: Japanese video cover ; Jenny is rescued by Riccardo ; In the film's funniest scene, Jenny loses control when she is sexually-aroused by the fatal phone. Spot the differences between the Dutch video release *(left)* and Danish video *(below)*.

hypnotised into killing themselves, or simply strangled by angry phone cords; and, best of all, a tone emanating from an airport courtesy phone causes a man's heart pace-maker to explode! This is laugh-a-minute stuff. At one point we even get to see a classic slasher-movie-style point of view shot... of a phone stalking its intended victim by climbing a spiral staircase (?!) The film's two stand-out moments of hysteria though, are saved for Ms. Lewis, who is hypnotised and seduced by the phone, writhing in erotic ecstasy, first in her bathrobe and secondly in a full black lingerie outfit, which she keeps on in the bath!...

The mystery is solved when it becomes apparent that the wrong number she dialled at the beginning of the film belonged to a long-disused Samaritans office. As Jenny was the first to call this *angst-ridden* telephone for twenty years, it formed a psychotic attachment to her. She calls the number again and says, *"I love you all. I want you to be free!"* The doves fly out of the office window and everything is alright again...

Deodato includes some misjudged comic-relief interludes, presumably not realising exactly how funny the film is anyway. Ultimately **Dial: Help** is such a wonderfully wrong-headed movie that trash fans will find it difficult to dislike. ***(Harvey Fenton)***

top: Charlotte Lewis gets steamy in **Dial: Help**.
above: Sales brochure for **Dial: Help**.

below: Deodato with Barbara Nascimbene and Massimo Ranieri in 1989, during the making of **Il ricatto**.
bottom: Filming **Il ricatto**.

top right: A classical portrait of Italian womanhood in **Ocean**.
bottom right: Ernest Borgnine adopts a typically expressive pose in **Ocean**.
opposite top: Deodato with Michael Berryman during the making of **Ocean**.
opposite middle: Deodato directing a scene in which Marisa Berenson is raped in **Ocean**.

opposite bottom: Deodato, seated next to Michela Rocco, with cast and crew on the set of **I ragazzi del muretto 2**.

IL RICATTO

1989 (TV)
Italy
directors: Tonino Valerii & Ruggero Deodato

produced by Sergio Giussani for RA.MA. 2000 & Reteltalia S.p.A.

Mini-series first transmitted in five episodes.
1st episode transmitted @ 20.30 on Canale 5 (Italy) on 23 April 1988

cast: Massimo Ranieri (Fedeli). Barbara Nascimbene. Luca De Filippo. Luigi De Filippo. Jacques Perrin. Barbara Ricci. P. Pepe. Leo Gullotta. Kim Rossi Stuart. Fernando Rey. Maurizio Berti. Jean Christophe Bretigniere. Kara Donati. Orazio Orlando.

story: Ennio De Concini & Massimo Ranieri. screenplay: Ennio De Concini & Luca Rossi. director of photography: Pasquale Rachini. music: Riz Ortolani. editor: Antonio Siciliano. art director: Lorenzo Baraldi. set dresser: Walter Caprara. costume designer: Bona Nasalli Rocca. production manager: Roberto Romoli.

Deodato took over from Valerii 40 weeks into the 50-week schedule.
A second series **Il ricatto 2 (bambini nell'ombra)** began in 1991 without RD's involvement.

OCEAN

1990 (TV)
Italian (production) title: **Oceano**
Italy, Spain & Germany
director: Ruggero Deodato

executive producer: Mario Sampaolo. produced by Giovanni Bertolucci for San Francisco Film S.r.l./ Cristaldi Film S.r.l./Cinecittà S.p.A./Socaem/Gobierno De Canarias. Presented by Franco Cristaldi.
filmed on location in Venezuela & Lanzarote (Canary Island)
in colour

cast: Irene Papas. Mario Adorf. Tom Patti. Gregg Thomsen. Ana Dieghez. Anna Kanakis. Andy J. Forest. William Berger. David Hess. Ron Maccone. Senta Berger. Martin Balsam. Lou Castel. Marisa Berenson (Muneca). Ernest Borgnine (Pedro El Triste). Alan Arkin Jr. Michael Berryman. Claudia Muzii.

story: Alberto Vazquez Figueroa; based on his trilogy. screenplay: Alberto Vazquez Figueroa & Ruggero Deodato. director of photography: Luigi Verga. music: Pino Donaggio. editor: Eugenio Alabiso. art director: Claudio Cinini. costumes: Millina Deodato. assistant director: Marina Mattoli.

Television mini-series advertised for sale in 10 x 52-minute episodes or 6 x 85-minute episodes

Ocean is unreleased and is the property of Silvio Berlusconi's company Mediaset. It seems that it serves as a guarantee, together with other films for the schedules.

I RAGAZZI DEL MURETTO 2

1991 (TV)
Italy
directors: Ruggero Deodato [8 episodes]
Ludovico Gasparri [6 episodes]

produced by Alessandro Canzio for Rai Due/Europool/ESSE. CI. Cinematografica

series 2
episode: **Fuga d'amore**
episode: **Si è svitato papà**
episode: **Il mestiere più antico del mondo**
episode: **Scelte difficili**
episode: **Chi ha paura del lupo cattivo?**
episode: **Una vita a metà**
episode: **Fuori dalla regola**
episode: **Ragazze in crisi**

cast: Michela Rocco [Di Torrepadula] (Elena). Claudio Lorimer. Barbara Ricci. Lorenzo Amato. Eleodi Treccani. Cecilia Dazzi. Massimo Di Cataldo. Alberto Rossi. Vincenzo Diglio. Francesca Antonelli. Paolo Pei Andreoli. Amedeo Letizia. Alberto Rossi. Elodie Treccani. Riccardo Salerno. Chris Childs. Aldo Barone. Mariangelo Giordano. Paolo Graziosi. Marisa Bartoli. Achille Millo. Fabio Traversa. Isabella Guidotti. Luciano Turi. Patrizia De Clara. Enrico Papa. Franco Oppini. Luisa De Santis. Ilaria Troncone. Orso Maria Guerrini. Delia Boccardo. Laura Troschel. Fiorenza Marchegiani. Sergio Fiorentini. Dagmar Lassander. Sergio Di Giulio. Fabrizia Castagnoli. Antonio Casagrande. Ruggero Deodato (photographer).

story: Patrizio Fassio, Marina Garroni & Domenico Matteucci. screenplay: Giovanni Lombardo Radice & Anna Stoppoloni. series creator: Enzo Tarquini. directors of photography: Sergio D'Offizi & Carlo Taffani. music: Stadio. editor: Gianfranco Amicucci. assistant director: Roberto Palmerini. script editor: Massimo De Rita.

distributor: SACIS

Television series aimed at an adolescent audience, which was very successful in Italy.

Below is the **Ocean** synopsis, reproduced direct from the (very plush) foreign sales brochure, printed by Filmexport Group:

"In the village of Playa Blanca, on the volcanic island of Lanzarote in the Canaries, lives a beautiful 16-year-old girl Yaiza Perdomo. She has inherited the gift of taming animals, curing the sick and communicating with the dead.

The son of the richest land owner of the island, Don Matjas Quintero, and two of his friends, have heard people talk about Yaiza. They want to meet the girl and travel to Playa Blanca, mainly with the intention of having a good time with her. When one of the boys tries to rape the girl, her brother Asdrubale rushes to her side to defend her from the aggressor. During the fight, unintentionally, he kills the son of Don Matjas with his dagger.

Aurelia, Asdrubale's mother knows Don Matjas to be a very violent man and she urges her son to go into hiding until everything has calmed down and justice can take its course.

Don Matjas's only wish is to see his son's murderer dead. The local police are unable to find Asdrubale as he has hidden himself on an island where there are more than 400 volcanoes.

Don Matjas therefore sends somebody off to get one of his exsubordinates, Damian Centeno of the Foreign Legion who, with seven hoodlums starts terrorizing the small village of Playa Blanca to find out where Asdrubale is hiding. The village's whole population and an old shepherd, Pedro El Trist, who all want to help Asdrubale, succeed in protecting him from his persecutors. It is then that Don Matjjas instructs Damian Centeno to kill both the girl and her other brother Sebastian.

The only way for Yaiza's family to save themselves is to flee from the island in a fishing boat. They hope to reach America but the crossing of the ocean is a real Odyssey during which Yaiza's father dies. Finally, Aurelia, Yaiza, Asdrubale and Sebastian land on the Venezuelian coast where they lead a miserable life of utter poverty.

Although near death, Don Matjas has not forgotten his revenge. He promises Damian Centeno to leave him all his fortune if Damian will give him his word to kill the Perdomo family.

The ex soldier of the Foreign Legion accepts Don Matjas's conditions. During the crossing to Venezuela he meets a beautiful prostitute, Muneca Chavez on the ship. Once arrived in Caracas he marries her immediately though he has not given up his aim to kill the Perdomo family.

They are mercilessly hunted down by Damian Centeno. The Perdomos flee into the interior of the country and are very lucky to be received and protected by Celeste, the owner of a big farm.

One day, Goyo Santana, a strange character arrives at the farm and tells the Perdomos he feels he is being followed by somebody. This somebody can only be Damian Centeno. The Perdomos decide to escape in Goyo's big boat in the direction of the Orinoco forests. They have heard that new diamond mines have been discovered. Although their mother is very much against their plans, the two brothers decide to join a group of adventurers and "desperados" in the hope of finally being able to solve all their problems and get rich.

Not far from the diamond mines a group of criminals have escaped from the prison "Eldorado"; they terrorize the whole area by killing and raping whomever they find on their way on their desperate flight to Brazil. The group of jailbirds run into Damian and Muneca. They rape and kill Muneca in front of the powerless Damian.

Damian buries Muneca whom he has deeply loved and for the first time in his life he himself feels the horrible pain he has always inflicted on so many others.

In the meantime Yaiza lives in the miners' village with her family; here she meets an old Indian who tells her that the only way to get rid of her "gift" which has caused so many problems for her, is to climb the sacred mountain of the "Waicas" from which descends the world's biggest waterfall called the "Saldo Angel".

In spite of the opposition of her mother and her brothers, Yaiza starts the climb of the mountain to meet her destiny. On the top of the mountain she is greeted by a second, more mature Yaiza.

This Yaiza tells her that the girl she has been, now will always remain on the sacred mountain and the one who will leave the mountain will be a woman who has lost her magic gifts.

The miners' village is besieged by the criminals who try everything they can do to take possession of all the diamonds so far extracted. The miners and the Perdomos are about to be overcome when Damian Centeno, in a towering rage, bursts into the place and kills, one after the other, the murderers of Muneca Chavez. After having finally taken revenge he finds himself in front of the terrified Perdomos. Without uttering a sound he puts away his arms and departs definitely thereby renouncing the persecution of the Perdomo family, the persecution which was the origin of all his troubles.

Yaiza descends from the sacred mountain and to her amazement she is holding in her hand a huge diamond given to her by the 'other Yaiza'."

all illustrations this page: **Mom I Can Do It**.
right: Deodato with young cast members and associate producer Andrè Koob *(on the left)*.
below: Original promo artwork, original title.
bottom right: Deodato in Caracas.

The original idea was to make a nasty, realistic film about a group of adolescents who are violent drug-pushers. For reasons of distribution the film was watered-down, mixing in comedy themes against the cruel and violent backdrop.

This is the **Mom I Can Do It** synopsis, reproduced direct from the Mifed sales flyer (promoted under the title **Los gamines**):

"Before he left Abilene on his summer vacation, Mark Stewart was a typical blond, all-American ten-year-old from the kind of family pollsters love – a businessman father, a stylish bridge-club mother and a romantic, much-admired big sister of 17, Kate. A nice middle-class kid whose life stopped being so average after Colombia. After living with the street kids of Bogotá – the vicious, feared mob of child delinquents aged three to fifteen called "los gamines" – to get his sister out of a drug rap that could have meant a thirty-year prison term in one of the country's hospitable jails.

Mark's adventure began in Cartagena, when the family rules loosened up in the hot, sultry atmosphere of the exotic tropical city brimming with curious little beggars who live in packs and have the run of the city, living off charity and thefts. And it was in Cartagena that Kate met Mike, the foot-loose young American traveler with a guitar and soft eyes.

In Bogotá things began going wrong from the start. Mrs. Stewart's purse was snatched right in front of the Hilton by some lightning quick gamines. And Mr. Stewart learned, much to his displeasure, that Kate's unkempt admirer had followed them and was seeing her on the sly. It looked like the trip was going to end early. Then in the airport the customs people took a look inside Kate's teddy bear (a gift from Mike) and found enough cocaine to jail her on the spot. While his father and mother started phoning lawyers, Mark realized their only chance was to find Mike again and make him confess – but how?

The street. Instinctively Mark took to the street, to the territory of los gamines, his only hope of saving Kate. And the ragged, starving, ruthless little gangsters put him to the test. Cuchillito, the twelve-year-old leader of the band, had the fair-skinned "gringo" stripped of his football jacket and money, but let him sleep in a corner of the courtyard that served as their evening refuge. Only to try to rape him during the night. But he defended himself. Cuchillito admiringly gave in, and Mark's initiation into the band was celebrated with a round of gasoline sniffing – stolen gasoline, of course.

The next days were filled with eye-opening experiences for the sheltered, over-privileged boy from Texas. He learned to eat scraps thrown out the back door of restaurants at meal times; he was shown the scars and deformities inflicted on the gamines by their parents before they ran away from home. Slowly Mark became an accepted member of the group. He was taught to steal hub caps and windshield wipers and escape from the police. There were territorial battles with other gangs, merciless violence, cruelty and sadism. Though part of the band, Mark found an unbridgeable gap between himself and the others, and not only because of the violence. It was as though he belonged at the same time to the world that victimized these lost children, that made them live the way they did.

At last Mike was located in a camp of gringos outside the city and – thanks to Cuchillito and his band – forced to turn himself over to the police and clear Kate. Or else! Los gamines didn't joke around. And the Stewart family was finally able to depart, after an ill-advised party to thank the "nice children" who helped Mark (and who systematically slashed their rented house to pieces in return). But the expression on Mark's face showed it had been more than just an adventurous vacation. He had grown up as fast as los gamines."

MOM I CAN DO IT

1992
Italian title: **Mamma ci penso io**, export title: **Mom I Can Do It**, French title: **Les petites canailles**, original title: **Los gamines**, shooting title: **I'll Do It Mom**
Italy & Colombia
director: Ruggero Deodato

Giovanni Bertolucci and Andrè Koob present a film by Ruggero Deodato. produced by Giovanni Bertolucci for San Francisco Film s.r.l.
©1992. San Francisco Film s.r.l.
negatives: Eastman Cinema e Televisione. laboratory: Cinecittà.
filmed on location in Venezuela

cast: Chris Masterson (Daniel Morris). Elizabeth Kemp (Jane Morris). John Rothman (US consul). Dolly Carroll (Pearl Morris). Carolina Brea. Aleksi Hecht. Yves Arispe. Giovanni Rodríguez. Verones Caicedo. Francisco Rodríguez. Gy Mirano. Ruggero Deodato (street photographer in yellow hat)

story by Ruggero Deodato. screenplay by Oddone Cappellino, Andrea Manni & Ruggero Deodato. director of photography: Roberto Forges Davanzati. music: Mario Raja; music publishers: Bixio C.A. BMG Ariola. editor: Gianfranco Amicucci. casting: Louis DiGiaimo. art director: Milton Crespo. costumes: Millina Deodato. associate producer: Andrè Koob. production manager: Mario Sampaolo. production supervisor: Filippo Deodato. production secretary: Anna Maria Severini. assistant director: Ottaviano Dell'Acqua. script girl: Egle Guarino. assistant cameraman: Dante Della Torre. assistant editors: Nadia Boggian & Massimo Cataldo. colour technician: Stefano Giovannini. technical supplies: Arco Due/MGM. insurance: Assitalia. Venezuelan production facilities: Vamos al Cine C.A. sound mixer: Marco Di Biase. sound editors: Michael Billinglsley & Alessandra Perpignani. sound effects: Cineaudio Effects & Union Sound. mixing engineer: Angelo Raguseo. music mixer: Goffredo Gibellini. sound studios, titles & opticals: Cinecittà.
the animated cartoon "I Soninghi" ™ © by DI.GI. International s.r.l. Cartoon Film through kind permission of the editor, Sabina Di Girolamo.
songs "Merengue del moro" & "Penelope" by A. Minotti & Mario Raja; "Furia" by A. Minotti, Mario Raja & Ruben Vilora, soloists: Ruben Vilora & Alvaro Atehortua; "Mariposa" by A. Minotti, Mario Raja & Ruben Vilora, soloist: Liliana Gimenez; "Danny's Menaito" by Mario Raja & Ruggero Deodato, sung by Chris Masterson; "Pepito Bananas" by Mario Raja & Ruggero Deodato. songs recorded & mixed by Enrico Chiaroni. music published by BMG Ariola and Bixio.

Italian theatrical release: none. running time: 98 minutes 11 seconds.
Export video running time: 94 minutes 15 seconds.

Mom I Can Do It is one of Deodato's more fascinating curios and the only film he directed for theatres that has seen virtually no release. Filmed entirely on location in Caracas in Venezuela, the story centres on 11 year old Danny Morris who is forced to join forces with a troop of children living rough on the streets in an attempt to clear his (single) mother of a smuggling charge. Danny and his sister Pearl are left in the care of the US Consul's girlfriend Rebecca but the boy escapes and has a variety of adventures before he is able to catch the real culprit and set his mother free.

The film was originally called **Los gamines** ('The Street Urchins') and an early plot synopsis reveals it to have been a far harder, much nastier piece of work than the one Deodato finally made. The synopsis lists the plot components as merciless violence, cruelty and sadism but Deodato's film is altogether different. It falls fatally between drama and children's fantasy and any political message it might have had (the boy belongs to the world that has victimised these children) is lost in lame attempts to be cute and humorous. The lightly ethnic soundtrack is obnoxious, all of the characters are broad stereotypes (especially the 'man in black', played with all the subtlety of a pantomime villain) and the thin narrative – consisting of a series of ridiculous contrivances – frequently just stops; in one case for Danny to sing a children's rap number when his pals are feeling down!

Technically the film is well made and some of the street sequences must have been extraordinarily difficult to capture. The acting by Americans Elizabeth Kemp (from Armand Mastroianni's two early eighties horror films **He Knows You're Alone** and **The Killing Hour**) and Chris Masterson (who appeared in Renny Harlin's **Cutthroat Island** (1995)) is fine and the (unidentified) actor who plays the children's leader Miguel is a natural. Shame about the story....
(Julian Grainger)

all images this page: **The Washing Machine**.
bottom left: Ludmilla seduces Alex in his own home, later leaving her red panties in his washing machine, where they are almost discovered by his girlfriend Irina.
above: Irina (Claudia Pozzi), Alex's girlfriend discovers red water leaking from their washing machine following Ludmilla's visit. Alex is quick to hide the evidence.
left: Publicity still showing some of the film's principal cast members: Kashia Figura (Vida Kolba) *(front left)*, Barbara Ricci (Ludmilla Kolba) *(right)*, Ilaria Borrelli (Maria 'Sissy' Kolba) *(seated on the washing machine)*, Yorgo Voyagis (Yuri Petkov) *(standing)*. The blonde lady on the far left stars in the part of Maria's (unnamed) blind girlfriend.
below: The Washing Machine.

THE WASHING MACHINE

1993
Italian title: **Vortice mortale**. Dutch video title: **The Washing Machine**. French shooting title: **La lavatrice**
Italy, France & Hungary
director: Ruggero Deodato

Eurogroup Films / Corrado & Alessandro Canzio / André Koob present a film by Ruggero Deodato. produced by ESSE. CI. Cinematografica (Rome)/Eurogroup Film (Paris)/Focus Film (Budapest).
©1993. ESSE. CI. Cinematografica Srl Roma.
colour by Telecolor. negatives: Kodak.
filmed in November/December 1992 on location in Budapest (Hungary)

cast: Philippe Caroit (Inspector Alexander Stacev). Ilaria Borrelli (Maria 'Sissy' Kolba). Kashia Figura (Vida Kolba). Barbara Ricci (Ludmilla Kolba). Laurence Bruffaerts (Nikolai, Stacev's assistant). László Porbély (music teacher). Claudia Pozzi (Irina, Stacev's girlfriend). Yorgo Voyagis (Yuri Petkov). Vilmos Kolba. Károly Medriczry. Sándor Boros. Támas Pintér. Agi Dávid. Ruggero Deodato (nosy neighbour).

story & screenplay by Luigi Spagnol. director of photography: Sergio D'Offizi. music by Claudio Simonetti; music published by Acquario S.r.l. film editor: Gianfranco Amicucci. costume designer: Adriana Spadaro.

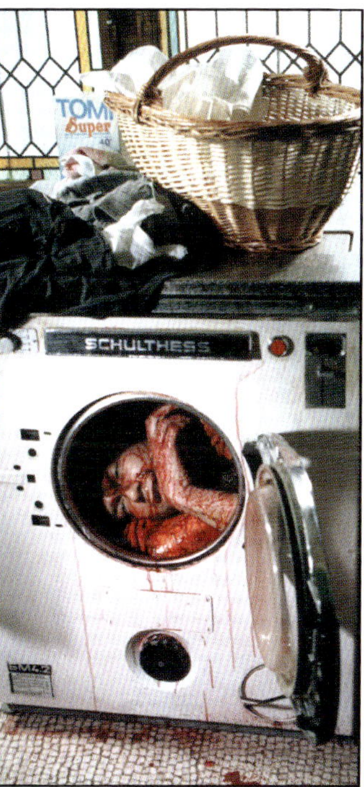

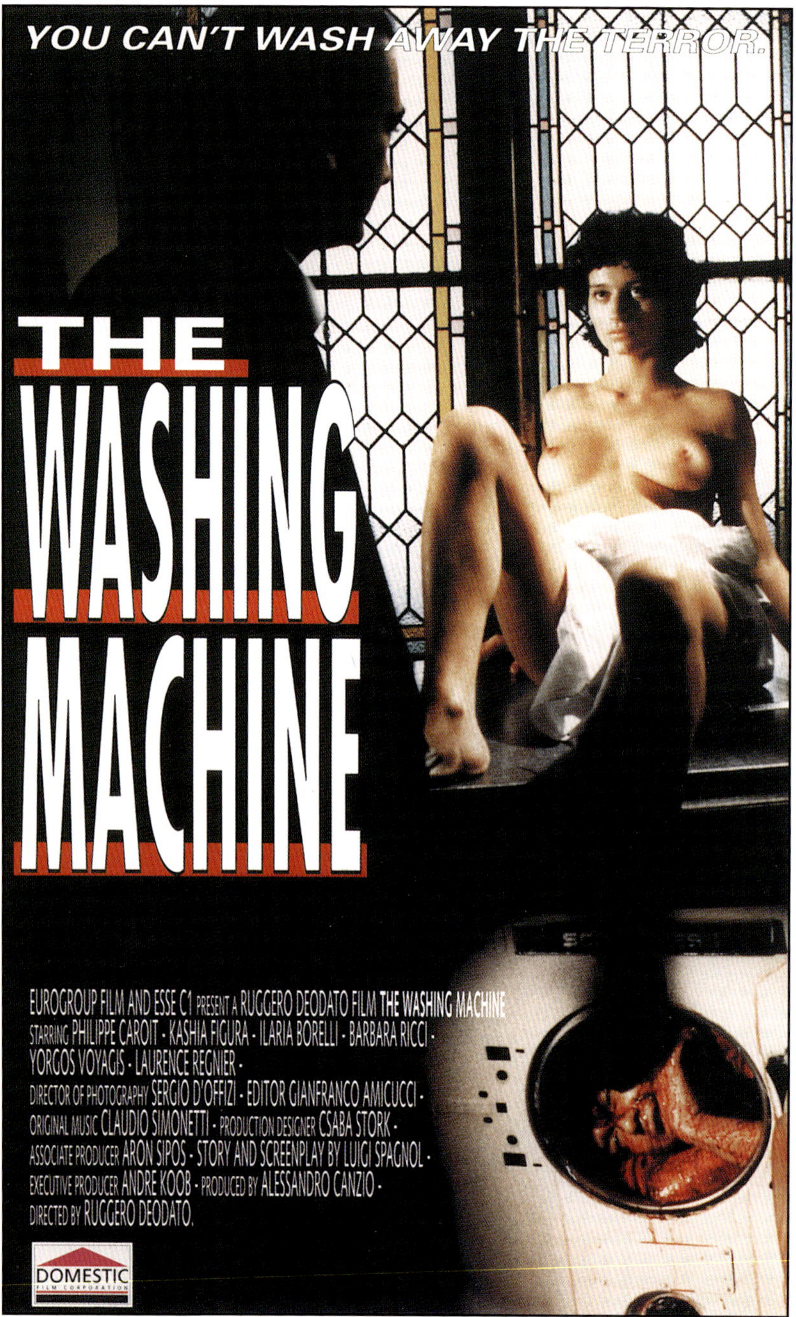

above: Sleazy Dutch video cover.

art directors: Francesca Pintus & Csaba Stork. executive producer: André Koob. producers: Corrado Canzio & Alessandro Canzio. associate producers: Aron Sipos & Denes Szekeres. production manager: Maria Ungor. assistant directors: Alberto Mangiante & [uncredited] László Porbély. script clerk: Egle Guarino. cameraman: Maria Elisa Basconi. production supervisor: Corrado Trionfera & Karoly Rozsnny. production assistant: Stefano Canzio. dialogue coach: Janine Koob. key grips: Gianni Gentili & Tibor Nyers. titles by Penta Studio. assistant editors: Maria Nadia Boggian & Giuliana Scalmani. custom jewelry: Airoldi. Cashmere knitwear: Malo. underwear & lingerie: Imec. shoes: Magli. sunglasses: Safilo. footwear: Veclamar; Flexability; Cristian Dior Men; Cori-Coriland; Chiara Boni. sound engineer: Elisabetta Trautteur. sound effects: Coop. Studio Sound; Renato Narinelli. sound studio: Fono Rete. mixing engineer: Franco Bassi.

bottom right: Sex in a fridge: appliance fetishism runs riot in **The Washing Machine**.
below: The three wicked sisters kick Yuri out of the house during the opening scene of **The Washing Machine**.

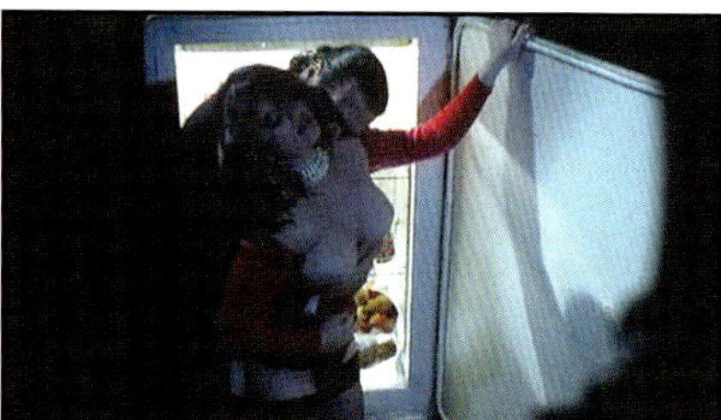

Italian theatrical release: none. running time: 89 minutes. (original version 104 minutes).

The Washing Machine is a sick and twisted minor gem. Despite Deodato's protests that this erotic thriller falls short of its potential due to a rushed production schedule and what he considers to be a less than ideal cast, it stands out from his other 90s films by virtue of its sexually-charged atmosphere and perverse scenario.

The opening scene sets the tone nicely. A fiery lady (Vida) with a fine eye for 'figure enhancing' basques fucks a guy (Yuri) in a kitchen fridge (!) The act is observed by another woman (Ludmilla) who sits on the nearby staircase with her legs apart, gently striking a triangle.

The clever combination of the open voyeurism (the two women make and hold eye contact) and the pure ringing tone of the percussion instrument has an immediately unsettling effect. Vida argues with Yuri over a bracelet engraved with the name 'Sissy' which he is carrying, and she kicks him out of the house which, it later transpires, she shares with her sisters, Maria (aka Sissy) and Ludmilla. Later that night Yuri's body is found by Ludmilla, dismembered in the washing machine at the house. The police are called, but find nothing and dismiss Ludmilla's story when it transpires she was drunk that night. However, one of the policemen (Alex) remains intrigued and is gradually drawn into a web of deceit which sees him become sexually involved with all three sisters, and which eventually costs him his life...

At the heart of it all is a suitcase full of cash and jewels. So once more, money is the root of all evil, but what makes these wicked sisters so special is their collective deranged glee as they go about their dastardly business.

The plot is fairly convoluted and, due in part to the fact that we are witness to several dreams and hallucinations, the narrative is at times confusing and apparently directionless, but the downbeat finale ties everything together in a most satisfying manner. (Note that release prints were cut down from the original 104 minutes, presumably to aid pacing.) The film's main handicap must be its title, but take a chance and check it out; you should be pleasantly surprised.
(Harvey Fenton)

WE ARE ANGELS

1995 (TV)
Italian television title: **Noi siamo angeli**
German television title: **Zwei Engel mit vier Fäusten**
export title: **We Are Angels**
Italy, Germany, France & Costa Rica
director: Ruggero Deodato

produced by Giuseppe Pedersoli for Smile Productions in association with RAI – RadioTelevisione Italiana/RTL (Germany)/M6 (France). executive producer: Pre-producciones Castin S.A. (Costa Rica). prints & processing: Fotocinema spa. stock: Kodak spa (Rome). filmed on location in Costa Rica

A series of six circa 90-minute comedy television films. Transmitted in Italy @ 20.50 on RaiUno from 16 February to 23 March 1997.
First episode transmitted in Germany on RTL, rated 14, on 6 July 1997.

episode: Facce da galera / Schwere jungs
episode: Il mistero delle cinque chiese / Das Geheimnis der fünf Kirchen
episode: La fortuna viene dal cielo / Alles Gute kommt von oben
episode: Dollari / Falsche Dollars
episode: Polvere / Die Abrechnung
episode: Finalmente si vola / Auf und davon

cast: Bud Spencer [Carlo Pedersoli] (Father Orso). Philip Michael Thomas (Father Zaccaria) <with> Kabir Bedi <as> (Napoleon). Philip [Philippe] Leroy (Duval). Richard Lynch (don Alfonso Santillana). Erik Estrada (Graziani). Renato Scarpa (Father Campana). Antonio Marsina (Rupert). Michael Berryman (Quesada). Andrew Taft (Wolfgang Galveston III). Carlo Reali (President Aneto). Marc Macaulay (Don Medina). Syd Brisbane (Father Celestino). Ty Hardin (the blind exorcist). Max Herbrechter (Caleste). Mike Kirton (Father Torment). Cesar Melendez (Father Rafael). David Hess (prison captain). Ellen Jacoby. Jeff Moldovan. Alfie Wise (McQuade). Michael Adenauer. Ronald Alfaro. Ivania Alpizar. Marlene Amador. Oscar Amador. Jean Paul Andrade. Mamma Jhonpaul Andrade. Vica Andrade. Laura Angulo. Dennis Atkinson. Joseph Azzara. Billy Bates. Nikhila Bedi. Ron Boston. Hellen Brenes. Giovanni Bulgarelli. Rita Campos. Pierluigi Camiscioni. Narda Campbell. Lance Carlson. Antonio Cardona. Antonio Casas Figueroa. Francisco Cordero. Wilbur Cruz. Thelma Darkings. Sacha Dark [Sasha D'Arc]. Andres De La Ossa. Guillermo Dufour. Rodrigo Fallas. Daniela Gallegos. Andres Garcia. Bernal Garcia. David Gatto. Sabryn Genet. Ramon Grado. Hernan Hidalgo. Jeff Horsfield. Anna Iztaru. Marcello Johnson. Joaquin & Luis. Rick Lane. Federico Lang. Roberto Leiva. Erwing Lewis. Richard Liberty. Roberto Lizano. Marco Martin. Max Maxwell. Mauricio McPhail. Tibor Mezsaros. Stephany Montero. Mariana Mora. Piero Musiani. Wesh Nash. Cesar Nieto. William Pena. Carlos Perez. Patricio Primus. Giancarlo Pucci. Javier Quesada. Ruben Rabasa. Gloriana Ramirez. Andrea Regass. Alicia Repeto. Eddy Rodriguez. Rodrigo Rojas. Ronald Russel. Freddy Salazar. Josè Antonio Sarol. Eduardo Silva. Mario Soto. Chuck Sweet. Claudio Taylor. Jim Theologos. José Pablo Torre. Enrique Torrent. Duenne Weshchuck. Edward White. Carlos White. Trevor Winacott. Luis A Zapparolli. Ruggero Deodato (man talking with Padre Zaccaria). Giuseppe Pedersoli (man talking with Padre Orso). Ruggero Deodato (appears in one episode). Sergio Fiorentini (voice of Padre Orso). Michele Gammino (voice of Padre Zaccaria). Jeff Moldovan, Carlos Perez, Billy Bates, Dennis Devaugh, Ronald Russo & Joe Hess (stunts). stand-ins: Pier Luigi Camiscioni & William Watson.

story & screenplay by Alessandro Moretti, Lorenzo De Luca, Alessandro Capone, Laura Curelli, Rosario Galli & Ruggero Deodato; based on an idea by Alessandro Moretti & Giuseppe Pedersoli. director of photography: Sergio D'Offizi. music: Enrico Riccardi; Peer Edizioni Musicali & Warner Chappell Music Italiana (Milan). editor: Rinaldo Marsili. art direction & set dressing: Osvaldo Desideri & Eva Dejna. costume designers: Vera Marzot & Lesley Herman. production supervisor: Luciano Balducci. assistant directors: Gabriele Polverosi & Elisabetta Trautteur. production manager: Victor Barriga. unit managers: Simona Scianniamanico & Filippo Deodato. production secretaries: Federico Foti & Rodrigo Rojas Aguilar. assistant production secretary: Bernal Delgado. secretary: Carolyn Markland Francis. administration: Maurizio Grazilsi. casting (Costa Rica): Pre-producciones Castin SA, (Germany): Risa Kess, (USA): Ellen Jacoby Casting International. continuity: Laura Curreli & Gaia Gorrini. dialogue coach: Ricky Sacco. stunt co-ordinator: Mike Kirton. special effects: Paolo Ricci. art director: Paolo Del Bravo. cameraman: Federico Del Zoppo. 1st assistant cameraman: Silvia Giulietti. 2nd assistant cameraman: Fernando Montero. still photography: Ezequiel Bezerra. set dresser: Eva Dejna. 1st assistant art directors: Gabrio Zappelli & Louis Valerio. 2nd assistant art director: Roberto Solano. property master: Carlos Urena. assistant costumes: Ernesto Rohrmoser. wardrobe: Elieth Navarro. costumers: Cecilia Quesada, Cecilia Fernandez & Gretel Cedeno. chief make-up: Stefania Sapori. make-up: Lorena Mora. hairstylists: Alfredo Montoya & Flory Mora. assistant hairstylist: Jeannie Del Rio. gaffer: Mauricio Trujillo. electricians: Julio Jimenez, Marcos Robles & Freddy Martin. key grip: Elio Bosi. grips: Gilber Valerio, Esteban Campos, Javier Serrano & Manuel Torres. generator operator: Jean Paul Andrade. drivers: Guillermo Costaneda, Guillermo Cano & Wilbur Cruz. sound re-recording: Danilo Moroni. dubbing recordist: Alberto Severini. music recording engineer: Charles Burgi. dialogue adaptation & dubbing director: Michele Gamino. dubbing assistant: Sabina Montanarella. dubbing recorded by C.D.C. colour timer: Ernesto Volpi. digital editing: Movie Republic s.r.l. recording equipment. R.E.C. technical equipment: Panalight; Image Devices. titles & animation: Medianet srl & Idee a Colori.
transport: Mudanzas Mondiales. catering: Bilbao. insurance: Cinesicurtà. costumes provided by Franco Carretti for ABC Costume Shop. production vehicles: Economy Rent a Car. transport: technical equipment aggiunti: Unique. travel agents: Rossini Travel. sound: Massimo Loffredi. boom operator: Carlos Mora. synchronization & re-recording: SEFIT. special sound effects: Consorzio Studio 16.

songs [opening credits] "Guardian Angels" composed by Enrico Riccordi & Paula Parfitt, sung by Bud Spencer & Philip Michael Thomas; [closing credits] "Love at the Mission" composed by Enrico Riccordi & Paula Parfitt, sung by Paula Parfitt; "Amen Blues" composed by Enrico Riccordi & Philip Michael Thomas, sung by Philip Michael Thomas; "Cachamba" composed by Ramirez Josè Del Carmen, sung by Kinito Mendez; "Brighter Day" by Cyrus & Koglin, sung by Kelly Lorena; "Everybody's Free (to Feel Good)" & "Faith (In the Power of Love)" by Swanston & Cox, sung by Rozalla; "The Key, the Secret" composed by Heath, Moratto, Persi & Rizzatti, sung by Urban Cookie Collective.

The Ruggero Deodato who directed six ninety-odd minute episodes of **We Are Angels** would seem to bear little resemblance to the man who made **Cannibal Holocaust**; however before we let natural prejudice take hold, it's worth considering that this was one of RadioTelevisione Italiana's most expensive-ever projects and was shown on the prime Sunday mid-evening slot in Italy. On TV at least, Deodato has hit the big time.

top: Deodato at the Taormina film festival, photographed together with Kabir Bedi, most famous as the star of Sergio Sollima's two-part TV show **Sandokan** (1975). Bedi appears in Deodato's **We Are Angels**.
above: Following its TV screenings, **We Are Angels** was issued in Italy as a two-part DVD set; this is the front cover of the second disc.

above: Deodato with Philip Michael Thomas *(left rear)* and Bud Spencer *(right)* during the making of **We Are Angels**.

Polvere (which literally means 'dust' but here 'gold dust') is a typical episode: the mission at San Rolando comes under threat when gold is discovered in the local river and crooked businessman Richard Lynch (**Cut and Run**'s Colonel Horne) succeeds in conning the land rights from the local Monsignor. To complicate matters, Lynch's maid Maria was once Spencer's girlfriend. Everything is sorted out in the end after Spencer has bashed Lynch into submission.

In a nice touch, Deodato peppers each episode with a cast of exploitation regulars that can mean little to the larger viewing audience in Italy but will delight fans of his theatrical films. Apart from the aforementioned Richard Lynch, a moustached David Hess (from **House on the Edge of the Park**) gets a good-sized role as a dastardly kidnapper, Michael Berryman (also from **Cut and Run**) shows up in a featured appearance and you can also find Erik Estrada (from **CHiPs**), Kabir Bedi (who played 'Sandokan' in Sergio Sollima's hugely popular TV series of the same name), the American Ty Hardin (who made several Spaghetti Westerns) and Philippe Leroy (in Cavani's **The Night Porter** and many others).

Deodato uses the Puerto Rican locations to startlingly beautiful effect – it looks like paradise – and Enrico Riccardi's music often underscores the visuals most effectively. Subtlety may be nowhere in sight – especially with regard to the acting – but there is a lot worse to be seen on TV than just good, simple fun.

(Julian Grainger)

Two title cards come up as the programme begins: RAI presents with the participation of... and the second card has the logo "Toys'R'Us". This gives us some sort of a clue about what we are about to see: light entertainment with lots of comedy, some action (but little violence) and a degree of sentimentality – and all in an exotic setting. With this in mind it should be said that **We Are Angels** is hugely entertaining. The set-up consists of two escaped prisoners who pose as two rather unlikely monks (Bud Spencer and **Miami Vice**'s Philip Michael Thomas – previously teamed in Enzo G. Castellari's **Extralarge** cop series) who live in the jungle at the beautiful San Rolando Mission along with several other (equally odd) brothers as well as a number of colourful locals. The enormous Bud Spencer plays Father Orso, a man over-fond of getting out of scrapes by thumping anything in sight. Thomas takes the Terence Hill part as Father 'Zac' Zaccaria, a man who has trouble maintaining his vow of chastity when there are so many beautiful, half-naked women around.

SOTTO IL CIELO DELL'AFRICA

1999 (TV)
German television title: **Unter der Sonne Afrikas**
export title: **Under African Skies**
shooting titles: **Pensando all'Africa/Thinking of Africa**
Italy & Germany
director: Ruggero Deodato
12 x 90 minutes

produced by Guido & Maurizio De Angelis for TPI – Together Production International S.r.l., Mediaset, Beta Taurus, Victory
filmed from 1997 for ten months on location in Zimbabwe and Botswana

cast: Carol Alt (Monica Marini). Rüdiger Joswig (Alexander Brandt). Hans von Borsody (Walter Brandt). Ingeborg Schöner (Lisa Brandt). Olivia Kolbe-Booysen (Sara Marini). Michela Rocco di Torrepadula (Kate). Robert Whitehead (Dr Henry Thompson). John Indi (John Mowanda). Adrian Steed (Professor Kohlmann). John Dennison (Dickerby). Warrick Grier (Henry Murch). Gina Borthwick (Angela Murch). Shane Bhatty

below and right: Behind the scenes during the making of **Sotto il cielo dell'Africa** in Zimbabwe.

(Jimmy). Peter Spyropoulos (Groovy). Andrew Whaley (Frank Morrison). Yvonne Peters (Maggie). Martin le Maitre (Dutoit). Tony Caprari (Bastiat). Derek Thixton (Anton Horvath). Godwishes Rusere (Aswahala). J.P. Bernard (Tobias Horvath). Keith Morkel (Van der Poel). Samantha Loaring (Mary Hamilton). Georgina Godwin (Mrs Hamilton). John Riber (Sam Russel). Mike Girvan (LKW driver). Brenda Ganda (Kristal). Diana Wilson (Sally). Lawrence Simbarashe (George). Yvonne Peters (Maggie). Michaela Merten (Alice). Michelle Donati (Chiara). Daniela Poggi (Sandra Vanucci). Karen Stally (Cindy). Paolo Lorimer (Paolo Mattei). Stefania Barca (Roberta Mattei). Gianni Williams (Marco Vanucci). Debbie Simmons (Elisabeth). Nicola Farron (Dr. Mattia Rosselli). Greg Latter (Captain van der Stel). Ian Wintersmith (Colonel Hill). Simon Shumba (Sanders). Dominique Bonarjee (Zoe). Gavin Colborne (Peter). Richard Lynch (Jim van der Oden). Wilson Dunster (David Osborn). Jennifer Stein (Agnes McCullen). Rossano Rubicondi (Eddy van der Oden). Jocelyn Broderick (Waldine van der Oden). Sara Jane Littleford (Allison Osborn). Sawna Del Chambre (Grace McCullen). Tomas Arana (Stefano). Valentina Lainati (Giulia, Stefano's wife). Burt Young (Oland). Ken Marshall (Steve). Linda Battista (Linda). Clayton Norcross (Pons). Ruggero Deodato (man with dog).

written by Luca Manfredi, Claudia Rittore, Alberto Simone, Massimo Torre, Dido Castelli, Luca D'Ascanio, Piero Bodrato. director of photography: Sergio D'Offizi. music: Guido & Maurizio De Angelis. editors: Gianfranco Amicucci, Gisella Haller, Jutta Neumann. art directors: Osvaldo Desideri, Eva Deyna [Desideri]. costumes: Ingrid Mignone. casting: Cornelia von Braun.

Italian television screening: 5 March 1999 (Rete 4)

Another major mini-series that seems to have received scant screenings or attention and hasn't as of this writing made it to DVD either in Italy or Germany.
(Julian Grainger)

above: Ruggero Deodato during the filming of **Incantesimo**, series 8.

INCANTESIMO 8

2005-2006 (TV)
Italy
directors: Tomaso Sherman and Ruggero Deodato

series 8 (27 episodes)
episodes 1 to 13 aired Fridays at 21.00 on Raidue, 23 September 2005 to 16 December 2005, episodes 14 - 27 aired Wednesdays at 21.00, 7 March 2006 to 14 June 2006

main cast: Walter Nudo (Antonio Corradi). Samuela Sardo (Giulia Donati). Paola Pitagora (Giovanna Medici). Giuseppe Pambieri (Diego Olivares). Delia Boccardo (Tilly Nardi). Linda Batista (Denise Nascimento). Fabio Fulco (Sergio Fanti). Duccio Giordano (Paolo Corradi). Alessandra Monti (Beatrice Balli). Paolo Malco (Giuseppe Ansaldi). François Montagut (Jean). Rodolfo Baldini (Cesare Gomez). Ivana Monti (Liliana Donati). Daniela Poggi (Cristina Ansaldi). Francesco Prando (Angiò). Antonio Tallura (Freddi). Giacomo Piperno (Renato). Luigi Diberti (Edoardo De Nittis). Carlotta Miti (Sara Segre). Benedetta Massola (Ludovica Segre). Emanuela Garuccio (Alice). Ivan Bacchi (Domenico Santi). Paolo Romano (Aldo Dessi). Fabrizio Contri (Maini). Corinne Clery (Viola). Barbara Tabita (Letizia). Emanuela Birocchi (Giada). Federico Russo (Michele). Guia Jelo (Costanza De Nittis). Patrizia La Fonte (Olga). Toni Garrani (Marchi). Alessandra Barzaghi (Monica). Vincenzo Alfieri. Eva Deidda (Gloria Piccoli). Cristina Pappa (Demetra). Daniele Petruccioli (Claudio Rondi). Luisa Marzotto (Elsa Scotti). Massimiliano Bellini Allocco (Renzo Moretti). Sofia Elmanjaui (Romina). Marco Tallone (Filippo Panini). Diana Collepiccolo (Emma). Denise Duchene (Charlotte). Eleonora Gaggioli (Clelia Colapinto). Paolo Lanza (Oscar Sensi). Samya Abbary (Samya). Alessandro Marrapodi (Gaetano). Francesco De Angelis (Francesco Forti).

produced by De Angelis Group (Guido & Maurizio De Angelis) and Smile Production (Giuseppe Pedersoli)

filmed from early June 2005 for 40 weeks on location in Rome and Florence (Italy)

distributor: De Angelis Group

A long-running soap opera set in the 'Life' beauty clinic in Rome, **Incantesimo** ('Enchanted') was originally conceived by Maria Venturi as a home-grown version of the hugely popular **The Bold and the Beautiful** (called simply **Beautiful** in Italy) which had been airing in Italy since 1990. The first set of 12 episodes began production in March 1997 starring Agnese Nano, Vanni Corbellini, Giovanni Guidelli, Paola Pitagora, Delia Boccardo, Daniela Poggi, Orso Maria Guerrini and Paolo Malco and the first-ever episode aired on Monday 8 June 1998. Originally running on Monday and Thursdays at 20.50, RAI appears to have struggled to find the perfect slot and the series moved to one episode per week on Tuesdays and then on Thursdays. By series 3, which began screening in 2000, each episode was attracting some 5 million viewers and series 4 (airing from 6 March 2001) moved to RAI's main channel Raiuno, eventually becoming RAI's longest-running soap opera.

By series 8, when Ruggero Deodato came on board (supporting veteran TV director Tomaso Sherman who in a previous life had co-written the Pier Ludovico Pavoni feature **Amore libero – Free Love** (1974) starring Laura Gemser), the beauty clinic had become a cutting edge private hospital and much of the drama was centred around control of this institution. The character of Sara Segre (played by Carlotta Miti) was introduced while Paola Pitagora, Giuseppe Pambieri, Linda Batista, Fabio Fulco, Francesco Prandi, Duccio Giordano, Antonio Tallura, François Montagut, Rodolfo Baldini, Daniela Poggi and Paolo Malco all returned from previous series. A massive undertaking, the series employed some 215 actors and a 40-week shooting schedule.
(Julian Grainger)

below: Carlotta Miti, whoi plays the part of Sara Segre in **Incantesimo**.

above: Italian DVD cover for **Father Hope**.

FATHER HOPE

2000 (TV pilot for unproduced series)
Italian television title: **Padre Speranza**
German television title: **Padre Speranza - Mit Gottes Segen**
export title: **Father Hope**
Italian subtitle: **Con la benedizione di Dio...** (With God's Blessing)
German shooting title: **Vater Hoffnung**
Germany & Italy
director: Ruggero Deodato

produced by Guido De Angelis, Giuseppe Pedersoli
De Angelis Groups Production in association with Smile Production present a De Angelis Production and Distribution Gmbh, Victory film Production and Distribution Gmbh co-production
©2000. De Angelis Production and Distribution Gmbh, Victory film Production and Distribution Gmbh
filmed on location in Crotone and Cropani in the province of Catanzaro in Calabria, Italy
film stock: Fuji Film. prints & processing: Fotocinema Spa

cast: Bud Spencer [Carlo Pedersoli] (don Carlo Vasari). Totò [Salvatore] Cascio (Nino Carbone). Giovanni/Gianni Caruso (detention centre deputy warden). Saverio Deodato (Attilio Venturi, taxi driver). Rodolfo Corsato (Mottola, coroner). Gianni Franco (Ettore Peluso). Laura Gualtieri (Doctor Rivelli). Vince/Vincent Riotta (Aldo Torrisi). Ines Nobili (Doctor Di Bilio). Lucio Rosato (Anastasio, prison doctor). Alberto Rossi (Episcopo). Paolo Triestino (Inspector Altieri). Valentina Lainati (Maddalena Carbone, Nino's sister). Alex Sandro [Alessandro Pess] (Vincenzo Torrisi). Mauro Ursella (Gegè). Angelo Infanti (Guido Fonseca). Marco Messeri (Father Leonardo). Marcello Arnone (Diotallevi). Ivna Bluck (Lulù). Alessio Casamassima (Darko Jacubi). Francesca Cavallaro (Vincenzo's girlfriend). Manuel Colao (Calabrian boy). Maurizio Comito (Franco, Torrisi henchman). Salvatore Corea (Marcello). Simona Corigliano (Luisa). Aleksander Cvjetkovic (Darko's father). Hadryan Darko [see note * below]. Anna Maria Lagani (little girl). Carmine Le Rose (tall boy). Antonio Leone (little boy). Alessandro Moretti (don Cesco). Paolo Napizia (Otello). Dario Natale (Inspector Batoli). Anastasia Sciuto (Darko's sister). Aiace Tugnoli (Rossi). Paolo Turrà (Cossi). Carmelo Viapina (Antonio, accountant). Luigi Malena, Fabrizio Lonetti (stunts).
uncredited: Ottaviano Dell'Acqua (pimp beating prostitute). Sasha D'Arc (pimp's associate).

below: A moment of high drama in **Father Hope**.

story: Alessandro [Sandro] Moretti. screenplay: Alessandro [Sandro] Moretti, Ruggero Deodato, Giuseppe Pedersoli. on-set sound recording: Marco Di Biase, Giulio Viggiani. costumes by Katrin Marras. art director: Antonello Geleng. music by Guido & Maurizio De Angelis. editor: Rinaldo Marsili. director of photography: Adolfo Troiani. line producer: Patrizia Tallarico. production manager: Gianfranco Pierantoni. unit manager: Francesco Morbilli. production secretaries: Angelo Lonetti, Sergio Lonetti, Ernesto Serleti. production assistants: Ludovica Valle, Angela Maria Rosati. publicity: Biamonte. still photography: Michele Lonetti. assistant costumes: Anna Liucia Cugusi, Emilia Aiello. set decorator: Fabrizio Riganello. assistant art director: Milo Geleng. 2nd assistant art director: Cristiano Iuorio. properties: Marco Priori, Francesca Sesito. art department assistant: Paolo Del Bravo. stunt co-ordinator: Ottaviano Dell'Acqua. 1st assistant director: Michele De Angelis. script supervisor: Laura Curreli. 2nd assistant director: Virginia Marasco. dubbing director: Novella Marcucci. assistant editor: Francesca Marsili. sound editor: Maurizio Moroni. sound mixer: Riccardo Canino. camera operator: Bruno Di Virgilio. 1st assistant camera: Marco Mazzoneschi. 2nd assistant camera: Antonello Sarao. key make-up: Marisa Marconi. assistant make-up: Maria Teresa Marano. key hairstylist: Sandro D'Angelo. assistant hairstylist: Carlo Allegro. boom operator: Giulio Viggiani. gaffer: Antonio Gasbarrini. electricians: Fabio Bolli, Valter Romoli, Ferrise Fernando. key grip: Elio Bosi. grips: Fernando Monti, Simone Bramucci, Carmelo Vitale. genny operator: Benedetto Stefanucci. drivers: Mario Vittori, Roberto Carrieri, Giorgio Marchio, Paolo Ruggero, Menno Adorisio, Domenico Pascuzzi. editing facility: Moviemax. steadicam supplier: Camera Works. technical & camera equipment: Fratelli Cartocci. production services: Maggiore; Avis. costumes supplied by Centro Costumi; Sorelle Ferroni; E. Rancati; Ascot & C. catering: Global Service Calabria; Ristorante Tonino Esposito. special effects: Ricci s.r.l. sound: N.C. s.r.l. Italian version: La BiBi.it. music publishers: Cabum s.r.l. shipping: Cecchetti Speed Coop. suppliers: Bud Spencer's wardrobe by Sarrocco Confezioni S.p.a. Bud Spencer's shoes by Valleverde. clothing: Bi-Brooks; Pierantonio Gaspari; Rosati Uomo. shoes: Bruè. luggage: Roncato. jewellery: Eliodoro. thanks to: Associazione Musicale Rossini; Cropani Marina; Maestro Mario Capelluto; A.R.S.S.A. for Villa Margherita; Costa Tiziana Hotel; DATEL; Acqua mineral "fonte d'oro"; Discoteca Focò; Bar Sax; Bar Italia; Cinema teatro Apollo; Ditta Greco Mobili s.a.s.; Archivio Audiovisivo del Movimento Operaio e Democratico; "Il Crotonese"; Associazione Treni Sorici e Turistici la Vaporiera Calabria Express; Praxsis Computers. title song composed by Bud Spencer & Nereo Foresti, arranged by Capranica & Lombardi, performed by Bud Spencer.

Premiere television screening in Hungary on RTL Klub on 20 March 2002
Italian television screening: Wednesday 28 December 2005 on Raidue at 21.00.

Father Hope is a feature-length television film starring Bud Spencer, made at the end of 2000, and executive produced by his son Giuseppe Pedersoli, who had also made **We Are Angels** and **Extralarge** as well as some of the later Hill/Spencer theatrical features. It seems likely that it was intended as a pilot to mirror what would become Terence Hill's long-running successful series **Don Matteo** (2000-2010), also 'incidentally' about a priest righting wrongs. Although purchased by Italian state broadcaster RAI in 2001, the film remained unseen in Italy until the 2005 Christmas season, and then screened on Raidue (the equivalent of UK's BBC2) rather than Raiuno. This screening garnered a barely respectable 3,550,000 viewers (an audience share of 14%). Bizarrely, the film's first-ever screening seems to have been on the 20th of March 2002, broadcast on Hungary's RTL Klub. Latterly there have been a number of DVD releases both in Italy and Germany although a version dubbed into English or with subtitles has yet to emerge as of 2011.

The story concerns unconventional priest don Carlo Vasari (Spencer), an ex-policeman tormented by his killing of a 16-year-old youth during street disturbances years before. After rescuing young streetwalker Lulù (Ivna Bluck) from her pimp (Ottaviano Dell'Acqua) and his scar-faced pal (Sasha D'Arc) and seeing her safely into the care of his cousin Father Leonardo (Marco Messeri), Vasari is sent by his superiors to Crotone in Calabria, in the south of Italy. Here he is to give moral guidance to youths held at a detention centre. When teenager Darko Jacubi (Alessio Casamassima) is murdered, 16-year-old Nino Carbone (Salvatore 'Totò' Cascio) is the prime suspect. Vasari thinks otherwise and investigates and, with the help of a journalist and a local taxi driver, he uncovers a conspiracy involving a vendetta by members of a local crime syndicate run by Guido Fonseca (the late, lamented Angelo Infanti, who also guested on **Don Matteo**) and brings the real culprits to book.

Spencer was getting on in years when he made this – he was 71 – and there is precious little action in **Padre Speranza**. With his eyes mere slits situated above huge bags, he comes across like a somnambulant Robbie Coltrane. The eyes matter because it is hard to judge the former action star's acting skills and while this is clearly an attempt at a 'serious' role, Spencer has never been considered an especially expressive performer. Nevertheless he is a substantial (in every sense) 'presence' and his work here is decent and deeply-felt. Spencer died in June 2016, aged 86.

One can't but wonder whether the character of don Vasari was considered a tad controversial for a prime time Italian television film: often described as a maverick, Vasari has little time for the rules of the Catholic church and embarks on his work with the dispossessed with gusto and dedication. Although it doesn't appear onscreen, the title for this pilot film is apparently **Con la benedizione di Dio...** which could be translated as "With God's Blessing..." Perhaps Vasari's belief in the Almighty rather than the structure and hierarchy of his Church had RAI executives worrying that Italian audiences might not find him entirely palatable but this is only speculation. Writer Sandro Moretti had previously co-created the big-budget Bud Spencer series **Extralarge** and the Deodato-directed **We Are Angels**. Intriguingly, an earlier credit can be found on Bruno Vani's bizarre and incompetent **Torino centrale del vizio** (1979) – co-written with Renato Polselli. In Italy as in much of continental Europe, a priest's status would allow him to question almost anyone, a useful set-up for an investigatory/procedural TV show. There is no reason to think that a decent series wouldn't have emerged if things had worked out differently. Perhaps the more sombre tone of **Padre Speranza** (contrasting, say, with the jolly atmosphere of **Don Matteo**) just wasn't sufficiently commercial.

The film is well-directed and edited, as well as beautifully shot by Adolfo Troiani, who takes advantage of the attractive Calabrian town of Crotone. The performances of the large cast are believable within the confines of the story and while the ravages of adolescence have left young Totò Cascio some distance away from his charming presence in Giuseppe Tornatore's **Cinema Paradiso** back in 1988, his work as the unfairly accused teenager is excellent. The guest appearance by a distinguished-looking Angelo Infanti is painfully brief and comes well over an hour into the story. Doing much of the driving for Spencer is Deodato and Silvia Dionisio's handsome son Saverio. Also of note is Mauro Ursella ('for the first time on the screen') as 'Gegè' (pronounced Gigi), a young actor with Down's Syndrome who shares many scenes with Spencer and at one point reveals important information that moves the story forward.

There is little here to attract fans dedicated only to Deodato's more disturbing works – although the shot of the naked and bloodied corpse of Darko Jacubi comes as something of a surprise – and in fact there is a scene of such jaw-dropping sentimentality that they may be actively repulsed. Suddenly we find Bud Spencer performing a song with a band consisting of a number of the inmates while their compatriots look on adoringly. If this weren't bad enough, this audience proceeds to join in as an impromptu, note-perfect choir while poor Nino sits alone in his cell crying. Even by Italian standards this is pretty hard to take, although Spencer does have a reasonable singing voice.

It is interesting to consider just how far into the mainstream Deodato has come; or more to the point, how close to the mainstream he has always been. His early apprenticeship included established directors like Roberto Rossellini, Carlo Ludovico Bragaglia, Mauro Bolognini and even Joseph Losey. As with all but the most artistically lauded auteurs, Italian directors are blown wherever the commercial cinematic winds take them. With the demise of popular genre cinema in the 1980s – made as much for export as internal consumption – many Italian directors either retired or moved into television. Apart from his work in drama, Deodato has directed well over a thousand commercials (some of which have won awards) and a number of documentaries the likes of the Italian Ministry of Foreign Affairs. Furthermore it shouldn't be underestimated just how big a star in Italy Bud Spencer is, and how enormously expensive such series as **Il ricatto**, **Ocean**, **We Are Angels**, **I ragazzi del muretto** and **Under African Skies** are to produce. In British television terms, think of prime time directors like Gillies MacKinnon (**Trial & Retribution**, **The Commander**), Ben Bolt (**Doc Martin**), Martyn Friend (**New Tricks**, **Rebus**) or Brian Percival (**Downton Abbey**). Deodato's more extreme films may eventually be seen – by Italian audiences at least – as just part of a varied career rather than as his only significant films.

Mention should be made of a few minor differences between the German and Italian DVD releases of the film: while the former ends with don Vasari and Nino leaving the prison to find a large crowd of well-wishers and a brass band (!) playing for them, the marginally longer Italian version continues on with several scenes clearly designed to establish the ongoing exploits of this unconventional priest and his small band of helpers, namely Father Leonardo, taxi driver Attilio, helper Gegè and the reformed Lulù. This shortening means that the initial credits on the end roller (displayed over pictures in the Italian version) are missing from the German release. Oddly, the opening credits on the German DVD – while in Italian and identical in content to those on the Italian DVD – are displayed on a differently-coloured background. The German DVD contains the alternative Italian ending.
(Julian Grainger)

Cast note *: The name Hadryan Darko has been attributed to both Ottaviano Dell'Acqua (who lists versions of the name on his own website) and also to actor/stuntman Sasha D'Arc, who's surname chimes with 'Darko'. In this case perhaps we may assume that the name is a joint pseudonym...

above: Bud Spencer plays the part of don Carlo Vasari, here being held at knifepoint in **Father Hope**.

below: German DVD cover for **Father Hope**.

top: Beatrice Deodato and Leonardo Capoccia in **The Bridge**.
above: Valentina Lainati in **The Bridge**.
below: The impressive location for Deodato's 2013 short film **The Bridge** (also known as **Kids' Game**), which forms part of the anthology film **The Profane Exhibit**.

THE PROFANE EXHIBIT (short 'THE BRIDGE')

2013
aka: **Kids' Game**
Italy
director: Ruggero Deodato

screenplay: Ruggero Deodato. cinematography: Gabrio Contino. assistant camera: Luca Valentino Paluello. production manager: Laura Ugolini. colorist: Filippo Corrieri. continuity: Francesca Spinozzi. post production facilities: Infinity Road Pictures. special effects equipment: Studio Laboratorio 51.

cast: Leonardo Capoccia (the boy). Beatrice Deodato (the girl). Valentina Lainati (the woman).

running time: 2 minutes 29 seconds.

The Profane Exhibit includes episodes by horror luminaries Uwe Boll, Anthony DiBlasi, José Mojica Marins, Sergio Stivaletti and Nacho Vigalondo. Ruggero Deodato's segment, called either **Kids' Game** or **The Bridge**, features a splendid location (it looks more like an aqueduct than a bridge) where a woman (Valentina Lainati) comes across two children (Leonardo Capoccia and Beatrice Deodato) and something dreadful happens. It's slight, of course, but effective. ***(Kim Newman)***

IO E MIA FIGLIA

2014
(translation: **Me and My Daughter/My Daughter and I**)
Italy (short)
director: Ruggero Deodato

Casa delle donne per non subire violenza ["Centre for Women Against Violence"], Video One produzione cine televisive present a production Associazione Video One.

produced by Mauro Baldanza. line producer: Marco Sermenghi. story: Mauro Baldanza. screenplay: Ruggero Deodato, Giulio Guarino. director of photography: Filippo Chiesa. editor: Michelangelo Longa. original music: Antonio Rimedio, Marco Biscarini, Luca Leprotti, Nico Dalla Vecchia. Recorded and mixed at Modulab Recording Studio in Casalecchio di Reno by Luca Leprotti and Marco Biscarini. assistant director: Michelangelo Longa. promotion office: Patrizia Stefani. chief engineer: Marco Buti. sound mixer: Alessandro Gaffuri. production director: Emanuela Zaccherini. production assistant: Carlotta Gieri. assistant operator: Enrica Balzani. makeup artist: Francesca Piani. electrician: Fabrizia Cacicia. electrician: Michela Marella. property master: Valerio Gnesini. assistant director: Chiara Baldanza. still photographer: Elvio Caria. post production audio: Luca Leprotti. color correction: Filippo Chiesa. effects: Jacopo Solmi. Thanks also. For the locations: Bologna Local Health Authority - Bentivoglio Hospital; Coka Club - Bologna - Fiore and Baldazzi families; Casa di Giulia - Malaguti and

Brunelli families; Restaurant Danilo e Patrizia; Granarolo Comprehensive Institute. The collaboration of the State Police and the patronage of the Province of Bologna; Region Emilia-Romagna; Comune of Bologna; Province of Catanzaro; Province of Reggio Calabria; Comune of Castel Maggiore; Comune of Granarolo; District Navile. With the support of: A.N.P.I. Bologna; Coop Adriatica; Camst; IMA Sfx; UIL Mobbing e Stalking; Centergross.

cast: Rita Rusciano (Giulia), Beatrice Deodato (Eleonora), Matteo Tosi (Antonio) <and with> Alessandra De Marco (Francesca), Andreina Sozzo, Emanuela Zaccherini, Roberta Constantino, Antonio Landi, Cristina Benfenati (teacher), Pierpaolo Paganelli. Extras in alphabetical order: Luisa Abate, Patrizia Albertelli, Alessandro Alberti, Cinzia Antonini, Alice Arcangeli, Arianna Arcangeli, Fabio Arcangeli, Chiara Baldanza, Francesco Baldanza, Sara Baldazzi, Silvia Baldazzi, Piero Barducci, Angelica Barletta, Erica Bichecchi, Irene Bonadia, Alessia Calzolari, Angelo Calzolari, Francesco Calzolari, Luca Carpano, Libero Casoni, Raffaella Ceddia, Claudio Cinti, Tommaso Cinti, Lilia Collina, Anna Cumani, Gabriella Dalla Ca', Alberto De Blasio, Fabi De Silva, Sofia Donini, Roberta Fiori, Tiziana Gentili, Hysen Hika, Juna Iargallo, Ennio Lambertini, Anna Lendinara, Loretta Levorato, Francesca Luppi, Monica Malaguti, Matilde Masi, Gabriele Mastromatteo, Stefano Mazzanti, Amedeo Orlandi, Gaia Orlandi, Auro Orsi, Bartolomeo Paleari, Laura Patrese, Flavia Piciacchia, Lauretta Rabbi, Valeria Ribani, Stefano Rimondini, Eugenia Rossi, Fiorinto Scirgalea, Paolo Serra, Laura Spimpolo, Lola Valgimigli, Franco Vandelli. The kids of the Matteucci State Middle School, Granarolo dell'Emilia, Bologna.

Premiere screening on 11 February 2015
running time: 17 minutes 54 seconds

Genre filmmakers have often dabbled in public safety or issue-raising short films. Terence Fisher's **To the Public Danger** (1948), from a Patrick Hamilton radio play, was made as a warning against drunk driving and George A. Romero's **The Amusement Park** (1973), commissioned by a church group, was intended to highlight neglect of the elderly. Full-on safety film horrors have stuck in the minds of the impressionable – Jeff Grant's **The Spirit of Dark and Lonely Water** (1973), John McKenzie's **Apaches** (1977) and John Krish's **The Finishing Line** (1977). Beside that little lot of nightmare fuel, Ruggero Deodato's **Io e mia figlia** is almost mild – though it certainly has one genuinely creepy performance from Matteo Tosi as unshaven Antonio, an apparent nice guy who Facebook friends widowed Giulia (Rita Rusciano), whom he hasn't seen since they were at school together – and then turns into a cackling pest, escalating from inappropriate gifts to additionally creeping after Giulia's thirteen-year-old daughter Eleonora (Beatrice Deodato)... which leads to an incident that puts both women in hospital and a resolution which isn't especially reassuring since it's possible Antonio hasn't even broken a law. Of Deodato's three recent shorts, it's the most accomplished bit of filmmaking – even subtle in ways his films often aren't – with one good chill moment as Giulia's mobile phone rings while she's sat in her car and she catches sight of Antonio in her rear-view mirror, calling from his own car.

(Kim Newman)

this page: Single mother Giulia (Rita Rusciano) is stalked by Antonio (Matteo Tosi) in the short film **Io e mia figlia**.
opposite top right: Promotional artwork for **Io e mia figlia** featuring Rita Rusciano, Matteo Tosi and Beatrice Deodato.
bottom left: **Io e mia figlia** was sold in Italy as part of a self-help/social awareness campaign package under the title **Stop allo stalking**... "Against all violence: a film, a course, testimonials". As well as the DVD – which has extras including talking head interviews discussing the film's subject – the slim package also features a booklet giving advice and coping strategies to aid people who are being harrassed by stalkers.

photo © Aldo d'Ambrosio

above and below:
Behind the scenes shots taken during the making of **Ballad in Blood**.

BALLAD IN BLOOD

2016
Working title: **Il giorno dopo...**
director: Ruggero Deodato

Pietro Innocenzi and Massimo Esposti presents A Ruggero Deodato Film. A Bell Film Production. Copyright 2016 BELL FILM SRL. Filmed in September 2015 on location in Orvieto and at the De Paolis Studios, Rome.

producer: Massimo Esposti. line producer: Umberto Innocenzi. executive producer: Raffaele Mertes. executive producer: Pietro Innocenzi. story by Ruggero Deodato. screenplay by Ruggero Deodato, Jacopo Mazzuoli, Angelo Orlando. sound engineer: Vittorio Melloni. sound editor: Claudio Marani DG Media. re-recording mixer: Francesco Tumminello. costume designer: Loredana Paletta. production designer: Paolo Innocenzi A.S.A. and Barbara Scambellone. music by Claudio Simonetti. director of photography: Mirko Fioravanti A.I.C. Imago. editor: Daniel De Rossi. production manager: Cristiana Badiali. unit production manager: Claudio Venneri. production secretary: Alessandro Espositi. production assistants: Fabrizio Collati, Massimo Mahieux. production accountant: Simonetta Emidi. dialogue coach: Laura Vergelli. assistant director: Mirko Urania. 2nd assistant director: Mario Di Caprio. script supervisor: Alessia Vincenzini. sound designer: Vittorio Melloni. boom operators: Stefano Tuderti, Pierpaolo Merafino. 1st camera assistant: Claudio Pagliarani. 2nd camera assistant: Luca Frondoni. Steadicam operator: Gian Piero Castellucci. drone operator: Massimo Gattobigio. data manager: Marlito Senolos. video assist: Elisabetta Petrocchi. still photographer and backstage: Aldo D'Ambrosio. Make-up key: Fabio De Stefano. make-up designer: Vittorio Sodano. sculpture artist and props: Antonio Alterio. make-up assistants: Eleonora Dessi, Stefania Piovesan, Giulia Riccardizi, Stefania Genco. hairdresser: Teresa Bellucci. special effects: Fabio Unger, Paolo Galiano. stuntman: Massimo Vanni. assistant art director: Marco Pittacci. 2nd assistant art director: Alba Lidia Tropeano. property master: Daniele Cianfarani. costume assistant: Maura Casaburi. wardrobe mistress: Maura Chiusolo. wardrobe mistress assistant: Naike De Lucia. assistant film editor: Saima Salazar Calzadilla. sound effects: OLTRE IL SUONO SRL. sound editor: Alessandro Giacco, Emanuele Giacco. foley: Mario Giacco. key grip: Roberto Moreschini. grips: Daniel D'Ottavi, Pietro Moreschini. gaffer: Alessandro Picchi. electricians: William Napoleoni, Danilo Di Palma. generator operator: Domenico Di Pietro. camera driver: Massimiliano Alvino, Fabio Sebastiani. electrician driver: Mario Fileni. grips driver: Luigi Aventini. laborers: Damiano Vinci, Alessio Vinci, Federico Trenta. financial advisor: Sic Data srl. medical advisor: Dott. Francis Spelar. post-production laboratory: Margutta Digital International. digital lab manager: Andrea Terilli. digital coordinator: Alessandro Pozzi. digital colorist: Fabrizio Conti. digital conforming: Leonardo Galeassi. digital artists: Marco Ruggieri, Michele Quassinti. key manager: Alfredo Longo. customer service: Cristiana Di Felice. re-recording dubbing: Federico Constantini. ADR director: Laura Vergelli. visual effects: Déjà Vu. visual effects producer: Daniele Tommasetti. visual effects supervisor: Fabio Tommasetti. 3D artists: Riccardo Jannelli, Teo Serapiglia. ORVIETO'S TROUPE. location manager: Elisabetta Spallaccia. hairdresser assistants: Semira Bekteshi, Virginia Bigornia, Elisa Maccaroni, Angelica Rossi. electricians assistant: Raffaele Prosperini. assistants art director: Carlo Brunori, Lorenzo Stramaccioni. film studio: STUDIOS SRL. picture vehicles: FCA Italy. camera, grip & lighting equipment: Panalight. production office: STUDIOS SRL. vans: 2001 RAINBOW. furnishings: CINE MOVIE, CINE ART di Alessandro Caruso, MUSEO AGOSTINELLI.

photo © Aldo d'Ambrosio

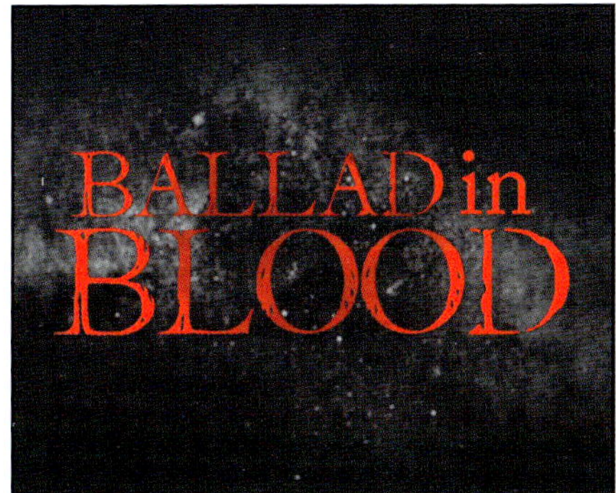

photo © Aldo d'Ambrosio

this page:
The drugs, sex and decadence of **Ballad in Blood**.

costumes and accessories: PELATELLI. insurance: STUDIO M di Massimo Forges Davanzati. technical support registration: MARCHEGIANI SRL. operator equipment: R.E.C. - Rental Equipment. sound designer equipment: NAGRIT. walkie-talkie: LATEL-COM. job security: RG Risorse di Leonardo Gammarota. catering: Sole Catering. Avid Media Composer: Tonys. Music composed, orchestrated, directed and produced by Claudio Simonetti. Recorded at ACQUARIO STUDIO - ROME. Published by Simonetti Productions s.a.s./ Emergency Music Italy © 2016. Soundtrack CD and LP available on DEEP RED RECORDS. "FLYING LIKE AN ANGEL" Artist: DR. FELIX. Music by Claudio Simonetti. Lyrics by Felix Imevbore. Publisher: SUGARMUSIC S.p.a. "FASAN TECHNO" Artist: Claudio Simonetti. Publisher: MEDUSA FILM S.p.A. "TECHNO TRAIN" Artist: Claudio Simonetti. Publisher: MEDUSA FILM S.p.A. "SWEETLY" Music by Riz Ortolani and Katyna Ranieri. Words of Katyna Ranieri. Publisher: ERREKAPPA. Master rights: COURTESY. Special thanks to Mrs. Katyna Ranieri for the courtesy of the song "Sweetly". International Sales: TVCO. Within the film appear the following products/brands. Thanks FCA Italy for the supply of cars. Fiat, Lancia; Ma.Ma Service. Product placement care of: Pubbli Level. Gianluca Vania Pirazzoli, Alvise du Chene de Vere; Petrone Antica Distilleria; Plose; Wiko Game Changer; 21 Nodi; Acqua Santa Croce; Oxiana; Pascucci; Smeg. Costumes and accessories. Thanks for the supply of high fashion clothes: Celli Centro Sposi; Electra. Scenography and furnishings. Thanks for the supply of paintings: jenniferdidomenico.tumblr.com; Ambra Nadalini; Jennifer Di Domenico; Barbara Fiume www.barbarafiume.wix.com/bidibibodibiboue. SPONSOR "ORVIETO". Fondazione Cassa di Risparmio di Orvieto; Cosp Tecno Service soc. cooperativa; Basaltite Guidotti Battaglini. Thanks to: Sonia Broccatelli UMBRIAFILMOVIE; Comune di Orvieto Sindaco Giuseppe Germani; Consigliere Comunale Flavia Timperi; Assessorato alla Cultura; Ufficio Cultura per il Pozzo di San Patrizio; Fondazione Cassa di Risparmio di Orvieto - Presidente Vincenzo Fumi; Pub Tavern Engel Keller - Orvieto; Maramao pane e birra - Orvieto; Servizio Catering Cramst - Orvieto; Bottega di Pittura Chioccia Tsarkova - Orvieto. Special thanks to: Daniele Malavolta; Pierfrancesco Campanella; Andrea Barni; Manuel Navati. Special thanks to the builders department of Theatre Studios Via Tiburtina, 521 - Roma. Thanks to: ARTIGIANCASSA SpA. Raffaele Cardinali, Franceso Adinolfi, Maria Rosaria Cucinella, Egidio Conti. BANCO POPOLARE DI SPOLETO - Branch of Roma Via XX Settembre. Bank manager Claudio Crognali. Any reference to real facts or persons is purely coincidental. The film has been recognized of cultural interest and has been realized with the contribution of the Ministry for Cultural Heritage and Activities General Direction for the Performing Arts. Direzione Generale CINEMA. This Picture has been produced with the assistance of the Italian "tax credit" provided for by law no. 244 of 24 December 2007. MiBACT. Direzione Generale CINEMA. This Picture has been produced with the support of Regione Lazio Regional fund for film and Audiovisual media. This Picture has been produced with the contribution of Fondazione Cassa di Risparmio di Orvieto.

cast: Carlotta Morelli (Lenka). Gabriele Rossi (Jacopo). Noemi Smorra (Elizabeth). Edward Williams (Duke). Roger Garth (Arden). Rita Rusciano (Francesca). Saverio Deodato (Remo). Ernesto Mahieux (Leo). Ruggero Deodato (Prof. "Roth"). Christiane Grass (old woman). Carlo Grotti (Lorenzo). Graziano Scarabicchi (Remo's friend). Adriano Paris (Remo's friend). Emiliano Martellini (Remo's friend). Mattia Biritognolo (boy in the car). Gianluca Adami (boy in the car). Mirko Delli Poggi (boy in the car). Federico Mandini (garbage collector). Flavio Lovisa (garbage collector). Rebecca Di Maio (girl on the cross).

World premiere at Lucca Film Festival on 5 April 2016 in Cinema Centrale.
running time: 94 minutes.

photo © Aldo d'Ambrosio

photo © Aldo d'Ambrosio

above and right:
Life and death in **Ballad in Blood**.

The end credits of Ruggero Deodato's **Ballad in Blood** include the standard disclaimer that 'any reference to real facts or persons is purely coincidental'. However, the film is blatantly based on the well-known Meredith Kircher murder case of 2007. The film takes the line of a great deal of tabloid coverage that those responsible for the death of the British exchange student in Italy were American Amanda Knox, her Italian boyfriend Raffaele Sollecito, and African immigrant Rudy Guede. The controversial case has gone through several retrials. Currently, Knox and Sollecito have had convictions annulled while Guede remains in prison. There are true crime documentaries on the case, including **Amanda Knox: Murder on Trial in Italy** (2011) and **Amanda Knox** (2016), and other fictionalised takes, Michael Winterbottom's **The Face of an Angel** (2014) and Tom McCarthy's **Stillwater** (2021). It's an irony that Deodato, who indicted the sensationalist manipulation of documentary footage by unethical filmmakers in **Cannibal Holocaust**, would make a movie which violates even more ethical codes – and sets out to do harm to actual people, living and dead – than the fictional exploiters who feature in the earlier film. A particular low point is the suggestion that the victim partially invited her rape and murder by being a racist, though presenting the drama as a sexualised mash-up of **The Hangover** (2009) and **Weekend at Bernie's** (1989) means that the film is pretty much calculated to appal. It focuses on speculating on what happened on the night of the murder, and doesn't get into the apparent hash made by the Italian authorities of several police investigations and trials … with the evident suggestion in the end that everyone here pretty much deserves what they get.

below:
That's a wrap! Traditional crew photo on the set of **Ballad in Blood**. The clapper board shows the film's shooting title **Il giorno dopo** ('The Day After').

photo © Aldo d'Ambrosio

photo © Aldo d'Ambrosio

Ballad in Blood also isn't terribly good, though it has some striking moments that show its auteur hasn't completely lost his touch. Near the end, Riz Ortolani's song 'Sweetly', from Deodato's **House on the Edge of the Park** is heard – augmenting a Claudio Simonetti score – and the tower in which the wild student party takes place is an impressive, well-used location. The day after a wild Halloween party no one can remember, drug dealer Duke (Edward Williams) wakes up in a student flat where Czech Lenka (Carlotta Morelli) has an intimate moment ruined when her boyfriend Jacopo (Gabriele Rossi) pukes on her breasts. In the next room, Elizabeth (Noemi Smorra) – who's English – is mysteriously dead, leaving a phone on which she recorded snippets of the Halloween party which serve to jog the blurry memories of the trio who apparently contributed to her death. The film loops back over and over to the night before, as Elizabeth becomes the victim of sexual abuse and violence perpetrated by her supposed friends, but also plays grotesque comedy as the foul-ups try to dispose of the naked dead body and also to prevent their guilt becoming known. When Lenka suspects that another friend has worked out what happened, she manipulates the two guys – as in the lurid myths of 'Foxy Knoxy', Lenka is depicted as a sex siren dragon lady manipulator who's the guiltiest of the trio even though she never lays a hand on any victims – into trying to murder her, though they mistakenly grab an old beggar who happens to be wearing a hood that looks like the intended victim's Halloween costume and throw her to her death. The girl who was supposed to be killed is saved because her abusive boyfriend turns up on a bike and bullies her into leaving with him – in a rare moment of believable human behaviour, Lenka is hypocritically appalled at the sexist behaviour of the boyfriend even though she was planning far worse for the girl. In typical things-get-worse fashion, others – including Leo (Ernesto Mahieux), a drug connection – get involved and try to finesse the situation to their advantage while the guilty parties continue to tear each other apart.

The horrors on display in vintage Deodato often depend on exaggerated performances from the likes of Giovanni Lombardo Radice and David Hess and he was never one for understatement – but the players here can't match that tone without provoking undue giggles. Morelli, who's also in Deodato's segment of **Deathcember** (2019), gets the most to do, and comes closest to giving a performance that works, but Lenka is written – by Deodato, Jacopo Mazzuoli and Angelo Orlando – as a Disney cartoon villainess domme. The use of mobile phone snippets to trigger flashbacks is reminiscent of the pioneering found footage aspect of **Cannibal Holocaust**, but comes along well after many, many other movies have gone for similar effects.

(Kim Newman)

above:
The prankster family take in the full horror of their mean-spirited folly in **Casetta sperduta in campagna**.

DEATHCEMBER
(short 'CASETTA SPERDUTA IN CAMPAGNA')

2019
Italy
director: Ruggero Deodato

cinematographer: Paolo Sodi. camera operator: Giovanni Raiola. assistant camera: Francesco Trecci. focus puller: Gabriele Coradeschi. grip: Luigi Migliardi. backstage video: Leonardo Bigliazzi. sound editing: Alessandro Fusaroli. music, sound design and mix: Boris D'Agostino. online editing: Domenico Calabrese. editing and color grading: Filipo Corrieri. post production supervisor: Andrea Bermani. post production facility: IRP Roma.

cast: Carlotta Morelli (woman 1). Valentina Lainati (woman 2). Gianni Franco (Father Christmas). Lapo Granchi (boy). Emma Duringer (girl)

running time: 3 minutes 23 seconds.

Deathcember is a multi-director project in the tradition of the **ABCs of Death** films, though adopting an advent calendar frame means 24 segments averaging 5 to 8 minutes in length makes for a gruelling 145 minute running time, especially since the tone tends to mean-spirited rather than macabre. Viewers won't easily forget the hideous claymation comedy child-rape/revenge episode ('Crappy Christmas') by Jürgen Kling, but too many other contributors present feebly miserable digs at Christmas, with much blood spattering ornaments, trees, gifts and cards. A few of the stronger segments come from Isaac Ezban, Lucky McKee (a b&w western) and Pollyanna McIntosh. Ruggero Deodato chips in with **Casetta sperduta in campagna**, an EC Comics-like anecdote about a prank gone wrong that serves almost as a pendant to his feature **Ballad in Blood** in that the hapless victim is played by former villainess Carlotta Morelli and what happens to her (though she's playing a different character) could be read as a come-uppance for what she did in the earlier film. Also in the cast is Valentina Lainati, from his episode of the earlier anthology film **The Profane Exhibit**.

(Kim Newman)

top left:
The orgiastic excesses of **Ballad in Blood**.

below and bottom right:
The tragic climax of **Casetta sperduta in campagna**, Deodato's contribution to the anthology horror film **Deathcember**.

CAROSELLI

A list of 'Caroselli' which Deodato directed for Italian television. Caroselli are advertising spots, often in the form of short stories, which were popular in Italy during the Sixties and Seventies. The brand advertised has been noted. Some featured well-known actors, the more notable of whom have been listed.

1967	Aperol (star: Nino Fuscagni)
1970-75	Philips
1970	Polenghi Lombardo (star: Alberto Lionello)
1971	Venus (star: Kaye Sanderson)
1971	Fornet (star: Ferruccio Amendola)
1971	Formaggino mio
1971	Ciao Piaggio (star: Micaela Esdra)
1971	Polenghi Lombardo (stars: Aroldo Tieri & Giuliana Lojodice)
1971	Personal G.B. (star: Arnoldo Foa')
1971-74	Kraft (star: Nino Ferrer; assistant director: Lamberto Bava)
1972	Birra Wuhrer (Isabella Biagini)
1972	Olio Topazio (Renzo Arbore)
1972	Esso (star: Gianni Magni; assistant director: Lamberto Bava)
1972	Brillantina Linetti (star: Nino Fuscagni)
1973-75	Amaro Cora (stars: Silvia Dionisio & Jean Sorel)
1973	Invernizzina
1974	Vecchia Romagna
1974	Pernigotti
1974	Philips (star: Teo Teocoli)
1974-76	Crodino
1975	Fanta (stars: Ilona Staller [Cicciolina] & Oriella Dorella)
1975	Abiti Monti (stars: Marino Mase' & Ivo Garrani)
1975	Cera Solex
1975-76	Sperlari (star: Gianrico Tedeschi)
1976	Cerotto Band Aid, Johnson & Johnson
1976	Bio Presto (stars: Franco Cerri & Jacques Stany)

OTHER WORK

Along with **Hercules, Prisoner of Evil** [listed in main filmography], Deodato has made notable contributions above and beyond the role of assistant director, to several further films:

1965
Django
Italy/Spain
director: Sergio Corbucci
Deodato noted that he was sole director on two weeks of exterior shooting on location in Madrid (Spain); for example the celebrated sequences in which Franco Nero drags his coffin through the mud.

1967
Pronto... c'è una certa Giuliana per te
Italy
director: Massimo Franciosa
When the original material proved impossible to edit, Deodato was contacted by production manager Luciano Cattania and hired to film substantial new scenes and re-shoots to allow completion of the film.

2006
Hostel 2
USA
director: Eli Roth
Acting role as 'The Italian Cannibal'.

2008
Dead Bones
Switzerland (short)
director: Olivier Beguin
Acting role as butcher.

2009
The Museum of Wonders
Italy
director: Domiziano Cristopharo
Acting role.

2010
Bloody Sin of Horror/Bloody Sin – Oltretomba
Italy
director: Domiziano Cristopharo
Acting role as inquisition cleric.

CREDITS AS ASSISTANT DIRECTOR

1958 **Nella città l'inferno** (IT/FR) FR: L'enfer dans la ville <Renato Castellani>
1959 **Il Generale Della Rovere** (IT/FR) FR: Le Général Della Rovere <Roberto Rossellini>
1960 **Era notte a Roma** (IT/FR) FR: Les évadés de la nuit <Roberto Rossellini>
1960 **Quelle joie de vivre** (FR/IT) IT Che gioia vivere ("collaboration") <René Clément>
1960 **Viva l'Italia!** (IT/FR) <Roberto Rossellini>
1961 **Vanina Vanini** (IT/FR) <Roberto Rossellini>
1961 **Pastasciutta nel deserto** (IT) <Carlo Ludovico Bragaglia>
1961 **Ursus nella valle dei leoni** (IT) UK: Ursus in the Valley of the Lions <Carlo Ludovico Bragaglia>
1962 **Anima nera** (IT/FR) <Roberto Rossellini>
1962 **Lo smemorati di Collegno** (IT) <Sergio Corbucci>
1962 **Il giorno più corto** (IT) US TV: The Shortest Day <Sergio Corbucci>
1962 **Il figlio di Spartacus** (IT) UK: Son of Spartacus <Sergio Corbucci>
1963 **RO.GO.PA.G** / **Laviamoci il cervello!** (IT/FR) episode title: Illibatezza/Pureté <Roberto Rossellini> [other directors: Jean-Luc Godard, Pier Paolo Passolini & Ugo Gregoretti]
1963 **Gli onorevoli** (IT) <Sergio Corbucci>
1963 **Il monaco di Monza** (IT) <Sergio Corbucci>
1963 **Totò sexy** (IT) <Mario Amendola>
1963 **La vergine di Norimberga** (IT) US: Horror Castle UK: The Castle of Terror <Anthony M. Dawson [Antonio Margheriti]>
1963 **Danza macabra** (IT/FR) FR: Danse macabre UK/US: Castle of Blood <Anthony Dawson [Antonio Margheriti] & [uncredited] Sergio Corbucci>
1964 **Anthar l'invincibile** (IT/FR/SP) FR: Marchands d'esclaves SP: Soraya, reina del desierto UK: The Slave Merchants <Anthony Dawson [Antonio Margheriti]>
1964 **L'idea fissa** (IT) US: Love and Marriage <Gianni Puccini & Mino Guerrini>
1964 **La vendetta dei gladiatori** (IT) <Luigi Capuano>
1964 **Romeo e Giulietta** (IT/SP) SP: Los amantes de Verona SP shooting title: Julieta y Roméo US: Romeo and Juliet <Riccardo Freda>
1964 **Genoveffa di Brabante** (IT/SP) SP: Genoveva de Brabante aka: Revenge of the Crusader <José Luis Monter & [uncredited] Ricardo Freda>
1965 **Su e giù** (IT) <Mino Guerrini>
1965 **L'età del ferro** (IT) (TV documentary) <Renzo Rossellini Jr.; supervised by Roberto Rossellini>
1965 **Madamigella di Maupin** (IT/FR/SP) FR: Le chevalier de Maupin SP: Mademoiselle de Maupin <Mauro Bolognini>
1965 **Johnny Oro** (IT) shooting title: Ringo cavalca ancora US: Ringo and His Golden Pistol <Sergio Corbucci>
1965 **Le lit à deux places** (FR/IT) IT: Racconti a due piazze US: The Double Bed episode title: Mourir pour vivre/Morire per vivere <Gianni Puccini> [other directors: Jean Delannoy, Al World [Alvaro Mancori] & François Dupont Midy]
1965 **I criminali della Galassia** (IT) US: Wild, Wild Planet <Anthony Dawson [Antonio Margheriti]>
1965 **I diafanoidi vengono da Marte** (IT) US: War of the Planets <Anthony Dawson [Antonio Margheriti]>
1965 **Il pianeta errante** (IT) alternative IT title: Missione pianeta errante UK: War Between the Planets <Anthony Dawson [Antonio Margheriti]>
1965 **Morte viene dal pianeta Aytin** (IT) US: The Snow Devils <Anthony M. Dawson [Antonio Margheriti]>
1965 **Navajo Joe** (IT/SP/FR) SP: Joe el Implacable US: Nevada Joe shooting titles: Un dollaro a testa/A Dollar a Head <Sergio Corbucci>
1966 **Il terzo occhio** (IT) shooting title: Bacio freddo della morte alternative title: The Third Eye (credited as 'Roger Drake') <James Warren [Mino Guerrini]>
1966 **I crudeli** (IT/SP) SP: Los despiados US: The Hellbenders <Sergio Corbucci>
1966 **Wanted** (IT) <Calvin Jackson Padget [Giorgio Ferroni]>
1966 **Un fiume di dollari** (IT) US: The Hills Run Ted <Lee W. Beaver [Carlo Lizzani]>
1967 **Riderà (Cuore matto)** (IT) <Bruno Corbucci>
1967 **Le plus vieux métier du monde** (FR/GER/IT) GER: Das alteste Gewerbe der Welt IT: L'amore attraverso i secoli UK/US: The Oldest Profession episode title: Nuits romaines/Notti romane <Mauro Bolognini> [other directors: Franco Indovina, Philippe de Broca, Michael Pfleghar, Claude Autant-Lara & Jean-Luc Godard]
1967 **Marinai in coperta** (IT) <Bruno Corbucci>
1967 **Peggio per me... meglio per te** (IT) <Bruno Corbucci>
1968 **Secret Ceremony** (UK) <Joseph Losey>

PROJECTS

The 1970 teen musical **Terzo canale – Avventura a Montecarlo** appears in some lists of Deodato's work. He was offered the film by producer / distributor Fulvio Frizzi (the father of musician Fabio Frizzi) but declined and the film was eventually made by Giulio Paradisi.

It was advertised in the May 4, 1983 edition of *Variety* that Deodato was due to direct a sequel to **Cannibal Holocaust** entitled **Cannibal Fury**, once again for Alessandro Fracassi's Racing Pictures.

In 1988 Luciano Martino offered Deodato his Dania Film-produced war film **Casablanca Express** to direct, however Deodato declined and the film was made the following year under the direction of Sergio Martino (Luciano's brother). Preliminary publicity material exists bearing Deodato's name.

In 1993 Deodato was touted as director for **I leoni del sole** / **Lions of the Sun** for Cine Vision TV. To star Franco Nero, Omar Sharif and Donald Pleasence, this action/adventure story was also promoted with Enzo G. Castellari attached as director. Not made.

INCIDENTALLY

Brazilian musician/composer Eumir Deodato is Ruggero's distant cousin. He wrote the score for Lewis Gilbert's 1970 film **The Adventurers** and Harold Becker's 1979 film **The Onion Field**. Lately he has worked as the orchestral arranger / conductor for Icelandic musician Björk.

CANNIBAL HOLOCAUST 2

Two films have been released as **Cannibal Holocaust 2** in selected territories. Neither has anything to do with Deodato's film.

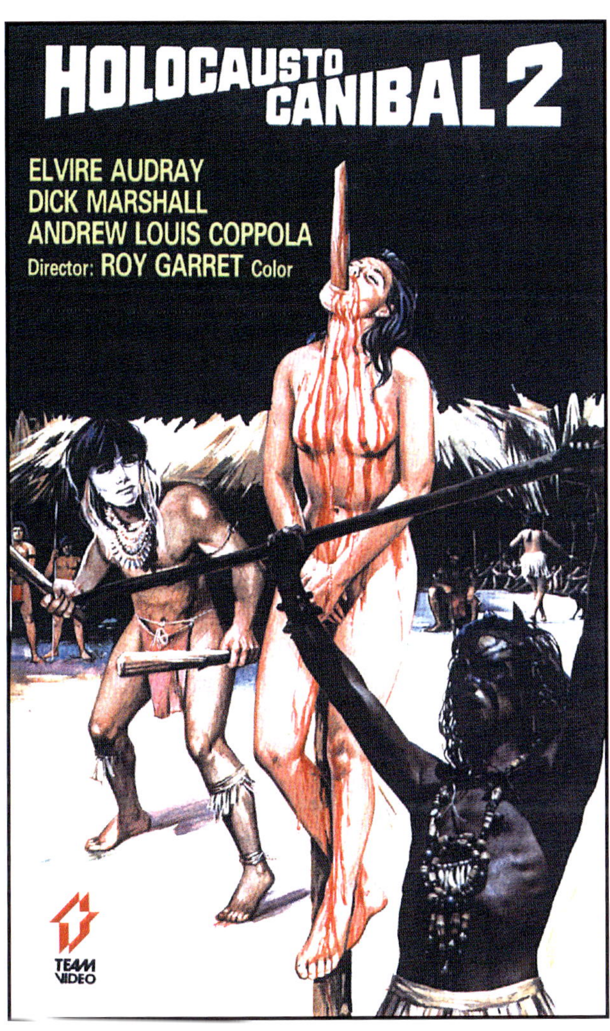

The poster below (note the spelling of the title: "**Cannibal Hallocaust II**") actually refers to the film also known as **The Green Inferno** and **Natura contro**. It was released in Italy in May 1988 as **Paradiso infernale (Yellow Dream)**. The director was Antonio Climati, who started out in the film business as a cameraman, most notoriously filming much of the footage seen in Jacopetti and Prosperi's **Africa addio** (1966). He went on to become a director in his own right during the Seventies, when he collaborated with **Cut and Run** editor Mario Morra to create a trio of Third World mondos: **Savage Man... Savage Beast**, (1975), **This Violent World** (1978) and **Sweet and Savage** (1983), all of which are packed with scenes of animal slaughter. **Natura contro** is also filled with wildlife footage, but the tone is much less abrasive; in fact this slick jungle adventure film is obtrusively glossy, hampered by slow-mo action scenes and TV-drama muzak. Despite being fobbed off as a sequel to **Cannibal Holocaust**, **Natura contro** is similar only by virtue of its South American setting. Climati's film is actually more of a traditional jungle adventure, ironically reminiscent of **Cut and Run** at times!

The advertising above actually refers to the film also known variously as **Schiave bianche – violenza profonda**, **Amazonia (The Catherine Miles Story)**, **Schiave bianche – violenza in Amazzonia**, and **The Forest Slave**. It was directed by Mario Gariazzo, who used the pseudonym 'Roy Garret' for this project. It was first released in August 1985 in Italy. Deodato's **Cut and Run** was released the same year, and was also known in some territories as **Amazonia**, which often leads to the two films being confused for one another. A white woman is kidnapped by Indios. Exploitable elements include mucho animal mutilation and a head-hunting theme gives Gariazzo an excuse to show several graphic beheadings. Competently made. Not bad of its type.

Japanese poster for 'Cannibal Holocaust'

A HISTORY OF VIOLENCE

Even before the release of **Cannibal Holocaust**, Italian cult film had a long tradition of subverting realist notions of actuality in order produce startling, and often controversial, imagery. Whilst this ambivalent tradition can be traced back to the Italian 'Mondo' tradition of movie-making,[1] which sought to stitch together connections between the industrial and developing worlds, this pseudo-realist dynamic was also seen in a variety of 1970s fictionalised Italian cult genres. Beyond the Italian cannibal film, I have argued elsewhere, cycles such the 'Black Emanuelle' series starring Laura Gemser utilized the manipulation of fake documentary footage to foreground controversial images of race and sexuality that these contradictory colonial cult texts often conveyed.[2] As seen in titles such as **Emanuelle in America** (1976) and **Emanuelle and the Last Cannibals** (1977), documentary inserts were used to connote primitive sexual ritual or regimes of female punishment at play within the non-Western sphere. Whilst many of the fictional Laura Gemser adventures have been subject to censorship (often for their violent sexual content), the cinema of Ruggero Deodato is indicative of the ways in which extreme cult imagery (and the controversy it ensures), can also convert into a fan following at a wider international level.

In Deodato's case, a background in actuality film-practice and commercial advertising helped him create **Cannibal Holocaust**, one of the most censored and controversial Italian narratives ever released. As with many entries to the late 1970s and early '80s Italian 'cannibal genre' with which the director is frequently associated,[3] **Cannibal Holocaust** charts the savage conflict between enlightened European 'adventurers' and the 'barbaric' third world environments they uncover as part of their expedition. Importantly, for a nation that continues to wrestle with a Southern region often defined as barbaric and Other, the motif of the Italian expedition to a savage, pre-industrial landscape carries a number of nationalistic nuances, which often get lost in the international receptions of these texts. Indeed, it is interesting to note that Deodato's own Southern Italian roots become a pointed topic of conversation vis-à-vis **Cannibal Holocaust** in the interview which follows.

In contravention to other movies in this cycle, Deodato skilfully manipulates audience expectations surrounding the disappearance of four documentary filmmakers in the Amazon jungle. Professor Harold Monroe manages to recoup the lost film footage the crew members has shot, and returns to New York, ready to screen the material for a national news network.

Ruggero Deodato

interviewed in 2011 by Xavier Mendik

above: Ruggero Deodato in one of several recent cameo acting performances, this time appearing as the Italian cannibal in Eli Roth's **Hostel 2**.

below: Deodato as the butcher in Swiss director Olivier Beguin's excellent 2008 short film, **Dead Bones**, which pays homage to both spaghetti westerns and the savage cinema of Ruggero Deodato.

above: The members of the film crew become ever more vicious as they impose their murderous will upon the innocent inhabitants of the riverside tribe in **Cannibal Holocaust**.

However, the footage reveals the western group as responsible for the rape and torture of local tribes, who fatally rebel after the three male members of the expedition violate a local maiden.

It is the gradual realisation of the Europeans' involvement in the brutal punishment (captured in the closing scenes of the found footage), that creates a series of moral ambiguities that have rarely been matched. However, what makes Deodato's film truly disturbing is the pseudo-realist manner in which he depicts the violence contained within these vicious lost reels. By mixing real footage of animal slaughter enacted by the film crew, with staged fictional inserts purporting to show their fate, **Cannibal Holocaust** occupies a purposefully uncomfortable space that exposes our tacit belief in the actuality of realist cinema. As a result, **Cannibal Holocaust** is a film that has to be endured, rather than enjoyed Importantly, it is Deodato's pro-filmic excesses that have dominated the international reception of this film. Comments by journalist Pierre Jouis are typical of the film's reception in this respect:

"Deodato's undeniable skill for movie directing enables him to give beauty even to the most horrific scenes; thus the execution of a young Indian woman who has committed adultery, although it is extremely violent, is still beautiful in its own way, as the whole thing is presented as a macabre ballet where visual elements (mud, blood and sun) as well as the soundtrack (electronic music) play an important part."[4]

It is this repeated attempt to conflate extremes of sexuality and death before the viewing camera lens (and to the subject beyond it), which confirms **Cannibal Holocaust**'s status as one of the most macabre pulp narratives ever released. Writer Pierre Jouis has rightly termed the film as "the pinnacle of voyeurism"[5], noting that the all-pervasive camera lens effectively robs the viewer of any moral position from which to view the atrocities we see depicted on screen. Even in the narrative's closing scenes of retribution against the white invaders, Louis notes that:

"Despite the dislike we have developed for these characters, the scenes that are shown to us are barely sustainable. Fay Daniels' death, after being raped, dismembered, beheaded and eaten uncooked in front of her friends who keep filming the event is particularly trying, especially as the bad quality of the pictures, shot from quite away of the action, increases the sordid aspect of the whole exercise."[6]

Whilst the director's controversial depiction of actual animal slaughter reignited debates about film moralities, the integration of these real-life inserts alongside the fictional footage of the explorers' demise added to the film's controversy, leading some campaigners to confuse **Cannibal Holocaust** with 'snuff' footage. This misreading of the film's imagery was particularly prominent in UK censorship campaigns, as outlined by theorists such as Julian Petley.[7] Arguably, one of the biggest victims of the reputation of **Cannibal Holocaust** remains director Ruggero Deodato himself. Not only did he face domestic prosecution and potential imprisonment for the shock imagery contained within **Cannibal Holocaust**, but the film also continues to cast a shadow over his career, often obscuring the other kinds of cult texts he created.

In the following interview, Deodato discusses the making of **Cannibal Holocaust** and how its images can be understood from both Italian cultural, as well as international, cult contexts. He also discusses some of his other seminal works, including the equally controversial suspense-thriller *giallo*, **House on the Edge of the Park**. This interview was conducted at the point where the 2011 UK director's cut of **Cannibal Holocaust** was in preparation, thus giving Ruggero Deodato an appropriate moment to reflect upon his status as an auteur with a history of violence.

opposite: The typically vibrant Thai poster for **Cannibal Holocaust**.

below: Cover for the first Italian special edition DVD release of **Cannibal Holocaust**, issued on the Alan Young label.

เรื่องจริงที่เกิดขึ้นที่ลุ่มน้ำ'อเมซอน'หฤโหด
ซึ่งนักถ่ายภาพยนตร์สารคดี 4 ชีวิต
ถูกฉีกเนื้อกินทั้งเป็น
ในขณะที่ช่างภาพคน
สุดท้ายยังลั่นกล้องอยู่...
Venezuela
Colombia
โหดที่สุด
ในประวัติศาสตร์จอเงิน
ไม่ใช่หนังผี
ไม่ใช่ภาพยนตร์
แต่เป็นเรื่องจริง!
เปรตเดินดิน
CANNIBAL HOLLOCAUST
ฉายที่
วันที่

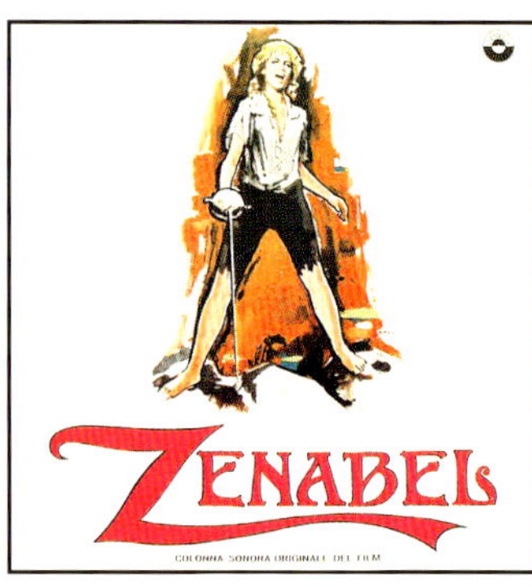

above and below: Ruggero Deodato's early film career was distinguished by his work in traditional Italian industry genres such as historical romps (**Zenabel**) and westerns (**I quattro del Pater Noster**), illustrated on this page by contemporary soundtrack LP covers for each film.

People often define you purely as a horror director, but you have stated that your key influence was Roberto Rossellini, who you described as your "master".

Yes, I have made many films, and as an assistant director I have worked with many Italian directors. And I have to say that I have taken influence from almost every one of them. But really, I always refer to three masters when talking about my greatest influences. Firstly there is Rossellini, because he gave me realism, he's the one I really took realism from. And then there is a another director who gave me cruelty. That's Sergio Corbucci. But a director who gave me elegance, and the associated skills for it, for the craftsmanship of his profession, particularly useful to me for making commercials – that has to be Mauro Bolognini. Nonetheless, Rossellini had the most decisive influence on me, particularly as the years go by, I feel more and more the power of his influence.

In many ways, Rossellini and the Italian realists do share a link with your cinema, by seeking to record reality in all its brutality.

Yes, they wanted to record a life so real, so true, and yet so shocking. It was a brutality born out of the realist directors I admired. My primary cinema was that of Rossellini's **Rome, Open City** (1945) or **Germany, Year Zero** (1948). Such films, along with Visconti's **Rocco and His Brothers** (1960) are the films that really impressed me. **Rocco and His Brothers** is for me a benchmark of excellence. There was a rape in the film, and it was the 1960s! The rape was carried out in such a strong manner. This is the kind of landmark I try to reproduce, from the powerful films of that time.

That said, you also worked with a number of 'fantasy' cinema directors in your early career, and I wondered if that also assisted the development of some of your later controversial works?

Well, I have to say that of all those directors, Riccardo Freda was the most imaginative, the most cultured. In my early career, I only made two films with Riccardo Freda, but we made those films in a very unique way. We shot two films at the same time: **Romeo and Juliet** (aka **Romeo e Giulietta**, 1964) and **The Revenge of the Crusader** (aka **Genoveffa di Brabante**, 1964).

Why was Freda so influential to you?

I found him to be a genius, really. He was a genius because he could do it all. He could do the editing, he could do the music, he could do it all. Riccardo was really, I have to say, sublime in his abilities. My skills could never match his. In my imagination I took on the roles of everyone, but really, I could not reach Riccardo. He surpassed the norm for all other directors. In terms of the other fantasy directors I worked with, Antonio Margheriti also had imagination, clearly, but I admired Margheriti more as a fine technical director, as a craftsman of the profession. He was a director who loved the technical challenge of shooting, but perhaps he was not so attentive to the narratives, or to the actors. So his influence on me was more technical, not so much one that inspired imagination.

When you were working with Margheriti and with Freda it was the peak of Italian Gothic cinema, why do you think the cycle was so important?

It was a period of considerable change in Italy, but let's be clear, the films that I made both with Margheriti and with Freda were not really Gothic, with the exception of **Castle of Blood** (Antonio Margheriti, 1963). With Margheriti I made all kinds of films. I made **Hercules, Prisoner of Evil** (1964), I made slave-trader films, I made science fiction films, and then I made the Gothic film **Castle of Blood**.

But these fantasy films were also significant because of their marketing strategies.

Yes. Those films taught me the technical means to exaggerate. If I make a love film, I exaggerate. If I make powerful horror film, I exaggerate. My technical knowledge helps me to exaggerate. I can think of a film that went very well, a film that I made in Iceland, it was called **Last Feelings** (aka **L'ultimo sapore dell'aria**, 1978). It was the story about a boy who swims, but who then falls ill, yet his illness then works to his advantage, and he becomes a champion. And in Japan they sell the film with a little handkerchief attached to dry away the tears. **Cannibal Holocaust** also used such tactics.

*One of your earliest cult films was the erotic thriller **Ondata di piacere** (1975), which was released in the UK as **Waves of Lust**.*

Waves of Lust seemed to me to be too sexy for a title. I was ashamed of that title as it misrepresented what was a thriller. **Ondata di piacere** is a film that I never liked, because of the personal investments involved. In my early career I began with comedy films. I love the comic stuff, it is how I am in real life. Then I married the actress Silvia Dionisio, who became very famous in Italy after I had discovered her. From that moment on, working became a real problem for me because in Italy, unfortunately, it is the woman who takes command more than the man. And although I had already directed five comedies by the time we married, it started to affect the way

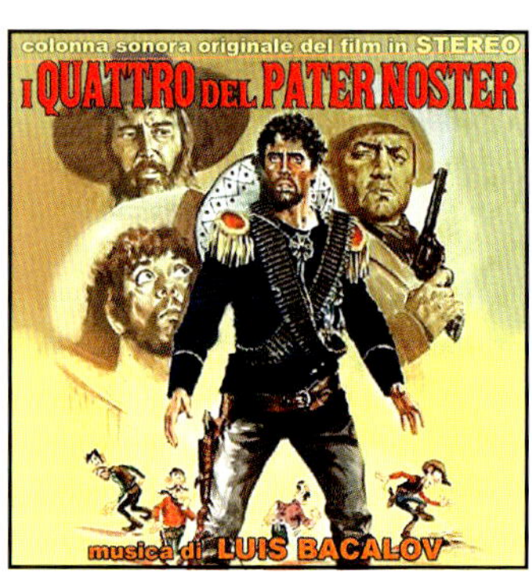

above: Silvia Dionisio (*right*) and Elizabeth Turner (*left*) in **Ondata di piacere** (aka **Waves of Lust**).

my projects would develop, as the first thing agents and producers would say was, 'Bring your wife along!' Or if I was making a film, they would call and say, 'Make sure that your wife is in it too!'

This implies artistic rivalries developed...

No, not at all. I just did not want to involve my wife in B-movies, because she had started to work for directors like Monicelli and Ettore Scola, who made a different class of film, so I did not want this. Also, I did not want to offend, though neither did I want to reply to these calls that were only about the availability of my wife. So I went to Milan to start making adverts. For three years I made adverts. Finally, after three years, they called me to make a film that did not involve my wife, and that film was **Ondata di piacere**, but it had a different title at the time. It was actually a thriller. I do not recall the title now, but it was a more noble title. So I said to my wife, 'They've finally called me to make a film!' An actress had already been contracted, she had made another Italian film already, quite a sexy one. But my wife said, 'No! You are not doing it! If I am not in this film, you are not doing it either.' I won't give you the whole story to the end, but finally the producers said, 'Look – your wife could do it.' Everyone was happy because my wife was famous. I said, 'OK, you do it'. And my wife did the film. So they paid off the actress who had originally been contracted. They paid her for nothing.

At the time, it was seen as an extremely risqué film for such an established actress to appear in.

Yes! But why was my wife asked to make this film? Because, at that time, she was number one. But just at that time Ornella Muti was emerging, and other actresses who would undress for the camera, but my wife had never undressed for a film. So my wife says, 'It is better that I start with my husband!' So I fell into a trap. And she accepted this film, despite the fact that she could command a sum of, say, 30 million lire, she took just 5 million lire to do my film. It was an embarrassing situation for me, because I had to oversee the undressing of my wife for the first time on camera. And this film really did not interest me very much. It was only good as an opportunity to bring me back into cinema. But thank heavens, I made a film of a certain quality... When I rewatch the film now, I say to myself, 'That's really not bad!' At the time though, I hated the film, but it did open up possibilities for me later.

What's interesting is that the international reception of the film favoured interpretations of the themes of intrigue and power play over its explicit images of sexuality. For instance, ***Continental Film Review*** *linked the film's enclosed exploration of erotic tension to Polanski.*[8]

[Looking at original copy of *Continental Film Review*] Yes – they did. Roman Polanski... not bad! But, I guess like Polanski, I was aiming for a sense of sexual tension. I remember the atmosphere of the movie was tense, very tense. This was because when I was shooting Silvia nude, I always tried to show her in the best way. Remember, I've done commercials, I'm like a composer, it is all about elegance. But she would say, 'Why are you positioning me like this?!' She would say, 'That's not right, that other American actress looks better.' I would say, 'No, I'm doing it just right, I want to make you look great.'

Interestingly this international reception seems to have been lost in Italian readings of the film, which emphasised ***Ondata di piacere****'s explicit nature, which I believe had an impact on your subsequent working practices.*

Very much so. The film created a number of problems for me. My wife and I did commercials at the time, for Amaro Cora. Mr. Cora was a gent from Piedmont, a very important figure. He was big operator, he made a fortune. I didn't think he would see **Ondata di piacere**, but he saw the film and said, 'Enough! Because of the nakedness of Dionisio that will be all!' And I thought that the film would just disappear without a trace. But I remember I was making commercials in Milan, and at Piazzale Loreto in the city, there was an enormous billboard poster of her from the film! I was ashamed of all this, because I was making commercials with Pirelli, with Phillips and others, while people were saying, 'Look! Look at the posters! YOUR WIFE! YOUR WIFE!' So I was dropped from doing

below: Giovanni Lombardo Radice plays the part of a somewhat befuddled accomplice to sexual terrorism in Deodato's divisive and challenging class conflict chamber piece, **House on the Edge of the Park**.

la F.D. CINEMATOGRAFICA presenta

DAVID A. HESS · ANNIE BELLE

in

LA CASA SPERDUTA NEL PARCO

con CHRISTIAN BORROMEO e con la partecipazione di LORRAINE DE SELLE

musica composta e diretta da RIZ ORTOLANI regia di RUGGERO DEODATO

colore LV LUCIANO VITTORI distribuzione ADIGE FILM 76

la F.D. CINEMATOGRAFICA presenta

DAVID A. HESS · ANNIE BELLE

in

LA CASA SPERDUTA NEL PARCO

con CHRISTIAN BORROMEO e con la partecipazione di LORRAINE DE SELLE

musica composta e diretta da RIZ ORTOLANI regia di RUGGERO DEODATO

colore LV LUCIANO VITTORI distribuzione ADIGE FILM 76

above and left: David Hess commands the screen in the role of unrepentant bully Alex, a terrifying misanthropist who extracts equal pleasure from acts of sex and violence in **House on the Edge of Park**.

commercials at that time due to **Ondata di piacere**. But because that film had great success, afterwards they called on me to make **Live Like a Cop, Die Like a Man**, in which I cast my wife in a regular part. And after that, I even did **Last Cannibal World**, because it was the same producer who called on me to do it. So it was a film that launched me into other projects. But at the time, I certainly did not like that film.

Just before we leave the film, there seems to be a link between ***Ondata di piacere*** *and say* ***La casa sperduta nel parco*** *(aka* ***House on the Edge of the Park****) in terms of class conflict. And I wonder why you connect sex to class-based violence in both films?*

Well, if it is present in **Ondata di piacere**, it is an underlying theme, while there was certainly more class conflict in **House on the Edge of the Park**, which is a film that always interests me. This film remains of interest because it is something that happens often, especially with the social hierarchies that are still present. And in **House on the Edge of the Park** the conflict between the powerful and the poor is very apparent. Although I did not have great expectations for this film, when I rewatch it now, with the years gone by, I think it's really not bad at all. Even if the film is very hard-hitting and rough, I find that it has aged better than Kubrick's **A Clockwork Orange**, which seems more dated today. I know that in Britain, this movie was very controversial, but I don't regret this film, even if it is one that I made in just three weeks, and even if it was shot entirely at night. Watching it now, I think –'Hey, this is really good'. There were certain things that I didn't like, but taking the film as a whole, it's not bad at all.

Both ***Ondata di piacere*** *and* ***House on the Edge of the Park*** *remain controversial for their presumed depictions of female sexuality and victimisation. How would you respond to these claims?*

I am often asked, 'How is the woman portrayed?' or, 'What was with the woman?' Well, I have to say, and I can promise you, that I was born into a family where the woman was the queen bee. Furthermore,

below: Alex forcibly undresses Cindy (played by Brigitte Petronio) in one of **House on the Edge of the Park**'s most distressing scenes of sexually-charged violation, made all the more disturbing as it is jarringly set to a saccharine lullaby theme composed by master composer Riz Ortolani.

above: A poster for **Cannibal Holocaust** that ironically uses scandalous media headlines to sell this tale of the consequences of unrestrained media exploitation.
below: American release poster from 1982.

the woman is dominant. I was not born into a patriarchal family, on the contrary, the woman is never overlooked. I have five sisters, all of them are liberated, and for this reason I never encountered the problem of the subjugated woman. For me, women were dominant. In my life women always have been dominant. That's how it is for me. My first engagement was with an English girl. She was the one who made me decide to leave Rossellini and go to work for directors who are more commercial. She did the PR for Dino De Laurentiis, important work, then she became the PA to Peter Sellers. So, I have only ever known women who have been achievers, women who have been my equal. I have never had subjugated women, that would not interest me. Therefore, I'm only interested in important women, I insist. Then, for the films, I don't know, what is there to say? – I was born in this very district, and suppressed women cannot be found around here. My father was Sicilian, but he married a Roman woman who had a Belgian mother, and Austrian grandparents, therefore they were liberated women, modern women, I never knew anything else.

*That is interesting. To expand on this, it seems that both these films and other works such as **Live Like a Cop, Die Like a Man** use the theme of women's bodies as sexualised or violated to express ideas of homoerotic desire.*

Yes, and casting helps with such themes. So in **Ondata di piacere**, I was helped a lot by the actor. Because the actor is a bit bisexual. One of the actors perhaps explicitly showed this.

*While I feel **Live Like a Cop, Die Like a Man** also deals with these same sex tensions, it also remains a fascinating index of the political and social conflicts of 1970s Italy.*

Yes. The *polizieschi* films very much reflected the extremes of the era. In these films the police are there not really to solve crimes, but more to put fear into people. And perhaps in the films we exaggerated, because the police at the time exaggerated too. There were some cases in Italy at the time where the police have had problems. There was a suicide, a politician killed himself after being interrogated by a prosecutor. Such things have happened. Indeed, consider the screenwriter in this case, the script was by Fernando Di Leo, and he was a tough, cold character! But when I took on this film, I just wanted to do the best job I could in a technical sense, as a craftsman. I did not think about any political agenda. Possibly Di Leo did, as he valued the film a lot.

In that respect, those critics who view the polizieschi film of the 1970s as just American rip-offs really seem to miss the Italian contexts of these texts.

Well, it may have been the case, but now Americans value that kind of film a lot. Quentin Tarantino is just one director who really loves **Live Like a Cop, Die Like a Man**. This is perhaps because the film is different from many American ones. It is not purely Italian or American, but combines elements of both cinemas. For instance, I incorporated American-style ballads into the film, alongside the exaggerated depiction of the police we discussed. So, every time there was a piece of action I would cue the ballad sung by Ray Lovelock. I rendered the films a little American in that way, a touch of the Western. There were training scenes done in style of the Western too. In terms of politics, yes. Those of us making such films were always hit hard by the critics not only for American influences, but also for the politics in the films. The critics said we were all politically very right-wing. But that was

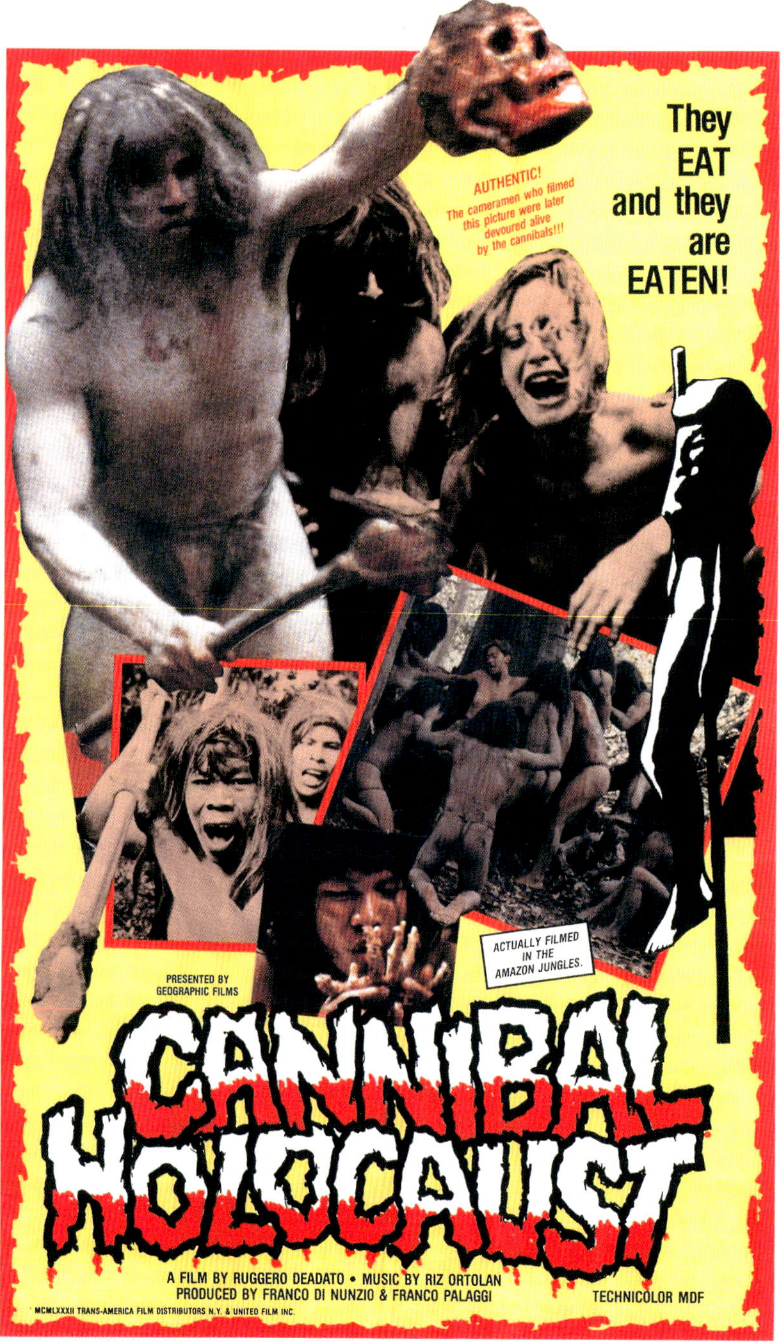

never true and do remember that directors such as Carlo Lizzani also made this kind of film, and he was clearly allied with the Left.

I am very interested in the political reception of your films. Have they retained a right-wing reading?

Well, the true barometer for me comes from Italian critics, and thirty years ago they condemned me very strongly for **Cannibal Holocaust** in their extreme left-wing journal *Manifesto*. But twenty years later that same journal did a three-page colour feature, finally declaring that it was time to praise Deodato for being the only person who dared to do such incredible things and to attack the Italian media in that film. So many years later, they saw the film differently. It was re-christened as a cult film, a film that went against mercenary journalism, against the abuses of natives, against the colonial.

It remains a film that garners multiple receptions then, was that political aspect part of your intention?

Yes, but **Cannibal Holocaust** was born from a combination of circumstances. I was invited by producers to make a sequel to **Last Cannibal World**. I tried not to do it, I never wanted to do it, because I didn't like the animal abuse, but in the end I gave in. Others convinced me to make another cannibal film. I did it because I was annoyed by what I was seeing on television at the time, in the evening papers and on the evening news. My son was complaining because the media was always full of dead and massacred people, it was the time of the Red Brigade's terrorism. A very troubled period. This is why I thought it was so strange, because journalists could show such terrible images on the evening news, when children were watching. Therefore I made a film against journalists, they are the ones who must have their scoop, and they will create a scoop if they cannot manage to find one.

above: German lobby still for **Cannibal Holocaust**. The literal translation of the title given here, 'Nackt und Zerfleischt', is 'Naked and Torn to Pieces'.

How did that political angle fit with the development of the project?

Well, when I began working on it I did not have a clearly outlined screenplay. The imagination I was born with makes me very creative on the set, I don't write out films, I don't use story-boards. I create the story aspect of a film on a day-by-day basis on the set. In this sense it is quite true that **Cannibal Holocaust** was a film created on a day-by-day basis. I had a few traces of ideas, and as they developed I sent samples of footage to my producer in Milan. At the time, Milan hosed MIFED, the biggest global film market and my producer kept calling me from there and saying, "They are buying your ideas, everything! They are buying the lot! Shoot what ever you feel like, slaughter whatever you like, do as you please!" So the day after, I started to make up what to do next, just on a whim. And that is how the most significant scenes in the film were created. I would think, 'OK, today I'll impale a village girl!' or, 'Tomorrow I'll kill a pig, because a crew member says she is fed up with eating fish!' So you see, the

left and below: The four murderous members of the exploitative fictional filmmaking crew in **Cannibal Holocaust**.

above: A blow-dart welcoming party threatens Professor Monroe and his guide as they risk their lives seeking the truth behind the disappearance of the Yates film crew in **Cannibal Holocaust**.

film was born like that, it was made up, and driven on by the buyers in Milan, and by the producer saying, 'Go on, go on, make it up, go ahead'.

In many respects, the film betrays the clear debt that your cinema owes to the traditions of Italian realist cinema.

Yes, through the idea of a film-within-a-film. The idea was born when I found myself so impressed by Jacopetti's films **Mondo Cane** (1962) and **Africa: Blood and Guts** (aka **Africa addio**, 1966); they were two films that made a real impact on me. Besides their outstanding and exceptional photography, I loved the realism of Jacopetti's work. For the first time, these films showed us stupendous editing and camera-work, all in an African setting, with those sunsets and that incredible realism. I said, 'What a shame, it's just a documentary!' So, when I hit upon the story for **Cannibal Holocaust**, and the story can be told in just a few words, that's important: 'A professor goes to search for four documentary-makers who have disappeared. He discovers that they have been killed, and he recovers the film that they shot. This film is then examined and the full truth of what the four had done is revealed...' So the story was very simple. My idea was to apply this simple story with the realism and truth of Jacopetti's film technique that I so admired. In fact it was also the cruelty, as well as the truth of the Jacopetti films, that I wanted to render in a film with actors. So I wanted to sketch out a story inside a kind of fictional container that would be like a Jacopetti film.

Another connection to Jacopetti's cinema is your use of his favoured composer Riz Ortolani. How influential were his previous compositions on your ideas for ***Cannibal Holocaust****?*

Very influential. Also, there was one thing that I really appreciated in Jacopetti films, and I did reproduce this most directly: I refer to Jacopetti's music, which I found so enchanting in his films. It was marvellous. These spectacles, these tragedies, some seen from aeroplanes, seen in hunts, scenes of firing squads, it was all accompanied by the stupendous music of Riz Ortolani. There was the song 'More', this was sung in the Jacopetti *mondo* films, it had been sung by Frank Sinatra, and by many others. And therefore I said that I wanted to apply the same thing. While editing the film **Cannibal Holocaust** I called up Riz Ortolani to say: 'I'd like soft, gentle music to accompany these ruthless images'. I had my doubts whether Riz would accept, but instead, he saw the film and said, 'Deodato, this is a masterpiece, I love it, I'll do the music for you.'

What remains truly incredible about the soundtrack to the movie, is that the music is so soft and deceptively beautiful, that it jars so dramatically with the brutal images that the film depicts.

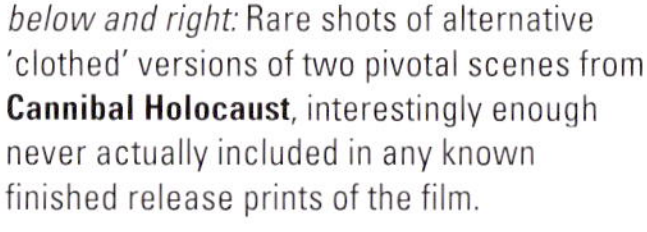

below and right: Rare shots of alternative 'clothed' versions of two pivotal scenes from **Cannibal Holocaust**, interestingly enough never actually included in any known finished release prints of the film.

Yes, this is one powerful aspect of the film. And I have to say that I even did this before **Cannibal Holocaust**, even in **Live Like a Cop, Die Like a Man**, I had the cruel and gripping sequences accompanied by soft, gentle music. I added a soft kind of ballad, because I loved the contrast. I saw that applying the sweet with the sour, the results could be stupendous. This is because it is more breath-taking to see these images accompanied by gentle music. You can feel both the pain and the pity.

This pain and pity certainly extended to your depiction of the natives in the film, who are subjected to extreme violence by their colonial media oppressors. One of the most infamous scenes being the woman impaled on a tree stump after she has been violated by Alan and the film crew.

Yes. I've made seven films in Venezuela, two films in Colombia, and so many others in South America. I've seen how those poor tribespeople are treated. They are put into awful areas. They are moved into shanty towns. They are badly treated. They are killed... I am on their side. I support their case. The film was made to support the natives. Remember the question asked at the end of the film: 'Who are the real cannibals?' Now that's the issue. In answer to the question, the film views the media as the real cannibals. Certainly, at the time a film like this upset those working for the press and the media, because it did not put journalists in a good light.

How was that notorious scene achieved?

I asked the set designer, I told him that we would be impaling the girl the next day. I said to him, 'Go and devise some way of doing it, work something out!' So he said, 'How on earth? For tomorrow morning?' 'Yes, for tomorrow morning', I said. So he gives it some thought, and the next morning he rings at the door of my room to say, 'It's Antonello, I've come to show you what I have prepared for impaling the girl.' So, I open up and he's there with a stick and a bicycle saddle mounted on a pole. Right? And I ask him, 'What's this?' ... 'It's for impaling the girl! We'll sit her on the saddle, which will be planted in the ground on a pole, we'll add blood, and we'll put a stick of balsa wood in her mouth.' So, it was all so simple. When I told Tarantino how we had done it, he said, 'No way, impossible, as simple as that!' But it really was like that. The whole film was like that, we just had fun. My great art lies in imagination. I am not like those intensely stressed directors.

*In terms of controversial elements of the film, we cannot discuss **Cannibal Holocaust** without considering the issue of violence against animals.*

The problem with **Cannibal Holocaust** was certainly the animals. I've still really got a problem with what happened to the turtle. But it's done now. In the film **Last Cannibal World** I did not want any animals to be killed. But my producer at the time, he killed some animals off the set, out of sight.Then they asked me to do **Cannibal Holocaust** and to use dead animals again, because this is what the Far East market wanted. At first I refused, but I finally said, 'OK, let's make this film.' My principle was to write nothing in the script about animals, but whatever we saw the natives killing and eating we would film. So what happened? Well, once I filmed a rat. The natives eat them. It is also a custom in Africa. There is a place called Gambela in Ethiopia where they burn forests to flush out the rats, which they then eat. So we filmed the rat sequence. Then there was the little pig, because our dressmaker on set said that she was fed up with eating fish every day. Then there are the monkeys, which are also eaten by the natives. The most unpleasant sequence for me was the turtle sequence. This turtle sequence derived from some trouble that

top: The casual subjugation of a stray indigenous Amazonian by one of Professor Monroe's military guides demonstrates the way in which native people are routinely repressed and humiliated by outsiders in the world portrayed in **Cannibal Holocaust**. *above:* A poster that bizarrely superimposes the head of an abused native woman from a completely different scene in the film onto the bottom left of this cannibal feast image. *below:* Tension rises in **Cannibal Holocaust**.

above: Professor Monroe (Robert Kerman) seeks the help of the military as he starts out on his quest to discover the fate of the missing film crew.
top right: A native hunter armed with poison darts is just one of the many hazards that can be encountered in the Green Inferno of the Amazon rain forest.

opposite top right: Explicit and graphic poster advertising a Danish release for **Cannibal Holocaust**.
opposite bottom: Yates lies dead after the natives take their final, devastating revenge for the murder and destruction that he has orchestrated in his desperate search for media spectacle.
below: The Yamamomo, totally integrated into their jungle environment, make their home in and amongst the trees.

our guide had. He said, 'When we find an animal that the natives would eat, we can slaughter it also.' And so it was. That is how the turtle sequence came about. It was one of my most tragic memories of the film.

You have often said in interviews that your experiences in the Italian South enabled you to deal with the issue of on-screen animal death, which I find an intriguing and fascinating statement.

Yes, despite the reputation of **Cannibal Holocaust**, I really love animals. Yet in my childhood, things were different all those years ago. I love the countryside and I have a house in the country at Spoleto. I spent my childhood with country-folk, and I know what those people did from time to time. Country-folk slaughter animals for food. I remember when they killed a pig, and suddenly there was lots of work for everyone to do. It is a horribly cruel thing to see. Little basins would be placed under the pig that had been strung up. With its head hanging down, the blood would be drained out of the pig, collected, and eaten immediately. Those drops of blood would be mopped up and eaten at once. Then there were peasants who would invite you over to do the capons, which meant castrating roosters. Otherwise a peasant neighbour might call us over to drown kittens because they had too many of them, so we would do the job with a sack. Thirty years ago, I saw things from a countryside perspective. So, if the natives ate something, what was I to do? I filmed them.

Beyond its controversial scenes of animal violence, you may be aware that the film was prosecuted in the UK, with many State officials and media commentators citing it as a snuff film!

Yes. In Italy the film was prosecuted too. I know that the UK has troubles with this film, but there is an ironic side to this. Do you know where I purchased the footage of gun-shot mutilation for the 'Road to Hell' documentary seen in the movie? It was in London! I bought it in London. So the UK has a very intimate relationship to my movie, even though it is controversial there too!

Final question. Having helmed such an influential movie that blurs the boundaries between real-life violence and fictional atrocity, I wonder what terrifies you more: the horror of fiction or the savagery of society?

For me the horror of society is definitely worse. But the incredible thing is that if I ask a youth the question today, 'Is it worse to see **Cannibal Holocaust** or to see those internet images of a decapitation in American-occupied Iraq?' – and we all saw those. And they all say **Cannibal Holocaust**!... I am speechless. There has been much talk of us doing a sequel to the film, and I think if there ever is a **Cannibal Holocaust II**, we should set it in Iraq. That's the kind of area to set it in because that's where the new media horrors lie...

I wish to thank Ruggero Deodato for his support and enthusiasm with this interview. My thanks also to Calum Waddell for assisting with the organisation of the interview and to Barbara Maio, Paulo Russo and Giovanni Memola for translating the questions during my sitting with Mr. Deodato. I would also like to express my thanks to Jon Wordie for translating the completed interview into English.

footnotes

1 For a detailed analysis of the Italian Mondo film, see the chapter 'Sensational Shock Scenes: Anti-Narrative in Mondo' in Mark Goodall *Sweet and Savage: The World Through the Shockumentary Film Lens* (London: Headpress Books, 2006), 69-91.
2 See Xavier Mendik's chapter 'Black Sex, Bad Sex: Monstrous Ethnicity in the *Black Emanuelle* Films' in Ernest Mathijs and Xavier Mendik (eds) *Alternative Europe: Eurotrash and Exploitation Cinema Since 1945* (London: Wallflower Press, 2004), 146-160.
3 For an extended analysis of the links between this film and the wider cannibal cycle, see the chapter 'Eating Italian' in Mikita Brottman *Meat Is Murder: An Illustrated Guide to Cannibal Culture* (London: Creation Books, 2001), 131-160.
4 Pierre Jouis *Fantasy Film Memory Shockers: Cannibal Holocaust* (Maisons-Alfont: Fantasy Film Memory Association, 1990), 9.
5 Ibid.
6 Ibid.
7 See Julian Petley's chapter '*Cannibal Holocaust* and the Pornography of Death' in Geoff King (ed) *The Spectacle of the Real: From Hollywood to Reality TV and Beyond* (Bristol: Intellect Books, 2005), 173-187.
8 'Crew of Four: A New Italian Sex Drama' in *Continental Film Review* Volume 24. No, 2 (Dec 1976) pp46-47.

CANNIBALS & CENSORS

Julian Petley discusses the process by which five minutes of cuts in the UK were finally waived by the **BBFC**.

When first distributed in Britain, **Cannibal Holocaust** rapidly became notorious as one of the first 'video nasties' to be successfully prosecuted, in August 1982, under the Obscene Publications Act. However, what was overlooked at the time was that the version distributed by Go Video was in fact a relatively toned down one – for example, the whole of the forced abortion scene was missing. Given the film's notoriety and legal history it would have been quite pointless to have submitted it to the British Board of Film Classification once the Video Recordings Act was passed in 1984, and indeed it was not until 2001 that this actually happened. Even then, however, the video was subject to over five minutes worth of cuts, in order to remove scenes of both sexualised violence and animal cruelty. I am extremely grateful to Craig Lapper of the BBFC for providing me with the full details of the cuts which the BBFC requested (the passages in square brackets denote the distributor's action in the light of each request).

Scene 1 – Killing of 'muskrat':-
At 18:18 – Remove all sight of 'muskrat' being killed. Resume on close-up of bearded man's face. [*Single cut made, 17 seconds.*].

Scene 2 – 'Ritual Punishment for Adultery':-
At 19:47 – Following long-shot sight of man holding naked woman's head as she lies on the ground, remove sight of woman dragged through the mud and having her legs forced apart. Resume on medium close-up of bearded man's face. [Single cut made, 19 seconds].
At 20:18 – In same sequence, and following long-shot sight of man preparing to attack naked woman lying on the ground, remove all subsequent sight of woman struggling and being raped with wooden dildo. Resume on medium-shot sight of men watching.
[*Two individual cuts made, totalling 18 seconds and 12 seconds.*]

Scene 3 – Rape of native woman by men from other tribe:-
At 32:04 – Following long-shot of tribesmen on river bank, remove all sight of woman being raped. Resume on medium-shot sight of men slicing corpse. [*Single cut made, 10 seconds.*]

Scene 4 – Killing and butchering of turtle:-
At 51:56 – Following sight of giant turtle being dragged from river, remove all sight of turtle being dismembered alive and disembowelled. Resume on medium shot sight of man filming. Reaction shots in which turtle or parts of turtle are not visible may remain.
[*Four individual cuts made, totalling 20 seconds, 12 seconds, 59 seconds and ten seconds.*]

Scene 5 – Killing of monkey:-
At 60:22 – Following close-up sight of blond man's face, remove entire sequence where top of monkey's head is sliced off and blood is drained into a bowl. Resume on medium shot sight of man running behind tree. [*Single cut made, 21 seconds.*]

Scene 6 – Shooting of pig:-
At 63:16 – Following long-shot sight of man approaching tethered pig, remove subsequent sequence showing tethered pig being kicked and shot. Resume on medium close-up sight of back of man's head as he says 'Things Like this happen all the time in the jungle'.
[*Single cut made, 19 seconds.*]

Scene 7 – Rape of native woman by film crew:-
At 76:47 – Significantly reduce rape sequence. [*Four individual cuts made, totalling six seconds, nine seconds, six seconds and ten seconds.*]

Scene 8 – Rape of Faye by cannibals:-
At 86:17 – After woman is partially stripped, remove all sight of her underwear being removed and her subsequent rape. Resume on shot of group watching in viewing theatre. [*Single cut made, 94 seconds.*]
At 88:16 – Remove medium shot sight of woman's genitals before she is dragged away by cannibals. Resume on sight of man's back.
[*Single cut made, two seconds.* NOTE: This final cut was an *additional* cut, required after the Board had viewed a version with all the other cuts made by the company.]

This was the version of **Cannibal Holocaust** in distribution on video and DVD in the UK until 2010, which is when the distributor Shameless decided to submit an uncut version of the film on DVD to the BBFC, in order to see what happened. Because both Xavier Mendik and I had written a good deal about the film over the years, Shameless asked us if we would both plan the extras and also submit the DVD to the BBFC for what is known as an 'advice screening'. This we did, and I have to say that we were extremely surprised, and, of course, gratified, to receive the following response from the BBFC:

> Our conclusion is that the film can be classified at '18' with a single cut, as follows:-
> At 18 minutes – Remove sight of man killing small mammal with a knife. Cut required from 0:18:21 - 0:18:35.
> This cut is required in accordance with BBFC Guidelines and policy on animal cruelty, which prohibit the classification of scenes orchestrated by film makers in which animals are cruelly subjected to pain or terror and/or cruelly goaded to fury. It is clear that the killing of the animal in this scene is quite protracted and that pain and distress are suffered by the animal.
>
> In terms of the other cuts required in 2001, it is the Board's view that the cuts previously required to four scenes of sexual violence are no longer required. In our view, the scenes are primarily horrifying and repugnant rather than likely to eroticise or endorse sexual violence.
> With regard to the other scenes of animal killing that were cut previously (namely the killing of the turtle, the killing of a monkey, and the shooting of a pig), our view is that in each case the kill is quick, clean, and humane and the animals in question did not suffer a level of pain or distress that warrants intervention under BBFC policy.

It should perhaps be pointed out that the Cinematograph Film Act (1937), passed in the wake of injuries incurred by horses during the making of **The Charge of the Light Brigade**, prohibits the exhibition of 'any scene … organised or directed in such a way as to involve the cruel infliction of pain or terror on any animal or the cruel goading of any animal to fury'. The scenes in which animals are killed are undoubtedly the most controversial in **Cannibal Holocaust**. The effect (and, one assumes, the intention) of these scenes is to intensify, by a process of association and osmosis, the already very considerable verisimilitude of the scenes in which it is made to appear that humans are being mutilated and killed. To point this out is not to justify the scenes of animal killing but simply to explain their function within the overall narrative. However, for those who do not wish to experience this aspect of **Cannibal Holocaust**, Ruggero Deodato has prepared an animal-cruelty-free version of the film, which is now included on the Shameless Blu-ray and DVD releases.

INDEX

Page references in **bold** refer exclusively to illustrations.

BIBLIOGRAPHY

Aramu, Daniele – 'L'Ultimo Cannibale: Intervista esclusiva con Massimo Foschi', *Nocturno Book*, 1997, pp 50-52

Balun, Chas. – 'The Last Cannibal Film You'll Ever Need To See', *Deep Red*, 4, 1987, pp 12-17

Balun, Chas. – 'The Strange Case of Ruggero Deodato: From Cannibals to Compromise in 10 Easy Years', *Deep Red Special Edition*, 1991, pp 43-50

Beine, Martin (2009) – *Tenebrarum number one: Cannibal Holocaust*

Bisette, Stephen R. – 'The Third World Cannibal Films', *Deep Red Horror Handbook*, 1989, pp 82-110

Bisette, Stephen R. – 'Animal Mutilation: Geek Show Gore', *Deep Red Horror Handbook*, 1991, pp 111-116

Bisette, Stephen R. – 'The Cutting Room Floor: Videos Restored and Compared: Cut And Run / Inferno in diretta', *Video Watchdog*, 1, 1990, pp 42-47

Brottman, Mikita (1997) – *Offensive Films: Toward an Anthropology of Cinéma Vomitif*, London, Greenwood Press.

Bruschini, Antonio & Tentori, Antonio (1994) – *Mondi Incredibili: il cinema fantastico-avventuroso italiano*, Bologna, Granata Press

Coxhead, Martin – 'So Gory It's a Crime', *Gorezone*, 17, 1991, pp 8-11

Gomarasca, Manlio & Aramu, Daniele – 'Il Ragazzo dei Parioli: Intervista a Ruggero Deodato', *Nocturno*, 1, 1996, pp 16-27

Jouis, Pierre (1990) – *Fantasy Film Memory Shockers: Ruggero Deodato's Cannibal Holocaust*, Paris, the FFM association.

Kerekes, David & Slater, David (1994) – *Killing for Culture: An Illustrated History of Death Film from Mondo to Snuff*, London, Creation Books.

Laborie, Guillaume – 'The Washing Machine', *Giallo Pages*, 4, 1994, pp 37

Palmerini, Luca M. & Mistretta, Gaetano (1996) – *Spaghetti Nightmares*, Florida, Fantasma Books.

Petley, Julian – 'Cannibal Holocaust and the Pornography of Death', *The Spectacle of the Real: From Hollywood to 'Reality' TV and Beyond*, Intellect, 2005, pp 173-186

above: A candid shot of Ruggero Deodato with Ernest Borgnine in 1990, during the making of **Ocean**.

below: UK quad poster for **Last Cannibal World**, which toured Britain's fleapits in the late Seventies under the title of **Cannibal** on a double-bill with American obscurity **Psychic Killer**. Those were the days...

ROBERT KERMAN
FRANCESCA CIARDI
GABRIEL YORKE

DIRECTOR:
RUGGERO DEODATO

EASTMANCOLOR

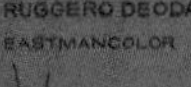